MW01122295

The Words and Music
of Patti Smith

THE PRAEGER SINGER-SONGWRITER COLLECTION

The Words and Music of Patti Smith

Joe Tarr

James E. Perone, Series Editor

Westport, Connecticut
London

Library of Congress Cataloging-in-Publication Data

Tarr, Joe.
  The words and music of Patti Smith / Joe Tarr.
      p. cm. — (The Praeger singer-songwriter collection, ISSN 1553–3484)
  Includes bibliographical references (p.   ), discography (p.   ), and index.
  ISBN-13: 978–0–275–99411–2 (alk. paper)
  1. Smith, Patti—Criticism and interpretation.   I. Title.
ML420.S672T37 2008
782.42166092—dc22   2008001444

British Library Cataloguing in Publication Data is available.

Library of Congress Catalog Card Number: 2008001444
ISBN: 978–0–275–99411–2
ISSN: 1553–3484

First published in 2008

Praeger Publishers, 88 Post Road West, Westport, CT 06881
An imprint of Greenwood Publishing Group, Inc.
www.praeger.com

Printed in the United States of America

The paper used in this book complies with the
Permanent Paper Standard issued by the National
Information Standards Organization (Z39.48–1984).

10   9   8   7   6   5   4   3   2   1

Contents

Series Foreword

Although the term, *Singer-Songwriters*, might most frequently be associated with a cadre of musicians of the early 1970s such as Paul Simon, James Taylor, Carly Simon, Joni Mitchell, Cat Stevens, and Carole King, the Praeger Singer-Songwriter Collection defines singer-songwriters more broadly, both in terms of style and in terms of time period. The series includes volumes on musicians who have been active from approximately the 1960s through the present. Musicians who write and record in folk, rock, soul, hip-hop, country, and various hybrids of these styles will be represented. Therefore, some of the early 1970s introspective singer-songwriters named above will be included, but not exclusively.

What do the individuals included in this series have in common? Some have never collaborated as writers. But, while some have done so, all have written and recorded commercially successful and/or historically important music *and* lyrics at some point in their careers.

The authors who contribute to the series also exhibit diversity. Some are scholars who are trained primarily as musicians, while others have such areas of specialization as American studies, history, sociology, popular culture studies, literature, and rhetoric. The authors share a high level of scholarship, accessibility in their writing, and a true insight into the work of the artists they study. The authors are also focused on the output of their subjects and how it relates to their subject's biography and the society around them; however, biography in and of itself is not a major focus of the books in this series.

Given the diversity of the musicians who are the subject of books in this series, and given the diversity of viewpoint of the authors, volumes in the series will differ from book to book. All, however, will be organized chronologically around the compositions and recorded performances of their subjects. All of the books in the series should also serve as listeners' guides to the music of their subjects, making them companions to the artists' recorded output.

James E. Perone
Series Editor

Introduction

In the summer of 2000, I was a slightly jaded reporter for an alternative weekly in Knoxville, Tennessee, when Patti Smith came to town. I rarely paid for music in those days; our office was bombarded with CDs from around the country (we would shamelessly sell the ones we didn't like back for ones we did), and the local promoters were always generous with complimentary tickets to the shows. In such an environment, music was cheap and easy—but also, at times, a revelation. The more barren the artistic landscape might seem, the more thrilling great music was when you stumbled across it, usually in hidden places but sometimes right in front of your face, notes that you at first took for granted, ignored, and dismissed, until they got under your skin and one day you finally noticed them—like a great pop song on the radio.

My favorite club was a little dive called the Pilot Light. I usually paid the cover there, because I wanted to support the cause. The owner, Jason Boardman, mostly ran it at a loss. He simply loved bringing in unusual and talented acts that you couldn't hear anywhere else. Sometimes the shows were a success, bringing in well over the number of people the bar was legally supposed to admit. At other times, maybe six people would show up, including the bartender. The air was usually thick with cigarette smoke. I would lean against a wall, holding a Pabst Blue Ribbon and trying to look cool. Most of the hip people scared me a little.

Some of the best shows I ever saw were at the Pilot Light, when I was elevated above cynicism to feel elation, joy, desire. At those moments, ambition was sparked. I marveled at the power of a performer to seize the moment. Moe Tucker blew me away with her encore rendition of "Bo Didley," where she played the guitar like she used to play the drums for the Velvet Underground, finding the primal rhythm of the song, which wasn't a stereotypical "tribal" rhythm, but more a human rhythm: a heart beating, blood flowing. Mostly, the magical moments came from unknown bands that were born, thrived, and, usually, died in obscurity: local artists like R. B. Morris, Todd Steed, Dixie Dirt, and Divorce; the avant-garde jazz group, Vandermark 5; or a punk rock band called the Gossip, whose lead singer, Beth Ditto, seemed to channel Bessie Smith, Mahalia Jackson, and Patti Smith with her deep booming voice and forceful delivery. Damo Suzuki, former singer of the German group Can, gave an intense three-hour performance, then hugged everyone in the audience during his encore. The British group Kaito made me feel like I was experiencing the late 1970s post-punk movement firsthand, even if their sound is something beyond that. I also caught Devandra Barnhardt, Deerhoof, and Shannon Wright, and the list goes on.

Sometimes the bands sucked and I would observe it all from a distance: detached, unmoved, and feeling slightly superior. But I was always a little in awe of even the bad acts—it seemed to take such courage to get on a stage and expose yourself for the love of or desire for something. At such moments, there seemed to be an unbridgeable divide: the world contained only two types of people, the performers and the audience. I have always been profoundly fascinated by that divide. Most people, I felt, wanted to engage the culture in some way, but so few people ever acted on it. Who hasn't, at times, fantasized about being a pop star? Yet only a few have the courage to step on a stage, risking ridicule, disdain, and embarrassment. What separates the minority of those who pick up a guitar and squawk into the microphone from the majority who stand there wishing they could?

The Pilot Light was my favorite place to see a show, but I also would check out music at larger venues: other dives such as the Longbranch, Patrick Sullivan's, and the Corner Lounge; a deli and pizza restaurant called the Tomato Head; fancier clubs like Blue Cats and the Orange Peel in nearby Asheville; historic theaters called the Tennessee and Bijou; and the outdoor venues Market Square and World's Fair Park. In these places, it was harder to be moved, even though the professionalism and sound systems were a step (or several) above the Pilot Light. But it was always possible to be moved, and it often happened when least expected.

On the night of Friday, July 28, 2000, I had a few drinks at a local brewpub on Gay Street in Knoxville, then walked a couple of blocks to the Bijou Theatre. Years before it had been a brothel and later was a segregated movie theater, with African Americans allowed only in the balcony. In 2000, it was a poorly managed playhouse with an occasional concert mixed haphazardly into the schedule. Although few concerts took place there, it was probably the best-sounding room in town. The acoustics were so crisp and clean that musicians didn't need amplification—the sounds of their voices and instruments floated right in front of you.

My exposure to Patti Smith at the time had been limited. I owned *Horses,* which I loved, and *Dream of Life,* which I liked. I also had taped copies of

Wave and *Easter*, the latter of which included the rousing (yet somewhat infuriating) "Rock n Roll Nigger." But I hadn't listened to her music much in years. I went mostly out of curiosity, because I had heard she was a phenomenal performer and because I was a sucker for rock legends, no matter how past their prime they might be.

A half hour into the show, I was unimpressed. She was floundering. This was no Sleater-Kinney, no PJ Harvey. She seemed out of her element, a pale imitation of her legend. Standing in the back of the theater, I felt a little bored. I wanted another drink. But I hung around, hoping maybe she'd play "Redondo Beach" or "Free Money." And then something happened. You could sense her finding her footing, feeling out the crowd, and suddenly she took off, careening with abandon, playing as if it was the last show she would ever play. Her recovery was all the more powerful because she had been having such a hard time finding a groove at first. She was a burst of manic energy, running around the stage barefoot, seeming to draw power from the crowd or the spirit world (two clichéd descriptions that seem so inadequate to describe her). The band—including long-time collaborators Lenny Kaye and Jay Dee Daugherty—seemed intuitively connected to her, anticipating her every whim and burst of inspiration, as she extended the songs, adding poetry or rants, wherever they felt appropriate. And they *did* feel appropriate, as though she had performed each song that way hundreds of times.

It's been too long now for me to remember much of what she played—perhaps because I was so caught up in the moment. She was touring in support of her latest album, *Gung Ho*. The newspaper I worked for later wrote, "In a ripped T-shirt and ripped jeans, reciting William Blake poetry, and even tossing in a free-jazz sax solo, she played rock 'n' roll like her life depended on it—which it probably does, considering that she's been doing this for nearly 30 years."[1] I only really remember being staggered, moved beyond words. All my cynicism and doubt had melted away. After a cathartic encore of "Gloria" and "Horses," I felt something I can describe only as affirmation—in life, in rock 'n' roll, in music, and in myself.

I walked out into the moist summer air and lit a cigarette, then wandered back down to the pub with my friends. Hipsters be damned. So what if her shaman routine sometimes felt a little canned or if she has struck some flat and false notes in her career—that was one hell of a rock show, one of the best I had ever seen. It instilled in me an urge to go out and do something, anything—to create, to shake things up, to take a risk. I can think of no higher compliment to give an artist.

Marveling at Smith's power onstage, I once again puzzled over the divide between artists and fans. Pop culture occupies a primary space in society. The majority engages it in a passive manner: we watch movies and television, we buy and trade music, we read, we look at art hung in galleries, we consume and absorb. Rarely do we perform or create art for public consumption. In the midst of passively consuming, we sporadically and perhaps randomly encounter art that is exhilarating, that wakes us up and makes us realize we don't have to be on the receiving end. Art shapes our lives, but how? Why don't more of us attempt to create it?

Smith knew the pleasures and thrills of being a fan. She had grown up during one of rock 'n' roll's golden ages. Radio stations sounded different from city to city (they weren't programmed from a corporate office), and weirdness ruled, in all its glory. Bob Dylan, the Rolling Stones, the Beatles, Jimi Hendrix, Marvin Gaye, Otis Redding, Janis Joplin, the Doors, Sly Stone, and countless others were all hitting creative peaks. It was a time when anything seemed possible and the soundtrack to revolution was being broadcast on the radio. These musicians were salvation to Smith as she grew up in a working-class New Jersey family. They pointed to a life beyond suburbia, a way to transcend the banality of everyday life. Art, for her, was religion, something sacred—especially as it blasphemed against tradition—that you were called to, that gave life meaning.

But in the 1970s, as Smith tried her hand at visual art and then poetry, the rock music that had so inspired her grew tepid, codified, and formulaic. Bands became bloated and bombastic. Groups like the Eagles, Elton John, Pink Floyd, Wings, Jethro Tull, and Yes tried to make grand statements and staged elaborate shows. Certainly, some great music came out of this period. But by and large, it was entertainment meant to be absorbed passively, feeding the audience's desire to be awed. The distance between the artists and the audience became as vast as it had ever been, as pop stars became populist, decadent versions of royalty, distinctly different from us ordinary folks.

As her beloved rock 'n' roll lost its edge, Smith started making her own music. It started as poetry blended with an electric guitar but soon evolved into a full-fledged rock band. Her early performances were marked by antagonism and defiance.

Smith was part of a movement that challenged the status quo, daring the audience to create, not just watch. Along with several other bands in New York in the mid-1970s—including the Ramones, Blondie, and Television—Smith helped create and inspire a new generation of musicians, what would later be called punk and new wave.

Even as a performer, Smith remained an adoring fan. Much of Smith's work has been a tribute to artists and musicians who have inspired her, building on their ideas and work, interpreting their classics, mourning their loss, imagining their epiphanies and dark moments. But most important, Smith reimagined these now-stereotypical rock 'n' roll archetypes in new ways, incorporating a female perspective.

Almost as abruptly as she had appeared on the rock 'n' roll scene, Smith vanished. She made four remarkable albums in the mid- to late 1970s, then got married and famously retreated to Detroit, Michigan, to raise a family with her husband. But after losing several close friends in the early 1990s, Smith reemerged on the rock 'n' roll scene. During her second act, she was both rocking and elegiac, but usually moving. Smith also spent a great deal of her energy prodding her audience, trying to engage them in the world artistically, socially, and politically—or just get them on their feet.

To say that it was remarkable that she did all of this as a woman sounds trite and patronizing today. As Gillian G. Gaar wrote in the introduction to her comprehensive *She's a Rebel: The History of Women in Rock 'n' Roll,* "Far from being a unique trend, women-in-rock have instead been a perpetual trend."[2] From the pioneering blues and country and western artists of the early twentieth century, to the soul singers of the 1950s, to the girl groups of the 1960s, the songwriters of Tin Pan Alley, and folk singers throughout the century, to the punk and post-punk female artists, to today's rock 'n' roll and hip-hop artists—women have always been there, making wonderful, engaging art. But they have not, until recently, been taken particularly seriously as Artists, with a capital A. Smith—perhaps because she came out of a literary tradition—was one of the first to be taken seriously as a rock 'n' roll auteur, if the film term could be applied to music; her work was not credited to some guy behind the scenes.

From one perspective, Smith is just one of many on the rock 'n' roll continuum. At the same time, it's hard to imagine the current crop of female artists without her; Smith is an integral piece, one of a handful of godmothers who paved the way. The pop culture atmosphere is much different today than in the mid-1970s. Until then, women artists, even those with the gumption and desire to take the stage, often found the doors closed to them. Rock 'n' roll, for all its revolutionary fervor, was remarkably sexist and confining in its gender roles. In a realm with many passive observers and a small number of active performers, women were expected to stay in the audience, gushing. The female artists who struggled to be heard often found themselves marginalized or shoved into a small number of very narrowly defined categories: folk singer, chanteuse, and girl group, each associated with stereotypical ideas of femininity.

Patti Smith changed all that. Her idols and avatars were conspicuously male. She so clearly identified with the masculine forms presented in pop culture—so much so that the cover of her first album cover showed an androgynous Smith, dressed in white shirt and suspenders, a coat draped over her back "Sinatra style."[3] In emulating and aping male rock stars, Smith freed pop culture from the tyranny of masculinity—demonstrating that all forms, styles, roles, and genres were open to anyone who dared appropriate them for their own use. By boldly pushing the boundaries of what was acceptable and redefining what music could be, she made it possible for both women and men to follow their muses.

Smith was hardly the first to suggest this heresy or attempt it, but she did it so well, made it so alluring and thrilling, that she became an icon herself. This was in no small part because she had learned well from her idols how to go about creating a myth for herself. Although it would take many years for this artistic freedom to spread and be embraced by audiences, it eventually did. In tapping into the ferocious side of rock 'n' roll as a woman, she opened up worlds of possibilities that countless female musicians—PJ Harvey, Sleater-Kinney, Kathleen Hanna, Courtney Love, Geraldine Fibbers, Lady Sovereign, and many others—would later explore. Even if her heirs weren't artistically influenced by Smith's music, they no doubt benefited from Smith's having proved to the record industry that women could be viable, commercially and artistically successful.

Patti Smith has been celebrated, mocked, revered, dismissed, and imitated in her more than 30-year career. If a single sentiment defines her music, it's that moment of affirmation—"there is a sea seize the possibility." She has seized many moments, many possibilities, in her years and continues to do so, when most artists her age would merely coast. She epitomizes the will to create, to take risks. Although her experiments have sometimes failed and she has at times come off as self-important or lost in the excess of her self-mythologizing, the high points have been ethereal, transcendent, and inspiring.

Throughout her career, Smith has remained remarkably earnest and hopeful about the possibilities of art. Her cynicism has been directed at institutions, governments, and people in power but rarely the people themselves. This lack of irony has opened her up to sporadic ridicule from the rock intelligentsia and hipsters. She never let it deter her or keep her from creating.

Today, Smith's best work remains *Horses*, a seminal album that continues to influence artists today. But there have been many other great moments along the way. Her music and lyricism have evolved, and in the process she became a visceral, engaging performer capable of moving even the most cynical of music fans. In recent years, she has continued to challenge, prod, and inspire, pushing political causes into the limelight and making moving art.

This book is not an attempt to define her. The music speaks for itself. Its high points have come in moments, forever gone. There were so many moments that I never witnessed and that are far more powerful than anything you will find in this book. But Smith has left a record and a body of art that is worth discussing.

This book is an attempt to make sense of what Patti Smith has done in her career, the touchstones as well as the missteps, her influence and impact on pop music, the direction in which she has pushed it. It is, in many ways, an odd project, like all music criticism. Although she is a poet in her own right, Smith's best work derived its power from the act of performance. It is one thing to read the lyrics to "Radio Baghdad"—quite another to hear Smith chant "sleep, sleep, sleep, run, run, run, run." How exactly do you convey the power of such a song? Or explain it? I don't think it's possible, but it's remarkable enough to discuss. The discussion about Smith's music has already begun and will continue, regardless of what is said here. I write the book because I enjoy the conversation and have something to say about it. Smith's art has moved me enough that I want to speak up.

Abstract Friends

In 1970, Patti Smith was living in the legendary Chelsea Hotel in New York City, trying to figure out how to be an artist or a writer. She would sit down at her old Remington typewriter, propped up on an orange crate, and write poetry and prose—including many fragments that would later end up in her songs. While she clacked away at the keys, a motley crew of infidels and renegades watched over her work. Pictures of the heroes she'd accumulated growing up were pasted on the wall above. "My 'hero wall,' I jokingly called it: Dylan, John Lennon, Camus, Genet, Hank Williams....I'd sit and write, grinning up at them, my abstract friends spurring me on," she has written.[1]

The sentiment is probably familiar to anybody who grew up in America in the second half of the twentieth century. I had my own shrine of fame that grew like mold over my bedroom wall, slowly evolving from the Doors and Lynyrd Skynyrd, to Bruce Springsteen and Bob Dylan, to R.E.M., the Clash, and the Replacements. Patti Smith found a spot there, along with Chrissie Hynde and Janis Joplin. On my school notebooks, I would scrawl my own rock and roll hall of fame of bands, musicians, artists, and whomever else I felt was worthy of emulation. In college, the wall grew more esoteric—the Mekons, Prince, Public Enemy, Diamanda Galas, and PJ Harvey—to reflect my evolving identity. Pictures were replaced with year-end album lists, which were hotly debated among friends (music geeks one and all), as we championed our selections for the year's best albums and songs.

One of the legacies of the recording industry and mass media is that they changed forever the relationship that people had with music. Professional musicians had long existed, but before recording technology, music was largely a populist endeavor: almost every family had someone who could play an instrument and playing music was a common pastime. As radio and records slowly took hold on American culture, people's relationship with music changed vastly. They became more self-conscious in the way they listened to music. For the average person, who might have once been an amateur player, music became a more passive pursuit, something you listened to but didn't create. Whether you listened to it alone in your room with headphones or with thousands of people in a stadium, the music itself became more and more isolated, while those who played it became more and more rarefied, at times even mystical. Music became a collective social fantasy. In the postmodern world, it's one way that Westerners imagined their lives. In a world suddenly cut off from and abandoning tradition, music became a social guide, as we identified with different models and searched for our role in the world. Or, as Dave Hickey wrote in *Air Guitar,*

> I used to wonder why there were so many love songs. More specifically, I wondered why ninety percent of the pop songs ever written were love songs, while ninety percent of rock criticism was written about the other ten percent. My own practice complied with these percentages....We need so many love songs because the imperative rituals of flirtation, courtship, and mate selection that are required to guarantee the perpetuation of the species and the maintenance of social order—that are hardwired in mammals and socially proscribed in traditional cultures—are up for grabs in mercantile democracies. These things need to be done, but we don't know how to do them, and being free citizens, we won't be told how to do them. Out of necessity, we create the institution of love songs. We saturate our society with a burgeoning, ever-changing proliferation of romantic options, a cornucopia of choices, a panoply of occasions through which these imperative functions may be facilitated. It is a market, of course, a job and a business, but it is also a critical instrumentality in civil society. We cannot do without it.[2]

I would expand Hickey's imperative to songs beyond the realm of love: pop songs teach us how to be people, decent people who can live with themselves, because learning how to be a decent person in this world is hard work. We learn how to take a stand, how to accept defeat, and how to mend a broken heart. Pop artists taught many of us how to pose in front of the mirror and later how to live with what stared back at us. When I look back at the pop songs scattered through my formative years, I know they taught me how to negotiate the world. They were little saints, heroes, cheering me on, offering consolation and abstract friendship; however isolated I might at times feel, music made me feel less alone, part of something larger, part of the human world. But this was not always the most obvious role music played. In premodern days, it also provided a social role, a means of worship, a social commentary, and a courtship lubricant. In today's world, however, pop music is more directly a guide, a means of connecting to the larger society, because that society has become too vast to comprehend on our own.

Pop culture has done some weird things to the world. Much has been written about how alienating the modern world can be; indeed, a great deal of pop music focuses on alienation. Whether contemporary society is more or less alienating than the world of earlier generations is a topic beyond the scope of this book. But to cope with modern alienation, the culture created a series of stars to speak for and represent the masses, the billions of lonely, confused, and misunderstood children. Or, put differently, artists began singing, writing about, and representing that alienation, while the masses rewarded the best of them by making them stars (and, as if in some cruel twist, further alienating them).

In such a culture, pop music—loosely defined—becomes a guide for how to act and talk, what to wear, what to believe in. Musicians, along with movie stars, comedians, artists, athletes, writers, and anyone else famous, become our role models, gurus, and spokesmen and -women. They helped us find our niche, be less alienated, and connect with the culture at large. Individuals contribute highly refined fantasies, but the collective fantasies define the culture and the boundaries of what is acceptable and ideal behavior.

A love affair with pop icons permeated Smith's thinking since she was a child. Throughout her life, she has revered many people, who acted as avatars for her. In her art, she built off of their work, feeding on their inspiration and attempting to channel them. "I felt the people I could learn from were the rock 'n' roll stars....I like people who're bigger than me. I'm not interested in meeting a bunch of writers who I don't think are bigger than life. I'm a hero worshipper."[3] In *Patti Smith Complete, 1975–2006*, she sprinkles the early pages with photos of some of her heroes: Johnny Carson, Rimbaud, Coltrane, William S. Burroughs, and Bob Dylan holding a magazine portrait of himself in front of his face. She also writes about some of the objects appropriated by these heroes that have resonated with her: Camus's raincoat, Ava Gardner's black capris, June Christie's "careless ponytail."[4]

In April 2007, she talked about how, even as a star, she has found herself engrossed by the work of others; "I've always been an iconographer. I don't think I qualify for icon status. I was always a big fan, so I never felt—I still don't—like a 19-year-old rock star. By the time I was enjoying a certain amount of popularity I was 29 years old and so had already tasted what it meant to be a devoted fan, a documenter or reviewer of other people's work."[5]

Smith was never content to merely admire, however. Her obsession with icons pushed her to become one herself. Although the imagining of fame has been played out countless times, it is mostly a fantasy of self-creation and identification. Rarely does the dreamer make it public through performance. It's even rarer that the dreamer creates music or art of any significance. In the twentieth century, as music became the realm of professionals, most Americans settled for vicarious thrills with no risk involved. But although pop art is an extremely elite club, anybody can force their way through the doors, if they have enough verve, talent, or chutzpah.

For most, the fantasy is not real life. Careers, families, children, personal struggles, desires, and health concerns consume our everyday lives. Even so, in a world bombarded by media, the fantasy is nurtured in countless ways. Subconsciously, we are always performing, in a range of styles that stretch from timid self-consciousness through conventional arrogance to the radically audacious. We wait for the cameras to focus on us, our 15 minutes, and, in some ways, we act as if we are always being filmed, documented. Should natural disaster strike or the next-door neighbor turn out to be a serial killer, we know our roles when the reporters show up. The fantasy remains within. But I don't think it ever vanishes completely. We imagine our life as a movie, a half-hour sitcom, where so-and-so will play you.

Smith practiced her lines from an early age. "Even as a child, I always used to imagine that I was being secretly filmed," she once said. "I'd pretend Bergman was shooting a movie. Or one of the saints, in shooting the whole earth, was doing a zoom on me."[6]

Like many baby boomers, Smith was a misfit kid who wanted something different and dreamed of being a star. She was born in Chicago on December 30, 1946; her family moved to Philadelphia in 1950.[7] Later the family moved to the New Jersey suburb of Woodbury Gardens. Her father, Grant Smith, worked in a Honeywell factory, while her mother, Beverly Smith, was a waitress.[8] The family were devout Jehovah's Witnesses, and as a child, Smith often accompanied her mother distributing religious tracks and proselytizing door-to-door. Although she enjoyed praying, the religion never seemed to offer much for her. The church teaches that art is a material thing of the world and, therefore, sinful. Smith gave up religion when "the elders of the church told me that art was a material thing that was not needed in Christ's world." If forced to choose between God and art, Patti picked art. [9]

There was much in the material world that Smith did find ethereal—magical things that seemed to offer their own salvation. She was jolted to the presence of rock 'n' roll at an early age. Walking to Sunday school with her mother one morning, she heard Little Richard's "Tutti Frutti" blaring from a boy's clubhouse.[10] "I didn't know what I was hearing or why I reacted so strongly. It wasn't 'Shrimp Boats' or 'Day-O.' It was something new and though I didn't comprehend what drew me, drawn I was. Drawn into a child's excited dance."[11]

Early on there was also a touch of mysticism, as she reportedly had both visions and hallucinations. "I didn't know the difference then, except that hallucinations were scary and visions weren't." Some of this was triggered by severe childhood illnesses: measles, chicken pox, Asiatic flu, mononucleosis, and scarlet fever. She had a lazy eye and sometimes saw double.[12] These dreams might have been frightening, but she saw them as a source of inspiration: "I had incredible dreams, incredible hallucinations, and I trained myself to memorize them and write them down—instead of just waking up disoriented. Or else I'd tell them to my brother and sisters [and] transform them into entertainment."[13] The fantasies were elaborate. Smith always felt different, unique. "I used to have this, this idea, that I was sort of like, part of, like, this alien race that were part Venus and part American Indian. Now this sounds kind of funny now, but I was very serious about it as a child."[14]

Despite her early revelations about Little Richard and the mysterious music known as rock 'n' roll, Patti did not set out to be rock star—but within her was a drive to be in the public eye, to be famous. Early dreams revolved around writing and art. "I decided I wanted to be a writer when I read *Little Women*. Jo was so great. I really related to her. She was a tomboy, yet guys liked her and she had a lot of boyfriends," he said in 1976.[15] She had a strong desire to create: "I was pretty creative....I would write a play and make everybody a part, with costumes. We didn't rely on toys and television sets for our pleasure. We relied on our cleverness."[16]

As a teenager, she was awkward and self-described herself as "homely."[17] Early on she was fascinated by masculinity. "I was really crazy about guys but I was always like one of the boys. The guys I always fell in love with were completely inaccessible. I didn't want any middle-of-the-road creep. I always wanted the toughest guy in school, the guy from south Philly who wore tight black pants. Y'know, the guy who carried the umbrella and wore white shirts with real thin black ties. I was really nuts over this guy named Butchie Magic 'cause he let me carry his switchblade. But I couldn't make it with guys."[18] According to Smith, she was so in tune with boys that she felt like one herself: "I was so involved in my boy-rhythms that I never came to grips with the fact that I was a girl. I was 12 years old when my mother took me inside and said, 'You can't be outside wrestling without a T-shirt on.' It was a trauma."[19]

It wasn't just that Smith emulated men, but she didn't see many women role models she could relate to. Had she grown up today, Smith might have found plenty of women to emulate—perhaps musicians PJ Harvey, Björk, M.I.A., Kelis, or Amy Winehouse; writers like Zadie Smith; actresses such as Sarah Silverman, Kate Winslet, Julianne Moore, or Scarlett Johannsson; or filmmakers such as Jane Champion or Sofia Coppola. But in the early 1960s, there wasn't much variety in female pop stars and artists.

> It was 1962. A time when roles were rigidly assigned. The boys had Bond and Brando. They beat off to Bardot. The girls had the pale range of Doris Day to Sandra Dee. All through childhood I resisted the role of a confused skirt tagging the hero. Instead, I was searching for someone crossing the gender boundaries, someone both to be and to be with. I never wanted to be Wendy— I was more like Peter Pan. This was confusing stuff. There were a few bright glimpses, mostly past tense: Jo March, Madame Curie, the brave mistresses of art. And there was always Joan of Arc.[20]

In 1964, Smith graduated from high school and took a summer job in a toy factory, inspecting toy beepers, steel sheets, strollers. She would later base her poem "Piss Factory" on the experience. During this period she was soaking up artistic influences, discovering books, art, and music. Her interviews are littered with anecdotes of discovering different artists and musicians. One day on her lunch break from the factory, she walked across the street to a small bookstore, where she found a copy of Arthur Rimbaud's *Illuminations.* "There's that grainy picture of Rimbaud, and I thought he was so neat looking I instantly snatched it up."[21] But the book got her fired, she claimed in one interview: "My supervisor got hold of it and because it was bi-lingual they thought it was a Communist book. She made a real big stink about it, such a stink that she got me fired. Which was a real drag, to go home and say 'I've been fired,' because it isn't easy to find work in South Jersey."[22] In another interview she claimed the book "almost cost me my job." Either way, *Illuminations* was immediately imprinted with an alluring subversiveness in Smith's mind. "I just left the factory in a big huff and I went home. So I attached a lot of importance to that book before I had even read it."[23]

Rimbaud immediately affected Smith's teenage writing, and he has remained a prime influence throughout her career. "First I wrote stuff that entertained. Then, as a teenager, I discovered Rimbaud and I realized that you can be entertained by words sexually in some place other than your sex organs. I discovered what I call 'brainiac amour'—when you fuck with the mind."[24]

In interviews throughout her career, Smith has recounted similar epiphanies involving the heroes she worshipped—stories of being transfixed by someone on the big screen, a song that crackled over the radio, a book or poem that felt transcendent or forbidden, the look of someone who made her melt with desire. "I've always been hero-oriented. I started doing art not because I had creative instincts but because I fell in love with artists....Art in the beginning for me was never a vehicle for self-expression, it was a way to ally myself with heroes, 'cause I couldn't make contact with God. The closest, most accessible god was a hero-god: Brian Jones, Edie Sedgwick, or Rimbaud because their works were there, their voices were there, their faces were there."[25] Her pop heroes were almost always men who were larger than life. Like many of her generation (and beyond), Smith sought meaning and significance in figures who populated the pop milieu she grew up in.

Another early inspiration was Johnny Carson, the legendary *Tonight Show* host. "My idea of how to relate to an audience really goes back to watching Johnny Carson with my dad when I was a teenager....He would come out and do his monologue, which was a new thing in those days, and you would feel that this was a guy who was actually conscious that there were people out there," she said. [26]

In the fall of 1964, Smith went away to Glassboro State College, where she studied to be an art teacher. The college was not the Philadelphia art school she had dreamed of, and she stumbled through more than two years there as a misfit, absorbing cultural influences in both writing and art meanwhile. She started listening to both Bob Dylan and the Rolling Stones. Dylan's "Like a Rolling Stone" hit the pop charts when she was a freshman; she wrote that "it helped me get through all those difficult adolescent times when you feel like a jerk and isolated."[27] Later she remembered it like this: "Dylan was somebody to be with, somebody to be. He gave voice to my yearnings. His urgency, his awkwardness, matched my own. I adopted his walk, his Way-farers, and his tarantula look, with just the right white tab collars and black jacket which he probably adopted from Baudelaire. I borrowed from him as he borrowed from others. I recognized him as one who had searched and suffered himself, who had taken another poet's name. He reflected Guthrie and Ginsberg and a little of us all."[28]

The Stones offered a more visceral thrill. Her father was watching the *Ed Sullivan Show* when Patti heard him screaming at the television. When she came to see what the fuss was, she saw the Stones in all their early bad-boy glory.

> pa was frothing like a dog. I never seen him so mad. but I lost contact with him quick. that band was as relentless as murder. I was trapped in a field of hot dots. the guitar player had pimples. the blonde kneeling down had circles ringing his eyes. one had greasy hair. the other didn't care. and the singer was showing his second layer of skin and more than a little milk. I felt thru his pants with optic x-ray. this was some hard meat. this was a bitch. five white boys sexy as any spade. their nerves were wired and their third leg was rising. in six minutes five lusty images gave me my first glob of gooie in my virgin panties.... I was doing all my thinking between my legs. I got shook. light broke. they were gone and I cliff-hanging. like jerking off without coming. Pa snapped off the tv. but he was too late. they put the touch on me.[29]

Smith's reaction to the Stones was not just physical but spiritual as well, as was her reaction to many pop figures. She heard from them something that seemed to offer salvation from the banality of her life. Smith felt destined to become part of this world. When Andy Warhol appeared at the Institute of Contemporary Art in Philadelphia, Smith went to gawk. She was in awe of the model, actress Edie Sedgwick. "She really got to me. It was something weird. Like, I really think you know your future if you want to. There I was—I had really bad skin, I was really skinny and really fucked up—but I knew I was going to do work for *Vogue*."[30]

It is perhaps important to remember that Smith, as a student of the world's finest self-mythologizers, learned well how to mythologize her own early life. This doesn't mean that these stories that appear again and again in interviews are invented or fake, but they are how she wanted to present herself to world. Whether she really believed it or not, Smith projected an admirable confidence and determination to be something and move beyond the confines of her world.

But in the summer of 1966, Smith's plans were temporarily derailed when she found out she was pregnant. She was expelled from college as a result, but the experience also seems to have reinforced her drive toward stardom. "It developed me as a person, made me start to value life, to value chance, that I'm not down in South Jersey on welfare with a 9-year-old kid. 'Cause every other girl in South Jersey who got in trouble at the time is down there."[31] She also said she gave up the child because "I wanted to create and re-create in my own way. I didn't want to create through another person—at that point in my life."[32]

In the spring of 1967, not long after she had her baby, Smith headed to New York City. She had promised her mother she would return when her money ran out. Some accounts have her living with friends, others on the streets. She soon found a job at Brentano's bookstore in midtown Manhattan.[33] As she later told one reporter, she wanted to be an artist's muse, so one day she wandered the campus of Pratt Institute in Brooklyn looking for one. "I was reading all the romantic books about the life of the artists so I went to Pratt, in Brooklyn, where all the art students were. I figured I would find an artist and be his mistress and take care of him. I found this guy, Robert Mapplethorpe."[34] The two became fast friends. Not long after they met, Mapplethorpe invited Smith to move in with him at his Brooklyn apartment.[35] A young art student at the time, Mapplethorpe would become a lifelong friend of Smith's and a pivotal force.

They dated for a while, but, more important, they encouraged each other artistically. They formed an enduring bond at a time when both were finding their identities as artists.

> We had nothing much to live on but we instantly became inseparable. We made art all the time together, out of anything, the cheapest materials. He was trained and very gifted and he shared many things with me and taught me things. He had the ability and I had the guts. We lived and worked side by side for years. We inspired each other, but his vision was fully formed. There was nothing I could teach him about his art. I read the books and he learned from me that way. We used to boost each other's egos in those early days. He'd say, "Patti, that's genius. But you wanna see something really genius?" We loved to laugh.[36]

She credits Mapplethorpe with pushing her to create: "I had all this powerful energy, and I didn't know how to direct it. Robert really disciplined me to direct all my mania—all my telepathic energy—into art."[37]

At the time, Smith's artistic interests were scattered, but she started producing a prolific amount. She gradually shifted from painting to writing. As she writes in *Patti Smith Complete,* "Standing before large sheets of paper tacked to a wall, frustrated with the image I'd draw words instead—rhythms that ran off the page onto the plaster. Writing lyrics evolved from the physical act of drawing words. Later, refining this process led to performance."[38] But it would take a few more evolutions before she would focus on songwriting seriously. In 1969, Smith and Mapplethorpe moved into the legendary

Chelsea Hotel, where she came into regular contact with many of the pop figures she revered. She became friends with Bobby Neuwirth, who would show her a world of possibilities.

> I was still kinda hoping to be a painter at that time, but it was beginning to become clear to me that it wasn't my beat and so I was writing quite a bit. I was in the lobby of the Chelsea and I had a notebook. "Hey poet," I remember him saying. "Well, you look like a poet. Do you write like one?" Defiant, very challenging. I thought, Whoah, Bob Neuwirth! He was in *Don't Look Back*. That's his leg on the cover of *Highway 61 Revisited!* So I gave him my notebook, and he read it and actually thought about it. He took me under his wing. He was a bit older than me, and really like a brother. He was very kind to me, but tough too. He taught me a lot, and helped me start to develop some sense of myself as a writer. At the same time he introduced me to a world that I hadn't been privy to. He introduced me to all kinds of people—Janis Joplin, the Grateful Dead—and introduced me in a way that they treated me respectfully.[39]

Smith suddenly found herself surrounded by some of the era's biggest countercultural musicians, artists, writers, and iconoclasts, all of whom treated her as an equal. She in turn was undaunted: "In the space of four days I think I had met every rock and roll star in New York through Bobby. And of course, I was acting real unimpressed then because, well—I think because I thought I was going to make it in the art world, and also I was so crazy over him."[40] She became friends with Joplin and the two would drink at the bar of the El Quijote, a restaurant next door to the Chelsea Hotel.[41] This new circle of people revolving around the Chelsea also included avant-garde filmmaker and musicologist Harry Smith, Kris Kristofferson, Allen Ginsberg, William S. Burroughs, Jim Carroll, as well as a number of people in Andy Warhol's crowd. "I got in my rock and roll period then 'cause I was hanging around [Neuwirth's] friends. Janis Joplin was alive then and Hendrix was around. I lived at the Chelsea and every night was a fuckin' party. Someone was always fighting or Nico was slashing some person. I got into that."[42] She started accompanying beat poet Gregory Corso to poetry readings. He would curse at the poets he didn't like.[43]

In 1969, Smith performed in *Femme Fatale,* a play at the Theatre of the Ridiculous.[44] Smith also provided the voice-over for an art film, *Robert Having His Nipple Pierced* by Sandy Daley, who also stayed at the Chelsea in 1970. She was also writing record reviews and articles for *Creem* and other rock magazines.[45]

Around this time, Smith met another person who would become a lifelong friend and her most enduring collaborator. Smith had read an article in *Jazz & Pop* by Lenny Kaye about a cappella music, which Smith had grown up listening to, and she contacted him soon afterward to tell him she liked it. Kaye had seen Smith hanging around at Max's Kansas City, a club popular with the New York underground. "After we met, she would come into

Village Oldies, the record store I worked in on Bleecker Street, and we'd drink a little beer on Saturday nights and pull records from the stacks and dance to them and hang out," he recalled.[46] A rock critic and guitar player, Kaye was a fan of 1960s garage rock, much of which remained obscure. He had helped compile a well-regarded record of forgotten guitar rock classics called *Nuggets,* which was released in 1972.

When Smith was scheduled to do her first poetry reading—with Gerard Malanga at St. Marks Church on February 10, 1971—she asked Kaye to provide guitar accompaniment. Now legendary (it is still referred to in articles about Smith), the event was attended by several artists, musicians, and writers, including Neuwirth, Mapplethorpe, Jim Carroll, Ginsberg, and Sam Shepard. Eminent rock critic and writer Nick Tosches wrote that the presence of the guitar and amplifier intimidated the other poets. "You might say they feared it, for none of them, once they had seen Lenny's amp sitting there like a dark Homeric vowel, wished to follow Patti's performance, and she was asked to close the show."[47]

Patti gave the reading in an in-your-face brand of beatnik cool, very much informed by rock 'n' roll and the counterculture. After asking the crowd, in a little girl's voice, whether they could hear her, she barked, "Because I don't want to beat off alone up here, it's really dumb." She then opened with Bertolt Brecht's "Mac the Knife," backed by Kaye. Dedicating the evening to crime, she lunged into her poems. Biographer Victor Bockris—who attended the reading—writes in his book on Smith that "it became obvious that Patti was not doing a poetry reading but rather delivering a performance." Bockris quotes another attendee, photographer Lee Black Childers, as saying, "Already her show wasn't like a poetry reading, even that early on. It had a cadence to it. The only thing you could compare it to today would be rap music. She repeated words, repeated phrases over and over and over. It bounced off itself and caught the audience up in the rhythm, which most poetry readings didn't do."[48] A more apt comparison might be to the poetry slams of the 1990s, where poets relied on the delivery and the physicality of language and performance to engage audiences. Smith's centerpiece of the evening was "Ballad of a Bad Boy," a poem about a young man who rebels against his mother by crashing his car. Kaye's guitar interpreted the crash.[49]

Many people who attended the event speak of it as groundbreaking: "There she was, perhaps a hundred pounds in all. She was clearly already a star; it was just a question of getting the message out to the world," said poet Aram Saroyan. "Patti was a breath of fresh air. There was something so liberating about her, in terms of her cocky attitude about life and poetry and who her heroes were," said Malanga. "She would virtually be possessed and transported."[50]

Thirty years later, Smith downplayed the event: "The Warhol people were there. Lou Reed was there. Robert brought his friends from the fashion world. I had met Sam Shepard by then, and he was there. It was a full moon. It was Bertolt Brecht's birthday. Lenny had an electric guitar. And I was in my beyond-gender mode. Maybe that had something to do with it."[51]

Her performance style and aesthetic were clearly taking shape, but it would be a few years before they would be fully realized in the form of a rock band. She was uncertain about which direction to take her art. "I realized at that time I didn't know what I was doing. I knew I wanted to do something, I knew I could read poetry—but I didn't know how to sing. I didn't have the skill . . . and so many people were asking me to do things."[52]

But Smith kept creating. With Shepard, she wrote the play *Cowboy Mouth*, which the two performed together at the American Place Theatre on April 29, 1971.[53] Patti said they wrote the play "on the same typewriter—like a battle. We were having this affair—he was a married man, and it was a passionate kind of thing. We were talking about two people—two big dreamers—that came together but were destined for a sad end."[54]

In the spring of 1972, Smith published her first book of poetry, *Seventh Heaven*, on the small press Telegraph Books. Dedicated to Mickey Spillane and Anita Pallenberg, the book paid tribute to many of Smith's idols: Joan of Arc, Marriane Faithful, Céline, Bob Dylan, Amelia Earhart, and others. It included the poem "A Fire of Unknown Origin," a tribute to Jim Morrison. Although the book did not sell many copies, it was well regarded in the rock press and among Smith's peers.[55] Two other books of verse quickly followed.

In 1973, Smith did a stint opening for the New York Dolls, pioneers of the punk and glam rock movement, reading her poetry at the Mercer Arts Center. In the fall, she asked Kaye to play with her again during readings. Soon after, they added a keyboard player. "I got the desire to sing—little blues songs, Billie Holiday songs. And we decided that we needed a piano player," Smith said. A friend recommended Richard Sohl, a "gifted, intuitive piano player—part Motown, part Mendelssohn."[56] A group was slowly taking shape, although it wasn't quite a rock band yet. Kaye said: "It was a cocktail trio with Patti out in front. She would do some poems and then we would play a few standards—'Speak Low,' things like that."[57]

Although she continued to see herself as a poet, Smith was increasingly drawn to the stage and performance. The thrilling possibilities of music were opening up to her, she told *Mademoiselle* in 1975. "My push is to get beyond the word into something that's more fleshy, that's why I like performing. The Word is just for me, when I'm alone late at night and I'm jerkin' off, you know, pouring out streams of words. That's a very one-to-one process, but I'm interested in communicatin'. I'm another instrument in the band."[58] But Smith was far from just another instrument. She was about to unleash herself on a world starving for something new and exciting, a world that Smith would help transform by rewriting the rules of what is possible.

On the cusp of fame, Patti didn't need her heroes anymore, but she held onto them like talismans, never forgetting the pleasure and purpose they had given her. In 1993, in an essay about her "wall of heroes," Smith wrote that she eventually understood that her hero worship helped her find her own identity and voice. "We go through life. We shed our skins. We become ourselves. Ultimately, we are not seeking others to bow to, but to reinforce our individual natures, to help us suffer our own choices, to guide us on our own particular journeys."[59]

Dreams and Limits

Fantasy is an intoxicating force in modern America. It is a means of escape but also a way of imagining what you could be and of defining yourself. Music can be the soundtrack to the fantasy or the fantasy itself. The fantasy could be a guiding light, or you could get lost inside of it. Two of the most extreme and haunting fantasies in American culture—perhaps because they seem so forbidden or unreachable—are those of the pop icon and the outlaw. You could lust after and emulate sexy, angsty James Dean or be confounded by and marvel at a cold-blooded killer like Charlie Starkweather, who, with his girlfriend, Caril Fugate, angrily gunned down people across the Midwest in 1958. Both fantasies offer their own kind of escape from the constraints of the banality of life. You could either be so talented and popular that you would escape the rules, or you could simply take aim at the world and shoot down all the patsies too stupid to see beyond the rules, the sick game.[1] (It perhaps requires a severe psychopathic mental illness to go on a killing spree, but not to have a passing thought of doing it.)

In June 1974, in the first single that Patti Smith recorded, "Hey Joe," she combined both fantasies to powerful effect. In it she honors one of her heroes, the late Jimi Hendrix, who made the song famous. In Smith's "Hey Joe," she also imagines the world from the eyes of a contemporary outlaw, Patty Hearst, the kidnap victim turned rebel (who then turned victim again when tried for her crimes and later found herself an iconoclastic place in John Waters's movies). With money borrowed from Robert Mapplethorpe, Smith recorded the single at Electric Ladyland, the recording studio Hendrix built in New York but was not able to record at before he died. "I felt a real sense of duty—I was very conscious that I was getting to do something that he didn't."[2]

Patty Hearst, the wealthy granddaughter of the newspaper mogul William Randolph Hearst, would seem to need no fantasy of escape. But she found herself lost in one, nonetheless. On February 4, 1974, members of the Symbionese Liberation Army (SLA) kidnapped her from her apartment in Berkeley, California.[3] The SLA demanded the release of imprisoned gang members in exchange for Hearst. When the swap failed, the SLA demanded the family provide food to the poor of California. On April 15, 1974, after months in captivity, a security camera recorded Hearst aiding the SLA in the holdup of a San Francisco bank. Hearst was caught by police in 1975 and tried and convicted for bank robbery (President Jimmy Carter commuted her sentence in 1979, and President Bill Clinton pardoned her in 2001).[4] But when Smith recorded "Hey Joe," Hearst was still on the run, wanted by the FBI, seemingly having turned her back on her rich white family, her fiancé, and her country, in favor of a life as a violent revolutionary.

Smith's version of "Hey Joe" opens with her yearning for the late guitar god who played his guitar with intuitive virtuosity. "Honey, the way you play guitar, makes me feel so masochistic... ," she moans, without any musical accompaniment. "The way you go low down deep into the neck," she sings, playing the double entendre for all it's worth. Her free-form prose then shifts gears to imagine the world of Patty Hearst.

The song slowly shifts into "Hey Joe," about a man who catches his woman cheating on him and kills her, then runs off to Mexico to escape the noose. Both Hendrix's and Smith's versions of the song celebrate the killing—"shoot her one more time for Jimi" or, in Smith's version, "shoot her one more time for me"—as just and righteous. In both versions, the music is expansive. Hendrix's guitar playing, punctuated by the thumping of Mitch Mitchell's deep, ferocious drums, carries the murderer off to Mexico. Smith's version lacks percussion. The guitar work of Lenny Kaye and Tom Verlaine doesn't swing the way Hendrix's playing does—it sounds stiff and flat. But it has a frenzy that complements Patti's growing ecstasy as she imagines a world where limits and laws don't apply.

At the core of the song is a brutal murder, but it is about much more than domestic violence. The victim is nameless and faceless, more or less a piece of property, notable for her absence as much as anything. In Hendrix's version, race and justice are subtle, omnipresent backdrops. Race is never mentioned, but it's hard not to see Joe, vis-à-vis Hendrix and the backdrop of the 1960s civil rights movement, as a black man, playing out stereotypes and subverting them. In a visceral way, the Joe in this song is rebelling against hundreds of years of racist American justice; liberation comes from standing up to rules that made African Americans property, nonhumans with no rights or recourse. The ugly sentiment of humans as property is shoved back in society's face: this is what you've created. If nothing else, it's a trashy detective tale with an antihero as protagonist.

For Smith, a woman regarded as the godmother of women rockers, it's a curious choice for a first single, despite her affinity for Hendrix. The song drips with misogyny, celebrating a man's ultimate authority over his woman—the right to kill her for choosing her own desires over him.

Smith further muddles the racial imagery, playing off modern-day stereotypes, when she brings Hearst back into the song. She imagines Hearst's family sitting at home, agonizing over what their sweet young daughter is doing out there, whom she's spreading her legs for. "Daddy, you'll never know just what I was feeling…I feel so free." For Smith, the revolutionary act is Hearst casting off her rich white heritage to have sex with a black man (never mind that the SLA had only one black member). It's a ridiculous stretch to imagine that either Hendrix or Smith was condoning murder or domestic violence. Their songs, in a sensationalistic way, glorify a world without limits, constraints, and rules. It was a celebration of rebelliousness and liberty that had been absent in rock 'n' roll for years, as most bands at the time only played the part of rebel. In *Patti Smith Complete, 1975–2006,* Smith writes that she holds sacred "the right to create, without apology, from a stance beyond gender or social definition."[5] Smith has always rejected gender constraints, preferring to imagine herself in whatever guise she wanted.

> A good writer can get into any gender, can get into any mouth. When I write I may be a Brando creep, or a girl laying on the floor, or a Japanese tourist, or a slob like Richard Speck. You have to be a chameleon when you're writing, and to get caught up with being a Jewish girl or a black girl or a divorced girl or a girl period, to me that's a big bore and a lot of silly bullshit. I've never felt grounded because of my ancestry or my gender. I think until women get away from that they're not going to be great writers.[6]

In the course of the song, Smith takes the identity of a man killing his woman, then that of a woman having sex with a black rebel and loving every minute of it. Although the narrator of the song is murdering a woman, Smith declares the right of women to imagine and feel whatever they want—a conceit that still sounds dangerously thrilling today. This sentiment burned through the punk movement that was about to ignite, and Smith was in tune with it.

The flip side to Smith's "Hey Joe" is "Piss Factory," an autobiographical prose poem that was all about the limits of Patti's origins—the world she fled to New York to escape. The song is about getting a job inspecting toys a factory. But she quickly runs afoul of the Catholic working-class women who run the floor. When Smith works too fast, messing up the quota, the floor boss warns her to slow down, or they'd shove her face in the toilet. What follows is a beatnik-style meditation on life in the factory, but there's little romance about it, no Jack Kerouac eulogies of the working class. It is a world of ugliness that drains the life from everything, making those who succumb to it equally repulsive. She longs for a radio, deliverance in the form of James Brown or the Chesters, and fantasizes about sex-starved young teenage boys. Unlike her repressed Catholic coworkers, Smith recognizes that her lust and desire are strengths: "I've got something to hide here, called desire."

One of the most personal things Smith has ever written, it also works as a statement of purpose, one that carried Smith through her entire career. She works herself into a frenzy, smothered by the closed, dead-end world of the factory, then lashes out against it—fantasizing about New York and being a big star. In 1976 she told writer Nick Tosches in an interview for *Penthouse* magazine, "To me that little 'Piss Factory' thing is the most truthful thing I ever writ. It's autobiography. . . . The stuff those women did to me at that factory was more horrible than I let on in the song. They did shit like gang up on me and stick my head in a toilet full of piss."[7]

Almost 30 years later, in 1996, memories of the factory still horrified Smith, who perhaps imagined what her life could have been, or what life is for many:

> I only worked there for two summers, but in that small glimpse I had of what some people considered a life, it was a real prison. I was at a time in my life when there was really no way out: my parents had no money, and while I'm not speaking against the local community, it wasn't a very culturally developed area. People were happy just to have this crappy job and live under the worst conditions—and that probably produced the most rebellion in me. . . . It felt like a lot of people were happy to be like cattle in the factory, and never rebel against the fact that it was 110 degrees and there were no windows. It was unhealthy, they were being paid minimum wage, they just sort of went along with it.[8]

Twenty years later, Smith was more sympathetic to the factory women. "I'd be a lot more compassionate now. Not necessarily for their stupidity, because some of their rules and codes I would still rail against. But being hard-working women . . . maybe their husband's dead, or their husband took off and they've got six kids to look after. So yes, much more empathy, compassion. Much more respect."[9]

Released on Mer Records with an initial pressing of 1,000,[10] many critics have called "Hey Joe/Piss Factory" the first punk record.[11] Setting aside the idea whether there could even be such a thing, this single, however groundbreaking, cannot lay claim to the title, as will be discussed later. But the song fueled the buzz surrounding the group and gave it momentum.

When she recorded the "Hey Joe/Piss Factory" single, Smith was still a nobody, some weird beatnik chick, a controversial poet known only by the scenesters in New York's underground. But when you listen to the song, her determination is ferocious. It's hard to imagine she would be anything but a star—and not just any star, but a star the likes of which we had never seen.

Building the Tower

In 1975, change was brewing in the pop music world, as unknown musicians began to resist the hubris of the music industry and stifling of culture. It happened at a time when Smith was finding her voice and honing her craft, and she was at the forefront of this movement, making rock 'n' roll feel dangerous and exciting once again.

In the mid-1970s, rock 'n' roll had become a very different beast from the one Smith had grown up with. Smith came of age when rock 'n' roll was threatening. It wasn't just that kids wore crazy clothes and grew their hair too long: the music represented the growing discord between the generations, between eras. It was modernism run amok, rejecting old ideas, questioning the consumerism that flourished after World War II, as well as the social order, people's faith in institutions, and the government.

By the mid-1970s, however, commerce had conquered that revolutionary spirit, channeling it into hard dollars. The musicians and the fans, disillusioned by (or tired of) the promises of the 1960s, turned inward. The threat of rock 'n' roll had been broken and tamed—as much by kids who invariably turned revolution into a consumer choice as by record company executives who refined market formulas.

In 1975, the top five singles of the Billboard Hot 100 were, in descending order, Captain & Tennille's "Love Will Keep Us Together," Glen Campbell's "Rhinestone Cowboy," Elton John's "Philadelphia Freedom," Freddy Fender's "Before the Next Teardrop Falls," and Frankie Valli's "My Eyes Adored You."[1] Four of these maudlin songs were covers. All of them, save Fender's weird slice of multicultural proto-Americana, felt manufactured, stripped of emotion. Pop charts have generally been dominated by the safest common denominators, and the search for authenticity in music is a dubious endeavor, as even the seemingly rawest songs are designed for effect. But this top five was particularly devoid of anything resembling danger, excitement, or passion.

Smith was depressed by how timid and tepid the music had become. "There is no way that singers like Elton John or Helen Reddy can ever transport people the way that Jim Morrison or Jimi Hendrix did. There's just no way. They just ain't there, y'know? I don't feel that people will allow this shit to go on much longer. They won't really let rock 'n' roll die or peter out or turn into Hollywood 'cause when you clear away the tons and tons of bullshit, the heart of rock 'n' roll is integrity."[2]

But most dangerous rock 'n' roll songs were created to make money—that is perhaps the source of their power—so the idea of integrity is as much in the minds of those who buy the hit singles and become devotees of the artists as within the songs themselves. In other words, a song with integrity is one whose fans believe in it. Integrity is something an audience bestows on a song, depending on what they are looking for and what resonates as true to their own lives, not something that a musical composition can possess on its own. The masses, after all, are the ones who decide what is cool and hip and what isn't, which is why subcultures have always flourished in pop music. In 1975, diehard rock 'n' roll fans like Smith were having a hard time finding songs they could be proud of, songs that spoke to them or represented their own experiences in the ways that Dylan, the Beatles, and the Stones did in the 1960s.

After releasing "Hey Joe/Piss Factory," Smith began playing live regularly. The group eventually added a bassist and second guitar player, Ivan Kral, and then a drummer, Jay Dee Daugherty, becoming a full-fledged rock band. Together with fellow New York band Television, the Patti Smith Group played a stretch of regular gigs at the burgeoning CBGB, a club in the Bowery on New York's Lower East Side. Opened in December 1973, the club would become a vital breeding ground for the punk movement and later post-punk movements.[3] Many now-legendary bands found an early welcome at the club, including the Ramones, Blondie, Talking Heads, the Dead Boys, and Sonic Youth. The Patti Smith Group and Television were two of the first bands to play there regularly, as the scene blossomed around them. When the club closed in 2006, Smith played the final show. "CBGB was the neighborhood—the artists and poets and musicians—and we all inspired each other. CBGB validated our mission," she said the night it closed.[4]

In the mid-1970s, the collective noise that the club and the bands generated began to attract attention from the music press and a generation eager for something new and exciting. Later, in 2007, Smith both downplayed and romanticized CBGB's place in history.

> When I think of CBGBs, I don't just think of CBGBs, but of when I was tour-
> ing during that period and all the new young bands and kids I met all over

Europe and America that wanted to do something different. It's more of a consciousness to me than a place. Any period which seems to breathe new life and freedom into the arts is often cherished by people. And it was one of those periods. At the time, we never thought about anything like that, we were still just figuring out new places to play, new ideas, and how to pay our rent and have enough money to eat.[5]

In this club Patti Smith found her voice and a new scene was born, one that would become as legendary as the 1960s counterculture movement that she emulated so much. Her early performances at CBGB transfixed audiences, a talent that has marked her career.

Critic Charles Shaar Murray described seeing Smith and Television in the spring of 1975:

> Patti Smith has an aura that'd probably show up under ultra violet-light. She can generate more intensity with a single movement of one hand than most rock performers can produce in an entire set....She's an odd little waif figure in a grubby black suit and black satin shirt, so skinny that her clothes hang bag-gily all over her, with chopped-off black hair and a face like Keith Richard's kid sister would have if she'd gotten as wasted by age seventeen as Keith is now. Her band...plays like a garage band who've learned a few '30s licks to go with the mutated AM rock. She stands there machine-gunning out her lines, singing a bit and talking a bit, in total control, riding it and steering it with a twist of a shoulder here, a flick of a wrist there—scaled down bird-like movements that carry an almost unbelievable degree of power, an instinctive grasp of the prin-ciples of mime that teach that the quality and timing of a gesture is infinitely more important than its size.[6]

For many rock critics, Smith embodied their fantasy: a tough, sexy, smart woman who liked loud rock 'n' roll and sang about sex. In some of the writing about her, there's a giddy expectation, as though she might be some sort of messiah, rock 'n' roll's revolutionary promise fulfilled with an artist beyond gender. Both male and female critics often responded almost sexually to her performances. "Her energy is so untrammeled, it fills the room; it pushes us against the wall in its intensity. Those wondrous salamander eyes move slowly, almost supernaturally. They embrace the whole of the activity around her," Marc Stevens and Diana Clapton wrote. "She is gracious, con-siderate, the essence of feminine charm, all the mannerisms of the sexually self-confident woman, the emotional largesse of the truly arrivée. There must be something bad about Patti Smith. Well, she doesn't play the guitar that well—yet...."[7]

John Rockwell wrote in the *New York Times* about a show where Patti ended up banging her head against a pipe organ. He described the show as performance art, "terrifying in its intensity, like some cosmic, moral struggle between demons and angels....She has always walked the line between genius and eccentricity, between the compelling and the merely odd, between art and insanity. The word 'insanity' may seem a little strong; this listener hasn't been inside Miss Smith's head. But she acts crazy sometimes, and if it's an act, it's an act that she plays so intensely that it's become its own kind of reality."[8]

Smith romanticized the Lower East Side club's seediness and felt inspired.

> I love playing bars. Hearing that pool cue really inspires me. When we used to play on the Bowery, I would almost burst into tears 'cause of all the stuff that was happening. I'd look out at that long line of neon beer signs over the bar and that dog running around shitting while I'm in the middle of a beautiful ballad. There'd be a bunch of niggers beating the shit out of each other over by the pool table and all these drunks throwing back shots. It was the greatest atmosphere to perform in, it was conspiratorial. It was real physical, and that's what rock 'n' roll's all about: sexual tension and being drunk and disorderly![9]

She was living the decadent fantasy of Rimbaud, the beats, Jim Morrison, and thousands of alcoholic poets, artists, and gutter punks, secure in the knowledge that she was creating something meaningful, even if the rest of the world had yet to catch on.

One spring night, Lou Reed reportedly brought Arista Records president Clive Davis to one of Smith's shows. He was impressed[10] and soon afterward signed her to a record contract—the first of the CBGB bands to get a record deal. The contract was unusual because it gave Smith artistic control, including power over the advertising campaign.[11]

In the summer of 1976, Smith and the band—along with Smith's then-boyfriend Allen Lanier, guitarist for the Blue Oyster Cult—began recording their first record. Once again, Smith selected Electric Ladyland Studios. She enlisted John Cale, former member of the Velvet Underground, to produce.

The recording process was contentious and combative, as Cale forced the band to do several takes of each song. "She struck me as someone with an incredibly volatile mouth who could handle any situation," Cale said. "She could also turn any situation around from a lethargic to an energetic one. But I think it was a very different experience for her going from being a band on-stage to working in the studio. It immediately throws you back on yourself. All her strength and instinct was there already, and I was trying to provide a context for it. It wasn't easy. It was confrontational and a lot like an immutable force meeting and immovable object. Still, something creative came out of it. There was push and pull."[12] Smith remembers long battles while making the record:

> I knew nothing about recording or being in the studio. We'd already done a single, but I didn't know anything. I was very, very suspicious, very guarded and hard to work with, because I was so conscious of how I perceived rock 'n' roll. It was becoming over-produced, over-merchandised and too glamorous.

I was trying to fight against all of that. We had a big, hard battle. John did everything he could to fight our fight for us, even in his sleep. But I made it difficult for him to do some of the things he had to do.

The tension, coupled with Smith's fiery desire and the energy of the time, produced remarkable results. Now regarded as one of the most important rock 'n' roll records of all time, *Horses* endures as a powerful work of art. There isn't a weak song on the album, which holds up after repeated listenings, offering the listener new insights. It remains her best work because it captures the energy, excitement, and possibility of rock 'n' roll in a way that few albums ever have. It broadened the landscape of what was possible.

The album is, in many ways, all about worshipping rock idols and being transformed by the music—or a tribute to how one fan was transformed by it. In these songs, she honors, rebukes, and becomes the avatars who inspired her. In a few of the songs, she slips into various guises, sometimes taking on the identity of her heroes (at their darkest moments as they drift off into the abyss), at other times an omnipotent narrator, directing the whole thing from above. In between, we get touching narratives from her own life. Many of the songs are based on Smith's poems, as she mixed and matched what fit to the music.

Having studied and worshipped the likes of Dylan, the Stones, Morrison, Hendrix, Coltrane, as well as earlier literary touchstones, Smith combined these personas to create one uniquely her own—postmodern rock 'n' roll that showed a new world of possibility. The album is a tribute to excess, decadence, liberty. It's a lusty homage to the masculine spirit that permeated rock music at the time, reflected back at the world from the eyes of a horny female fan, too proud and talented to settle for being a mere groupie. By paradoxically embracing rock's masculinity, Smith delivered a crushing blow against the tyranny of masculine rock.

The album has been written about and deconstructed extensively. Smith herself has explained the inspiration behind the songs in several interviews, as well as in her lyrics compilation, *Patti Smith Complete, 1975–2006*. Several of the songs were interpreted in ways that Smith did not intend. That only adds to their power, as each takes on meanings beyond what the artist intended, with the listener becoming an active participant in the art. This is possible because the songs resonate with universal themes—loss, love, death, and sexual ecstasy—without becoming generic or bland. Smith created the landscape and vivid details, yet never rigidly defined a meaning.

Horses begins on a soft note with Richard Sohl delicately opening with his keyboard on "Gloria (in Excelsis Deo)," but discord quickly follows, as Smith drawls the album's most famous line: "Jesus died for somebody's sins, but not mine." The words are not necessarily, as they might seem, a rejection of God. Rather, they reject the need for salvation from "sins" of the world, because those sins offered their own salvation. In her Rimbaud view, Smith was proclaiming her earthly desires as good, pure, and completely hers: Jesus didn't need to die for her sins, because she was happy to commit them: "they belong to me," as she sings a few lines later. His blood wasn't on her hands. The song's title, "Gloria (in Excelsis Deo)," is a play on the Latin phrase, "Glory to God in the Highest." It could be read as a blasphemous pun or as a praise of the God manifest in the world, in some hot young chick named Gloria, in the pleasures of sex, in the joys of being in love or being young.

In 1996, Smith said that she wasn't rejecting Christ with that line but instead searching for freedom. "I happen to believe in Jesus. I never said he didn't exist. I only said that I didn't want him to take responsibility for my actions. Because I was young, I perceived myself as an artist, and the artist as a sort of cerebral criminal. I wanted the freedom to pursue all the things I imagined. Things within my art, not in life. In my art, I wanted the right to be misguided, misdirected, slightly criminal, utterly promiscuous, even a murderer. Within the realm of my work."[13] In 2007, she reiterated this sentiment:

> When I wrote "Gloria," it wasn't really anti-Christ—who I really admire—it was anti the idea that everything was set up for us and we had to fall into a certain behavior based on how things were organized for us. If I was going to do things wrong, I didn't want anyone having to die for my sins—I was going to take responsibility. It was really about personal and mental liberation. A writer called it a declaration of existence. To this day, I think that's the best description of that song, although I probably would not write the same lyric now because I've gone through a long process of evolution.[14]

Smith certainly was not the first to reject Christ in a rock song—John Lennon's "God" was the most famous (and more earnest) renunciation until the Sex Pistols' nihilistic "Anarchy in the UK" came along. Even so, rejecting God carried plenty of shock value in 1975 and continues to in pop culture. Smith herself later squirmed away from the sentiment, altering the lyrics in the late 1970s to "Jesus died for somebody's sins, why not mine?" In recent years, she has sung both lines in performances. The revised line feels like a prodigal daughter recanting. It also feels older (in the "My Back Pages" sense): the defiance of youth grows into an open question, uncertainty.

But in 1975, the original line captured the new defiance and rebellion that Smith was harnessing and that would soon erupt in the music world. The Jesus line introduced "Gloria," one of the great rock 'n' roll songs, written by Van Morrison and originally performed with his group, Them. It is one of two rock standards that Smith uses on the album to reconnect with rock 'n' roll's roots, tapping into the music's original energy and building her own music off of it, as if she had dusted off all the clutter and bombast it had accumulated to find what is really important.

The theme is that of countless rock songs—a sexy young woman whom the singer is in love with. What made the original so great was Van Morrison's lusty growl and innuendo—he's not just longing after this woman, he's nailed her, and she continues to thrill him as he brags of his love to the world. One of rock 'n' roll's incomparable singers, Van Morrison brought to life not just ecstasy and desire but also the thrill of being young. The song was one of a handful that defined garage rock. Listening to it, you're easily transported to a drunken party.

Smith and the band picked these simple rock classics to merge with her poetry and give her a landscape to play in. " 'Jesus died for somebody's sins but not mine' is from a poem. I used to read this poem, but I wanted to go from it into something simplistic. I loved three-chord songs, and 'Gloria' is the quintessential three-chord song. . . . We used to call it 'fieldwork'—Lenny and Richard would give me three-chord fields. Even though I wrote the poem at the beginning of 'Gloria' in 1970, it took all those years to evolve, to merge into 'Gloria.' "[15]

As a singer, Smith is simply out of her league compared to Van Morrison—in her version of the song, she couldn't even manage to sing the chorus, "G-L-O-R-I-A," and instead just chants the letters, while her band sings backup. She cannot evoke the range of emotions with her voice that Van Morrison does. No matter. Her version works on the energy and audacity with which she declares her supreme right to be on the stage and sing this rock classic. In keeping with her philosophy of imagining the world however she saw fit, Smith sings the song the way a man would, with aggression and keeping all its phallic imagery, except that she is much more raunchy than the guys ever dared to be, seeing the woman "humping on a parking meter." There's no irony or shift in meaning. The song is about desire, and you're not left baffled by the song the way the Kinks (and, later, the Raincoats) left you on "Lola." Smith adds several lines, including a verse that puts her on the rock stage in a stadium with thousands of women groupies lusting after her.

It is not, as many assumed at the time (and continue to), a lesbian love song. Smith has confessed to having rather vanilla sexual tastes—even to being a bit bothered by gay male sex—and has said she was merely imagining the world as a man desiring women. "Sexually I'm really normal. I always enjoyed doing transgender songs. That's something I learnt from Joan Baez, who often sang songs that had a male point of view. No, my work does not reflect my sexual preferences, it reflects the fact that I feel total freedom as an artist. On *Horses*, that's why the sleevenote has that statement about being 'beyond gender.' By that, I meant that as an artist, I can take any position, any voice, that I want."[16] That carefree abandon in choosing her voice had a staggering impact. From that opening song, Smith completely shattered old ideas of what a rock musician should be and forged a new model of cool. Musicians had been defining their own model of cool for decades, of course, but Smith pushed the boundaries further.

Smith follows "Gloria" with a very different kind of song, "Redondo Beach" (which also was interpreted as a lesbian love song by some, an easy leap with only the lyrics to go on). Intensely personal, it counterbalanced the role playing and hallucinatory narratives in Smith's other songs, presenting listeners with a life in all its precious fragility. Using a reggae beat that foreshadowed reggae's influence on punk, the song is about a quarrel that Smith had with her sister, Linda, who stormed off into the city. After several hours, Smith goes looking for her and comes across a young girl who killed herself on the beach—and a sense of foreboding about what might have become of her sister grows in her. "The hearse pulled away and the girl that had died it was you." It's a morbid fantasy but also a song of longing for something dear, something she may not ever touch again, something she knows will one day pass on. The song mourns not just the ephemeral nature of life but also the impossibility of controlling and containing the ones we love: our love cannot necessarily keep them from fighting us, from disappearing, or from killing themselves.

On the next song, "Birdland," Smith dives back deep into fantasy, inserting herself into the visions of Peter Reich, the son of renegade psychologist Wilhelm Reich. Smith has said she was inspired by Peter Reich's *Book of Dreams*, in which he recounted seeing what he believed was a spaceship at a family gathering not long after his father's death. He at first thought it was his father coming to take him away, but as he cried out to the spaceship, he realized it was a flock of birds.[17]

Smith's "Birdland" is a hallucination, an extended poetic sequence. More than nine minutes long, the song is a close relative of Jim Morrison's poetic passages performed with the Doors, such as "The End," "When the Music's Over," and "Soft Parade" (except that Smith is the better poet, capable of subtlety and range that Morrison never managed). It's an intense moment to capture—the cataclysmic moment of mourning for a loved one, especially a parent. Smith nails it; in her delivery we can feel Peter writhing on the ground, screaming out to his father, "No daddy, don't leave me here alone."

There are no drums on the original recording of "Birdland," which breaks it free of rock beat structure, allowing Smith to follow the rhythm of her verse. Lenny Kaye goes berserk on the electric guitar, fueling the celestial fantasy. But Smith has said she felt most connected with Sohl while playing the song: "I can still picture Richard, his eyes like saucers, following, then staying in step, anticipating my next move." Part of the song's intensity is due to Cale, who "had me so nuts I wound up doing this nine-minute cut [of "Birdland"] that transcended anything I ever did before."[18]

On "Free Money," Patti again indulged her outlaw fantasies, picturing herself as a thief bringing money to a loved one—but it's such a common fantasy that it feels completely genuine. Smith said she wrote the song for her mother, who "always dreamed about winning the lottery. But she never bought a lottery ticket! She would just imagine if she won, make lists of things she would do with the money—a house by the sea for us kids, then all kinds of charitable things."[19] The specifics don't matter much; the song could just as easily be about a lover or child.

Despite its implication of law breaking—"I know they're stolen but I don't feel bad"—the song feels completely righteous. Richard Sohl's tender piano intro seals it within a righteous sentiment. The money cannot be dirty if it goes to the narrator's love, which is pure and not of this world. But more than that, it's a working-class fantasy; increasing the tempo, Smith sings how, she imagines lying in bed each night in a pile of money. It's a fantasy that has been played out billions of times around the world, as dreamers picture a world where money, the magic elixir, is available to make things happen, ease burdens, and create opportunity. Smith tips her hat to such a fantasy, to anyone who ever bought a lottery ticket, and to those, like her mother, who dreamed of winning the lottery but never got around to buying a ticket. Much of Smith's art was inspired by artists of privilege—drawn to the New York art scene, she was always interested in transcending the banality of everyday existence and escaping the factories, dead-end jobs, suburbs, and closed minds. There is a loftiness to her work, and she has never been much of a working-class hero. But she remains connected to her working-class roots and understands what it means to work your ass off for a living. "Free Money" is perhaps the finest example of that righteous empathy at work. Once she had escaped Jersey, she would never go back, but she also would never forget where she came from. "Free Money" remembers the feeling of wanting to escape where she'd come from.

"Kimberly" was also inspired by family, this time her younger sister. Based on a memory of when Kimberly was a baby and Smith was holding her, watching a storm roll in, the song describes the violence of the universe colliding with the innocence and vulnerability of a baby. But it all seems part of the grand scheme: "Little sister the fates are calling on you."

The album's final three songs revolve around rock stars, utilizing mythical imagery and grand sentiments about the struggle to make art, to live. The first is "Break It Up," written from a dream Smith had about Jim Morrison, in which she saw him stretched on a marble slab. He was alive, with wings, and partly merged with the slab.[20] The song doesn't make much literal sense: it reads like Smith pleading with the gods to release some innocent boy from their clutches. There's a wonderment about where he went, how someone so precious and dear could have succumbed to the void, how such power could be suddenly silenced.

"Land: Horses/Land of a Thousand Dances/La Mer (De)" is an epic song that lasted 9 minutes 25 seconds on *Horses*. In concert it often stretches to 20 minutes as Smith improvises new verses, inspired by whatever ghosts are possessing her. The song is riddled with allusion and symbolism, but to pull a single meaning out of it is futile; it works more as an intoxicating hallucination, with meaning clouded and beside the point. Obvious antecedents are, once again, Jim Morrison's extended poetic songs. There are also literary references: Rimbaud, Blake, Whitman, the beats. Smith has pointed to the character Johnny in William S. Burroughs's *The Wild Boys* as one ancestor of the song's main character, Johnny.[21]

The song begins with Johnny drinking a cup of "tea," as another boy creeps up on him in the hallway. When Johnny sees him, he is frightened, but freezes. The rebel boy smashes him into a locker, laughing. It's a typical adolescent confrontation, one that boys both thrived on and were terrorized by, and one that Smith must have fantasized about as she grew up idolizing and fixated by everything boyish. The fight progresses, as Johnny suddenly feels horses surrounding him, running around him. The horses might be a girl's sexual metaphor for force and power, but here they twist into formation, running the classic rock 'n' roll dance tune, "Land of a Thousand Dances."

Smith's "Land of a Thousand Dances" is thick with homoerotic nuances. Sung by the too-cool sexy tomboy, the song allowed guys to feel safe to indulge in the fantasy. Smith could embody the masculine sexiness of Keith, Mick, and Jim, but retain a feminine allure, making it safe for both sexes to desire her.. In this way, she liberated men to be completely passive fans, worshipping their idols. "Land" evolves into male rape fantasy and violence. As Johnny lies in his sperm, Angel looks down and says, "Can't you show me nothing but surrender?" The encounter collapses into murder or suicide—the ultimate surrender or aggression—as Johnny picks up a knife and feels it harden against Johnny's throat, pushing it in. It's all about embracing your darkest fantasies about murder, rape, and suicide and feeling good about it, masturbating to it.

Sexual fantasies are largely about power, either the surrendering of your power or seizing power over others. "Land" is remarkable in that it takes both perspectives simultaneously, as Smith puts the listener in the heads of rape victim and rapist, murderer and corpse, both of whom are thrilled to be there. The fantasy is, of course, not literal. It is a means of getting off, of feeling alive—enjoying the thrill of committing a thought crime.

For me the climax of the song comes when Patti screams, "When they built that Tower of Babel they knew what they were after," another thought crime against God. For if there's a point to the song, it is the celebration of people's attempts—in all their miserable limitations and pathetic fragility—to climb out of the grit and grime of life, of people's struggle to transcend death, heartbreak, and hunger in order to become something larger than life and create a thing of beauty. In building the tower of Babel, the humans of the Bible were simply emulating God and trying to be like Him. They wanted the heavens, and who can blame them?

The attempt, however noble, is doomed to failure. The song closes with Johnny alone, screaming a cry no one hears, his pituitary glands spitting out of his throat. In the final moments, however, as his world unravels, he sees Gloria humping a parking meter, hears a Fender guitar, sees the dancing of a simple rock song. Smith has said that the Johnny who dies at the end of the song is Jimi Hendrix, who died vomiting in his sleep.[22] It's a comforting thought to imagine such a brilliant talent experiencing a moment of affirmation as his life was fading away.

Horses ends with a tribute to Hendrix, "Elegie," borrowing lines from the late musician's song "1983 (a Merman I Should Turn to Be)": "Well it's too bad that our friends can't be with us today." It was recorded on September 18, 1975, the anniversary of Hendrix's death.[23] In recent years, the song has become something of a requiem for the fallen angels of Smith's generation. Often, she gives a roll call of the casualties, as she did on the night CBGB closed.

Accompanying this startling music on *Horses* was a distinctive cover, which has been written about as much as the music has. The black-and-white photograph was shot by her old friend Robert Mapplethorpe and is regarded as one of the greatest rock album covers ever. It shows Smith leaning against a white wall, on which she casts a slight shadow. She's dressed in black pants and a white shirt, open slightly at the collar and sleeves, which are frayed. Suspenders wrap over the shirt. Draped over her left shoulder is a suit jacket. Pinned to its lapel is a small pin of a horse, which is upside down to the viewer. Her hands touch slightly across her chest, her left one holding the jacket in place. Her coal black hair stretches down to her shirt collar. The right side of her face is partly in shadow, as she stares out at the camera. No smile. Not a mean look exactly, but it's cocksure, intimidating, as though she is the Johnny in "Land," saying, "Come and get me man."

Smith later wrote that she had overslept on the day of the photo shoot and simply tossed on her usual clothes, which she wore both onstage and in the streets. As Mapplethorpe was shooting, the light he liked began to fade, and he asked her to take off her jacket to highlight her white shirt. "I tossed the jacket over my shoulder Sinatra-style, hopefully capturing some of his casual defiance," she said.[24] In another interview, she said of her attire, "I liked to dress like Baudelaire."[25]

Her pose is reminiscent of not just Sinatra, but many other poses—Keith Richards is there, Bob Dylan, James Dean. It is distinctively male and impossible to look at without thinking about men. Smith absorbed all the sexy masculinity of her heroes and reflected it back in a style that was even sexier. She certainly wasn't the first tough female rock star, but she was the first to look tough, haggard. She made masculinity feminine, merging the genders in pop culture. When the album was released, Smith suddenly found herself an icon, irresistible and unique.

The critics—many of whom knew Smith and Kaye from their rock critic days—understandably gushed. "For some of us, Patti Smith is the girl of our rock and roll dreams. As a performer she doesn't merely flirt with danger, she seduces it, trying at the same time to be both audacious and ingratiating, to challenge an audience and win it over," wrote Mitchell Cohen.[26]

"Each song builds with an inexorable seethe, a penchant for lust and risk that shakes you and never lets you forget you're listening to real rock 'n' roll again at last. Meanwhile, every song contains moments that go beyond raunchy into emotional realms that can give you chills," Lester Bangs wrote in *Creem*. "Patti's music in its ultimate moments touches deep wellsprings of emotion that extremely few artists in rock or anywhere else are capable of reaching."[27]

In *New Musical Express,* Charles Shaar Murray called Smith's album better than the first albums of Dylan, the Beatles, the Rolling Stones, and Roxy Music. "It's hard to think of any other rock artist of recent years who arrived in the studios to make their first major recordings with their work developed to such a depth and level of maturity," he wrote.[28]

In retrospect, it can be hard to measure the impact *Horses* had on the culture. Smith said not long after the album appeared, and throughout her career, she and the band were on a mission to shake things up with *Horses*.

> We were on a mission. But we were also making it up as we went along. I mean, I was never a singer, I can't play any instruments, I had no training. Plus, I was brought up in a time when all the great rock stars were male. I didn't have any template for what I was doing. I did what I did out of frustration and concern. I felt like rock 'n' roll was disintegrating. We'd lost Jimi Hendrix, Jim Morrison, Bob Dylan was in a motorcycle accident, the Rolling Stones were shifting into a new phase. I was concerned about what was going to happen to rock 'n' roll. I had no ambition to make records, nor even thought that I had the ability, or even deserved, to do so.[29]

In another interview, she said, "The reason why I came to rock was 'cause I saw the art was in a bad position. I felt that for a long time I had depended on rock 'n' roll for my life's blood, and it was about time that I started payin' it back. I owe much more than I could ever hope to give."[30]

The altruism is a bit hard to buy and feels like self-mythologizing. Personal desire, ambition, and an artist's urge to create surely had more to do with this fiery music than a desire to save rock 'n' roll. Still, her disgust with the state of music undoubtedly nudged her forward and gave her confidence to make rock the way she knew it should sound.

Smith was the first CBGB band to release an album, but many others soon followed suit: Television, the Ramones, and Blondie. This New York scene didn't yield huge commercial successes but raked in critical plaudits and, more important, influenced hundreds of bands, both in America and Europe. For serious rock fans, the music began to thrill again. "Patti Smith was, and is, pure experience," guitarist Thurston Moore wrote for *Bomb* magazine in 1996. "Her reign in the '70s as a street-hot rock 'n' roll messiah seemed to exist from a void. No past, no future—'the future is here,' she'd sing. I'd hear tales of romance, the girl with the blackest hair hanging out at recording session writing poetry. But I didn't know her. I could only embrace the identity I perceived. I was impressionable and she came on like an alien."[31] Michael Stipe remembers getting *Horses* after it came out when he was 15. "It pretty much tore my limbs off and put them back on in a different way....It was like the first time you went into the ocean and got knocked down by a wave. It killed. It was so completely liberating."[32]

Many consider it the first punk rock album; today, Smith is often described as the godmother of punk. There are some similarities, evidence that the group was in tune with the times. Smith's music utilizes a simple chord structure—"field work," as her band called it—which was a defining element of punk rock. But Smith's music used the structure as a means toward improvisation, a launching point to go places, both lyrically and musically, a tendency that was less evident in punk. Many punk groups scorned straying outside the simple three-chord structure and extended guitar solos.

There's also a tone of reverence toward the past in Smith's work, a reclaiming of the revolution that rock once promised, whereas many punk rock groups (especially in Britain), despite their emphasis on basic rock 'n' roll structure, scorned the past as corrupt. "Phony Beatle Mania has bitten the dust," the Clash famously declared in "London Calling."

If anything, the Patti Smith Group played a transitional role. Lenny Kaye has said, "Sometimes I think of us as the last of the Sixties bands. We liked those long rambling songs, we liked 20 minutes of improvisation....We had a lot of that revolutionary 'kick out the jams, motherfucker' fervor."[33] The group was an essential bridge between the two eras, distilling the more powerful elements of the 1960s and foreshadowing the later movement.

Others, like her former lover and sporadic collaborator Tom Verlaine, saw her influence in punk. Talking about the English punk rock bands, Verlaine told a journalist: "They all sounded the same to me. The sound was copped from the Ramones and the lyrics, the attitude, were taken from Patti Smith. Not the manic side, but the 'fuck off' side. I know what her style was like at the time she first toured there. I think a lot of people were struck by her attitude—especially bands."[34]

The Patti Smith Group was certainly a kindred spirit to the punk movement, looking to get back to basics and inspire daring actions. By deliberately trying to shake things up, trying to create a sound that felt dangerous and exciting, the group helped create a space where punk could flourish. The group fits squarely on a continuum of primitivist rock bands: from 1950s rockabilly to the British Invasion to 1960s garage rock to the urban rock of Velvet Underground, MC5, the New York Dolls, the Modern Lovers, and the Stooges. After Smith and the Ramones came the landslide of punk rock, in Europe and America, with far too many bands to mention.

Smith often came off as a mentor and mother figure to the punk rockers. "Well, I love the Clash, and I really love the Sex Pistols. I think Johnny Rotten's great, I have a real crush on him. See, all those kids were my friends before they had bands, so it's real gratifying to me to see them up there."[35] When the punks became more vitriolic toward their predecessors, Smith lectured, "Part of the style of these kids is to dump on the heads of anybody over 19. Sometimes I get real mad and want to give Johnny Rotten a spanking...but I understand them, I think it's cool."[36]

In 2005, on the 30th anniversary of the release of *Horses,* Patti Smith and her band performed the album in its entirety at the Royal Festival Hall in London. The concert was released as a CD, coupled with the original recordings. After 30 years, the songs continue to thrill with the idea of possibility. Listening to Smith sing, it's striking how she seems to have lost none of her fire. As with all anniversary celebrations, there's a whiff of nostalgia for the memories the songs evoke, both in musicians and the fans, but that is not what gives the music its power. The album still feels daring, and Smith hasn't lost her conviction, her belief in rock 'n' roll, despite the genre's obvious failures and disappointments. Eminent rock critic Sasha Frere-Jones called Smith's performance of *Horses* in 2005, "one of the most viscerally affecting things I have ever seen. Her enthusiasm as a performer is never mere crowd-pleasing, and her lack of cynicism is never empty cheer."[37]

In concert Smith is prone to improvising, tweaking each song to make it contemporary or following whatever whims inspire her. She has honed this talent over 30 years. "I'll never do a number in which I don't have to put myself on the line. By that I mean that I'll always enjoy putting myself on the spot, always enjoy playing with fire. That's what 'Land of a Thousand Dances' is for; that's the one where I always hallucinate a long story at the end. And sometimes it's really frightening, it's like boxing: go crazy or go down."[38] These moments can be powerful as the song is reinvented. Occasionally, they fall flat. In the 2005 live recording, Smith somehow turned "Land" into a rant against technology and parents who don't speak to their children (Would Johnny have been spared some measure of pain if his parents had talked to him more? Didn't he really want it, after all?).

More often than not, Smith finds fertile ground in her live musings. Her recent performances of "Elegie" are always touching as she recites a list of the dead. The 2005 performance of "My Generation" (which was recorded during the *Horses* sessions—with Cale on bass—and released as a B-side to "Gloria")—ends with a condemnation of Smith's own generation: "my generation ... created George Bush. New generations, rise up, rise up.

Smith has always felt proud of *Horses* and her place in rock 'n' roll history. Ultimately, however, she understood that she is part of a long tradition and hoped the tradition—of scraggly young people making rebellious, sexy art—would continue.

The Lost Tongue

When Patti Smith was a little girl, her mother showed her how, at night, she could talk to God. The idea that she could open up a line of communication to the higher powers immediately resonated with her. "It was the greatest gift she could ever have given me. It was the idea that no matter how bored you may be, you can still go to bed early and you can pray—which means that you can talk to the Ultimate Place all you want: tell your troubles, ask for stuff, and receive."[1]

This spirit world was exciting but could also be terrifying, with dire consequences. When Smith was 12, she was given a school assignment to report on the news of a specific country. She chose Tibet and prayed it would become newsworthy. Sure enough, that year, China invaded. "I felt tremendously guilty. I felt that somehow my prayers had interfered with Tibetan history. I worried about the Dalai Lama. It was rumored that his family had been killed by the Chinese. I was quite relieved when he reached India safely. I vowed to always say prayers for his safe-keeping, which I have done."[2] (Years later, she would sing about Tibet and the Dalai Lama's escape.)

Patti Smith may have abandoned the religion of her mother (the Jehovah's Witnesses) for art in her early teens, but she didn't stop believing in God. Instead, she started finding God in unorthodox places—museums, British rock bands, decadent poets, abstract paintings, and the scribblings of alcoholic homosexual writers. She continued to pray and look for spiritual connections, even as she blasphemed, an act she also saw as a kind of spiritual discovery, an argument with God. Throughout her career, her work has been infused with the idea of communicating with the higher powers, stretching from the extremes of sacrilege to suppliant cries for mercy.

In fact, Smith has consistently viewed art as a type of prayer, reaching out to the spirit world and God. "The highest thing an artist goes for is communication with God. Which is universal communication," she said early in her career[3]—which is to say that if you can connect with or move God, you can certainly touch mere mortals, and if you can touch God but humans won't listen, it's their loss: you did all you can do. "If one went through all my albums, every single one of them, including the first, is, is littered with Christian imagery, I think," Smith said in 1996. "It's because I've been reading the Bible since I was a child and always found it, inspiring not only spiritually but poetically. And I have a tendency to do that. I think, there's hardly, I don't, I can't think of any piece of work I've done that doesn't have some at least abstract allusion to the scriptures."[4]

Some religious references were more obvious than others. On her two albums after *Horses*, Smith delved deeper into spiritual and biblical metaphor. This was not Christian rock or religious rock in any sense. No proselytizing (at least not proselytizing for God) or religious dogma can be found in her work, no specific creed or God to whom she is praying. Her beliefs, viewed through her art, are vague liberal Western ideals embracing whatever moves her—Jesus Christ, the Dalai Lama, Genet, Mick Jagger, William S. Burroughs—and dedicated to exploration and the search. It's an inclusive New Age–style philosophy of connectedness, emphasizing biblical metaphor and the struggle for good. The goals were transcendence, ecstasy, art, and rock 'n' roll. Whatever moved you had to stem from some higher power. Ecstasy and pleasure were forms of being moved, of praying.

> An artist is somebody who enters into competition with God. The guy who built the Tower of Babel was the first artist. If I had to check out where I was in other centuries, I was his old lady. If I wasn't the guy, I was his chick. He knew that there was more and God got jealous. Even gods get uptight. Women make gods uptight. Everyone thinks of God as a man—you can't help it—Santa Claus was a man, therefore God has to be a man. But a man comes once. A woman never stops coming.[5]

Her artist-outlaw heroes are kinds of saints through whom Smith prays to God and seeks guidance. "I started doing art not because I had creative instincts but because I fell in love with artists....Art in the beginning for me was never a vehicle for self-expression, it was a way to ally myself with heroes, 'cause I couldn't make contact with God. The closest, most accessible god was a hero-god: Brian Jones, Edie Sedgwick, or Rimbaud because their works were there, their voices were there, their faces were there. I was very image-oriented."[6]

RADIO ETHIOPIA

On the liner notes to *Radio Ethiopia*, Smith's 1976 sophomore effort, Smith wrote that when she was little she "got stoned on the Bible" (the drug comparison perhaps calculated to outrage mainstream America or curry favor with the atheistic rock 'n' roll intelligentsia who were her core audience). But one story didn't quite fit with her as a little girl: the story of how God destroyed the tower of Babel and divided the human race with language, so that they could not all communicate with each other. She wrote, "To rob us of communication...of the universal tongue because we sought to create beyond the landscape...the artist in me was already aroused." Later in the liner notes, she calls rock 'n' roll "the highest most universal form of expression since the lost tongue (time: pre babel)." This new art religion was a populist one, without hierarchy or doctrine—a religion of the people.

Her views are a bit paradoxical. To worship God, we must blaspheme and challenge his rules and authority. In this, her spirituality viewed God not just as a being to be emulated and searched for, but also an equal to be argued with. "I think blasphemy is just a form of exploring, y'know, it's just a, y'know, youthful exuberant manner of exploring the whole, the whole concept. I think I've often found the people that are the most blasphemous are often the, wind up to be the truest believers, because they've taken the time actually to question, pull things apart, be angry and then, either submit or, y'know, or find certain answers."[7]

By 1976, rock 'n' roll had, for Smith, become a religion—the thing that gave her a taste of divinity. It was capable of saving people, and she yearned to show others the light. Smith was dedicated to spreading the word.

To help achieve this on *Radio Ethiopia*, Smith selected Jack Douglas as producer. Having worked with John Lennon, Aerosmith, and Alice Cooper,[8] Douglas was much more associated with popular rock than with underground or avant-garde rock, the way Cale was. Considering her desire to spread the word of rock 'n' roll to the masses and to fight for the soul of the music, her choice made sense. She has said she wanted it to be a "hit record."[9] The album ended up being slightly schizophrenic, striving for both rock standards and experimental breakthroughs.

"Ask the Angels," the song that opens *Radio Ethiopia*, is about being redeemed and called to action by the angels: And honey honey the call is for war." But it wasn't a call for literal war. Her writing was thick with metaphor. Excited by the New York music scene, and seeing that same energy bubbling up in places like California, Smith saw the potential for change and was calling others to join her crusade. "This song is about new things happening, new energy rising and rock and roll happening again."[10]

The good fight was to have a meaningful culture and good art. She wanted to free music from the control of corporations and evil record companies.

"The reason why I came to rock was 'cause I saw the art was in a bad posi-tion. I felt that for a long time I had depended on rock 'n' roll for my life's blood, and it was about time that I started payin' it back. I owe much more than I could ever hope to give."[11]

On the album's second song, the obtuse "Ain't It Strange," Smith sings about feeling the "Hand of God," which makes her "whirl" and "move in another dimension." She turns away from the temple and the pagoda, which she says look "like the inside of any one man." The implication is that the spirit moves within people, not institutions or buildings. So, too, does the energy of rock 'n' roll.

On "Poppies," Smith again sings about the tower of Babel, wondering, "Oh God are you afraid/Why did the tower turn you off babe," then hoping to hear God through the radio, through rock 'n' roll, the universal language restored. Smith has called the song a prelude to "Land," with "five differ-ent things goin' on in the song." She has said the song is about heroin, about how Edie Sedgwick horded her stash, and how she heard on the radio that drug fields were being burned.[12] But for Smith, getting high is just another attempt to reach the gods, an outgrowth of the longing for transcen-dence. Reading Smith's description of the song, the concept sounds absurd:

> "Poppies"—is like parallel visuals. That's one thing goin' on, and then there's background singing and the other thing that's going on is the awakening of a woman, not as victim, but just awakening...trying to find out who she is. Like I've swum through the centuries and so many centuries are calling to me.... Hey Sheba, Hey Salome, Hey Venus, connect...eclipse in my way....Then there's another one that is this weird vocal that I don't believe I did, it sounds really like Jim Morrison to me, and that's like me, myself. It's like three parts of me, one is a victim, one is like all the aspects of being female, and then one is totally strong. Like if you want to go as far as me you have to look God in the Face.[13]

Her idea of rock on "Poppies" is a far stretch from "96 Tears" and "Wooly Bully." Fortunately, the song doesn't sound so absurd. Besides, the way Smith growls and mumbles the vocals shows that she was learning how to use her voice effectively within the context of the music—you can hear a desperation in her voice that was certainly inspired by Edie and imagining a life on the brink.

Religious metaphors are littered throughout the album. Some of them are a bit silly, such as on "Pissing in a River," when Smith sings "my bow-els are empty excreting your soul," but even so in keeping with Smith's graphic beatnik style. It would be a mistake to tie all these strands of reli-gion into a conscious concept unifying the work. The words found their way into Smith's lyrics because at the time she was viewing the world in grand, biblical terms. A battle was being waged for the soul of rock 'n' roll, and

Smith felt called to arms. As she writes on *Radio Ethiopia*'s liner notes, "i got to polish up my weapon...my fender duo-sonic w/a maple neck and the original pick-ups....rock n roll is royal warfare...the universe is our battleground...the fender—all guitars—straining for the note of nobility—our weapons."

Throughout the album, Smith mumbles and mutters, as though obscuring her meaning—perhaps a pop art form of speaking in tongues. *Radio Ethiopia* climaxes with "Radio Ethiopia/Abyssinia" (Abyssinia is the former name of Ethiopia). It's a more-than-12-minute song of noisy electric guitar and feedback that Smith tried to match with her muttering and screaming. Intended as an experiment in improvisation, it also gave Smith a chance to play her guitar (since the song was more about capturing a mood and feeling than skill), plucking wildly at it in a free-jazz-like frenzy, enjoying the noise and sound of it, freed from any structure or rules of song craft. Attacked by critics, it was one of the group's favorite songs on the record.

The song begins with feedback from a strumming guitar, and bits of noise burst in randomly—a drum roll, keyboards—with a few breaks in the music, and then finally the music builds and Patti begins singing incoherently. The lyrics read, "Oh, I'll send you a telegram/Oh I have some information for you." But it's as though she's trying to send that information telepathically, because it's almost impossible to hear what Smith is singing on the track: she blurts the words out in a frenzy.

This makes some sense aesthetically, mirroring the music, but doesn't make for a particularly coherent or enjoyable listening experience. Whatever her grand vision for the song was, Smith completely failed to draw most listeners into her world. Repeated listenings bring little reward or understanding. The only pleasure I draw from it comes from imposing my own meaning: it sounds like a madwoman's rant, which brings its own kind of pleasure, but not the kind Smith intended. The image I get is of a crazy, homeless woman on the streets in some third-world urban nightmare (suggested perhaps by the title), drooling and babbling at the rich Western tourists who step over her. The meaning comes from Smith's guttural moans and the agony of screeching guitars: a woman's nightmare thrown back on those who created the conditions where it can flourish.

My interpretation, it turns out, is completely wrong (even though I prefer mine to the real one). In fact, the song is more about one of those rich tourists, feeding off the chaos of the third world and losing his mind. According to Smith, the song is about Rimbaud, who wrote a letter to his sister the day before he died. He was in Marseilles, searching for a way to get back to Ethiopia (then called Abyssinia). "The song was exploring Rimbaud's state of mind at that moment when he experienced perhaps the last bit of excitement in his life—the hope of returning to Abyssinia—while realizing that he wasn't going anywhere except where God was going to take him."[14] The song closes in mourning, as Smith imagined Rimbaud's final moments, passing on in agony—something that was becoming a stock approach in her work, the attempt to merge with her fallen heroes and strengthen her connection to them.

The song was intended as much as improvisation as any sort of coherent narrative. It was a springboard for Smith and the band to go wild and see where it would lead them. Smith wrote in *Patti Smith Complete* that the song was recorded in New York City while a hurricane sent fierce rainstorms their way, flooding the outside of the studio. "Unity was our drug. By the last take we were completely lost yet all there. My guitar felt fantastic in my hands. The neck like a mallot [*sic*]. . . . A storm was coming but I didn't feel nothing, just groping for the right note."[15]

Kaye described the song as an attempt by the band to find "mental telepathy" onstage: "We try to have, like, levels and depths, so that someone who wants to plunge into us can plunge to whatever level they want and find something to take out with them and, hopefully, it will lead them to the next level, which is 'Radio Ethiopia.'"[16] Finding a connection with your bandmates is certainly an admirable goal while performing, and as a practice it might lead to good music, but that is a weak justification for the value others are supposed to glean from a piece of music. If a song sucks, why should any listener care that the musicians got off on it or communicated with each other? You might as well be watching someone masturbate, which is how many responded to the song.

Even as a cathartic rave up, the song falls flat. Noisy, cathartic rock songs can succeed in different ways. They can infect you with a hook that drones on and on, and the uncontrollable noise, feedback, and screeching never disrupt the groove but instead only amplify or accentuate it. The Velvet Underground did this with "Sister Ray," the Stooges did it on "L.A. Blues," and the MC5 on "Kick Out the Jams." This style of song can also operate as an emotional catharsis, crossing some mental dark line of fantasy that is taboo, as in Smith's own "Land," Sonic Youth's "Death Valley '69," which imagined Charles Manson's gang in a frenzied killing, or the Doors' "The End," the classic rock oedipal and parenticide fantasy (which, to be fair, wasn't all that noisy and drew its power mostly from Morrison's dark fantasy, although Robbie Kreiger's frenzied guitar playing didn't hurt. It seems to me, nonetheless, to share the spirit of epic noise anthems.). In these kinds of songs, the guitars and drums pound you over some dark, forbidden line, which is an undeniable thrill, even if you only cross it in your head. Other noise assaults can be used in more melodic, formal three-chord rock song structures, working on a righteous level; the music is a hammer, smashing something or someone who is evil and must be brought down, for example, the Sex Pistols' "God Save the Queen," the Clash's "Know Your Rights," Creedence Clearwater Revival's "Fortunate Son," Sleater-Kinney's "The Last Song," Jay-Z's "99 Problems," or PJ Harvey's "Rub 'Til It Bleeds." In the righteous songs, the music really is a weapon that attacks: Sleater-Kinney

shrieking against a rapist, PJ Harvey tearing against the tyranny of a relationship, CCR against the fortunate ones, the Johnny Rotten against British
aristocracy, Jay-Z against racist cops. Then again, there is the pure joy of
hearing a virtuoso coax ethereal sounds from their instrument: Jimi Hendrix, John Cale, Eddie Hazel, John Coltrane, or even just smart, accomplished musicians, like Yo La Tengo or the Grateful Dead in concert. These
sonic assaults often work on several levels at once. "Radio Ethiopia," unfortunately, works on none of them. Its vision was never fully realized, though
it is an admirable experiment, as Smith dared to stray from familiar, safe
ground and take a risk.

A much more engaging song from the sessions that wasn't released until
the album's reissue on CD in 1996 is "Chicklets," compelling because of
Smith's intoxicating vocals, which are much more evocative than any of her
sonic experiments. The song opens with Smith instructing the guitar player
(presumably Kaye), "Don't worry, we'll find it, Keep it really sexy and dark,
like in a damp cave." Smith's voice perfectly matches the bluesy acoustic guitar playing, as though she is serenading the guitar, trying with all her might
to coax it into that damp cave. Her singing on the song is so infectious and
shows she was gaining confidence in her voice, the skill of which she would
demonstrate later in her career.

During this period of her career, Smith felt called to arms, imbued with
a sense of purpose. She took to calling herself the "field marshal of rock
'n' roll." As she began to see herself in the role of rock 'n' roll's savior, she
drew the wrath of many critics, particularly in Britain, who tore apart *Radio
Ethiopia*, relishing in picking apart her failed experiments. Mariane Partridge
wrote for *Melody Maker*, "Patti Smith certainly has one hell of a lot to answer
for. Not only does she unashamedly use her band as a backcloth for her pretentious 'poetic' ramblings, but she simultaneously comes on as the savior of
raw-power rock and roll as it struggles to survive the onslaught of esoteric
rock. In other words, she's into the myth-making business. And in this, her
second album, the myth is exposed…as cheap thrills."[17]

Critics in her own country were somewhat more sympathetic, but few
praised her second effort. "Smith seems to lack the direction necessary to
live up to her own best ideas—the song-poem structure of the first album
wasn't completely effective, but here there's no structure at all," wrote Dave
Marsh in *Rolling Stone*. "Even her lyric writing, the most captivating and polished part of her work, seems depersonalized—there's nothing as moving as
'Redondo Beach' or 'Kimberly' on this album. And if there were, one would
hardly be able to hear it in Jack Douglas' overpowering mix."[18]

But others championed her work. "When it works, which is just about
everywhere but the (eleven-minute) title track, this delivers the charge of
heavy metal without the depressing predictability," wrote Robert Christgau.
"Its riff power—and the riffs are even better than the lyrics on this rock-
poet experiment—has the human élan of a band that is still learning to play"
(www.robertchristgau.com). Even her attacked opus found some admirers.

The Italian critic Piero Scaruffi went so far as to rank "Radio Ethiopia" among the greatest songs of all time, at number 35 on his list, providing Smith some vindication (www.scaruffi.com/music/sings/html). And *Circus Magazine* wrote that "there is still *no one* making records like Patti Smith's. Much of the lyrics sound like they were recorded while Patti was asleep; someone installed a microphone in her brain."[19]

There are some bright moments on *Radio Ethiopia*. The critical backlash against it is overblown and clichéd. "Distant Fingers" is an infectious melody, and Smith's vocals are a high point; "Pumping (My Heart)" is an energetic surprise, merging pop sensibilities with punk rock energy, although it seems to end just as the band takes off on a wonderful tangent (as though Smith and company picked the wrong moments to let loose and cut the right ones short). Yet *Radio Ethiopia* is not a particularly engaging album. It doesn't get under your skin or carry you away the way *Horses* does. Although in parts she musters some of the intensity she did on her début album, its pleasures are mostly subtle. You have to be sympathetic to her and patient to root out anything inspiring.

This is probably, at least in part, the inevitable sophomore slump. After making an album so intense and original as *Horses*, one heaped with praise, how do you follow it up? No matter what you make of *Radio Ethiopia*, Smith can be complimented for trying something different and pushing herself in a new direction. But noble intentions, unfortunately, don't always make for enjoyable or inspiring listening.

Some of the critical scorn might result from *Radio Ethiopia*'s being less honed than *Horses*. *Horses* had been developed and realized over many years. It was the culmination of her youthful ambitions and fantasies, and the songs evolved first from poems written alone in the dead of night to performance pieces, then to songs that were collaborations with her band—with Smith revising and perfecting them and getting feedback at each step. In contrast, when she set out to record *Radio Ethiopia*, Smith was faced with a blank page. "The flow of language that seemed infinite, that poured through my hand onto sheets of paper onto the wall and into the air, seemed to dry up as we created *Radio Ethiopia*."[20] In this context, it's not surprising that she found herself singing about the rebirth of rock 'n' roll and a dead universal language. She was confounded by a need to communicate and a desire to recreate for others the liberating experiences that her own rock heroes had created for her. To some extent, she probably overthought the process. Smith had not yet honed the skills of her craft well enough to simply write good songs with less inspiration, as someone like Dylan could do.

She told one interviewer that the record was inspired by the fans she had met and seen on the *Horses* tour.

> We've been on the road for a year. The first record really reflected exactly what we knew then. Being alone by ourselves, fantasizing, playing in small clubs, the fragile adoration of the people who believe in ya. But then you go on the road

for a year and it's real maniac. There aren't 40 people who love you but 4,000. You have to really project. You can't be as fragile. It's the power of projection that you learn on the road. So the new record reflects what we learned from the kids. Before I was a fan, an artist, or whatever. If I'm a fan of anybody these days, I'm a fan of my audiences.[21]

That attitude was in keeping with Smith's desire to spread the gospel of rock 'n' roll, so to speak, as she saw herself as a mentor to a new generation of rebels, artists, and freaks. It was likely fueled by the punk generation, which was coming into its own at the time. The British punk rock groups—most notably, the Sex Pistols, the Clash, the Buzzcocks, and the Jam—were just gathering steam, and they had drawn much inspiration from the New York art scene, now a few years old and already legendary. Of the New York scene, the Ramones deserve most, if not all, of the credit for punk rock, but Patti Smith and others helped.

Smith's search for heavenly inspiration and self-definition as a role model for rock 'n' roll brought scorn from plenty of critics, who found her quest arrogant, boring, and preachy. But they didn't just attack her music; much of the criticism was vitriolic and contemptuous of her. Smith seemed to take a lot of it personally, even as she dismissed the criticism and claimed she didn't care.

In an unflattering article about a press conference that Smith gave at London's Intercontinental Hotel in 1976, *Melody Maker*'s Allan Jones wrote that Smith went on unprompted rants against the media and the media's belligerent response to her music, saying at one point, "If everybody's hung up about poetry there's a long...there's a big [fucking] poem in the record. Tell them if they're hung up because there's no poem in the record that when they buy the record it's got the longest poem in the history of man. It took me four months." Jones continued, "Now this left everyone somewhat nonplussed. What on earth was the woman ranting about?"[22]

Some of her comments were in fact quite difficult for any critical thinker to swallow, and "arrogant" is really the only apt description. Taking a cue from John Lennon, Smith compared herself to Jesus Christ. "Like Jesus says, when two people are gathered together in my name. Well, I feel the same way. I like performing in an interview situation or for 4,000 people or in a club. As long as all the energy is directed toward the same place."[23] While she is not literally saying she is Christ, Smith's lack of self-knowledge and humility shines through in the comment. It is hard not to imagine that she sees herself as an object of worship or as a divinity, deigning to admire and observe all the "little people" as she shows them the light.

In other interviews, her statements seemed designed for maximum shock value.

Because I think if Jesus was around, if I was a groupie, I'd really like to get behind that guy, you know what I mean? That's why I think Mary Magdalene was so cool, she was like the first groupie. I mean she was really into Jesus and following him around and I wish she would've left a diary. It's too bad she repented because she could have left a really great diary. I mean all this stuff about Jesus, how wonderful he was, and how he's gonna save us. All I'd like to know is if he was a good lay.[24]

The tour for *Radio Ethiopia* continued in this vein, with Smith and the press pushing against each other. It was, apparently, a grueling schedule, so much so that Smith's good friend, Richard Sohl, quit the European tour, which certainly must have taken a toll on her. Complaining about Sohl's departure, Smith told the same London press conference, "Like, I don't know if you guys are aware of this but rock and roll is like very hard work. Like being on the road is like really [fucking] hard work. It's like worse than being in the army. You have to be an athlete. You have to be an army guy. And it's, like, really rigorous. And you know, like, the pain and the physical exhaustion of touring was too much for [Sohl], because he's a very sensitive guy."[25]

Back in the United States, Smith was banned from New York's WNEW, an alternative rock station, because of her belligerence during this period. The program's host, singer-songwriter Harry Chapin, had told Smith before an interview on November 29, 1976, not to use any profanity. Smith responded with a rant against the station, during which she used the word "fuck" or "the people's slang." "I want to know how alternative this radio is. The first thing that happens when I walk in is that you tell me you don't have a bleep machine and to watch what I say—that's no alternative, that's the same old stuff."[26]

Smith later wrote a manifesto about her experience, which was printed in the March–April 1977 issue of *Yipster Times:* "We believe in the total freedom of communication and we will not be compromised. The censorship of words is as meaningless as the censorship of musical notes; we cannot tolerate either. Freedom means exactly that: no limits, no boundaries...rock and roll is not a colonial power to be exploited, told what to say and how to say it. This is the spirit in which our music began and the flame in which it must be continued."[27]

In this increasingly combative and hyperbolic atmosphere, Smith literally took a dramatic tumble. On January 26, 1977, in Tampa, Florida, Smith played a show at the Curtis Hixen Hall, a sports arena that seated 6,000 people, opening for Bob Seger and the Silver Bullet Band, a pairing that made some aesthetic sense, given both performers' working-class roots, but in reality bridged two vastly different audiences. It was the largest arena she had played in up to that point.[28] The show reportedly was not going well, with an unresponsive audience. While the band was playing "Ain't It Strange" and Smith was doing her usual dance routine, she tripped over a sound monitor and fell off the stage, 15 feet to the ground. Her brother, Todd, who was heading her stage crew, tried to catch her but failed. Smith hit her head on some two-by-fours and then on the ground.[29]

Smith broke two vertebrae in her neck. It could have been much worse. "I'm so lucky. The doctors can't believe it! [And] I feel just like the Field Marshall, down in the line of duty. I know I'll be standin' soon, and in the meantime, just tell the troops to keep fightin'," Smith said shortly after the accident.[30] She romanticized the accident to the press:

I feel like I've done it. I've seen the Angel of Death, and wrestled with it. Maybe the other guys wrestled and lost and I won....it happened when I was spinning like a dervish—you've seen me do that—and just as I stopped spinning, I reached for the mike, and just went off the stage. It was the most amazing thing that's happened to me. I'm like the kind of performer that courts risk, I court death, but the way I kept it together was totally relaxed. I saw, like a spiral tunnel of light, and I felt my consciousness draining through it. I felt myself going and I said—GET BACK HERE! I gripped my consciousness by the throat....the biggest battle was in my head, and I won.[31]

A year later, the angel of death had mutated into God:

When I perform, I always opt for communication with God, and in pursuit of communicating with God, you can enter some very dangerous territory. I also have come to realize that total communication with God is physical death. The part of the song that I fell in was on "Ain't It Strange": "Go, go on, go like a dervish/Come on, God, make me move." I was opting for communication with my Creator, and it led me down the most nondisciplined path I've ever taken. Disintegrating and going into a black tube, that's what I felt like. I was losing consciousness, and then I was in a tunnel of light, a classic Jungian dreamspace. I felt like I was being pulled and it was not at all unpleasurable. But it was a leap out of this state of being, which I happen to be very fond of, so I made a conscious decision not to pursue that kind of communication while in performance.[32]

Others speculated she was simply drunk or high and lost her balance when the accident happened. But Smith has consistently denied that. The band had to play in front of Bob Seger's equipment, which left little room for Smith to move around and dance, which has always been a trademark of her performance. "Y'know, people said all kinds of things. They said I was totally stoned and fell off the stage, and all these things are, y'know, a total lie. It had nothing to do with that. If I, if I was in any special state, it was more of a, y'know, we would really drive ourselves to some kind of fever pitch or spiritual state in that particular song, and, as a band, we were in the top of our form."[33]

"It was an accident," Smith said 25 years later. "I wasn't drunk or fucked up, no matter what anyone says....It was an accident on a practical level, but on a spiritual level it was time for me to assess what I was doing and where I was going. Which I did. I was laid up for four or five months."[34]

Her injury was serious and caused blurred vision (her eyesight was permanently damaged),[35] and one doctor warned that she might not regain full use of her legs. After doctors gave her conflicting recommendations—one called for spinal surgery, another for extensive physical therapy—Smith chose the latter, more grueling treatment.[36] She also fractured her jaw and eventually lost two of her teeth from the fall.[37]

Such an accident would have been traumatic for anyone. But for a fledgling rock star obsessed with fallen rock idols, the injury must have given Smith pause to wonder whether she would soon be another rock 'n' roll casualty (comments about wrestling with and beating the angel of death, notwithstanding). For the time being, Smith was out of commission, which turned out to be a blessing for her. She spent much of the next year wearing a neck brace and in physical therapy, which was paid for by Sam Wagstaff, a friend of Mapplethorpe's.[38] She used the time off to collect herself and write.

"Probably it was the best thing that ever happened to me. I was in a period of constant motion and it forced me to stop. I was just moving, ya know, just going. I had no direction. My period of immobility gave me the time to reassess myself. I've reaccepted certain responsibilities. We really care about kids, we care about rock and roll, we care about the future and we work as hard as we can. We aren't always great, but our motivations are clear, and they've never altered."[39]

FIGHTING THE GOOD FIGHT

While recovering from the injury and the pitfalls of stardom, Smith's thoughts turned toward recovery and redemption, as she became more focused on what she wanted rock 'n' roll to be. Again, she sought inspiration from both God and art. She reread the New Testament and watched Pier Paolo Pasolini's film, *The Gospel According to St. Matthew,* which accentuated the Marxist and revolutionary aspects of Christ's life. She worked on her third book of poetry, *Babel* (with the assistance of Andi Ostrowe, who took dictation, an arrangement that was mocked in the music press), and her third album, appropriately titled *Easter.* The religious metaphors continued to run through her music.

As the music scene began to explode and burst with new energy, Smith yearned to be back in the game. "The following months of recovery and rehabilitation were a difficult time for the band. But we stuck it out together. In this period of I was able to resume my studies, reclaim my relationship with language.... It was in this period that the punk movement came to the forefront," Smith wrote in *Patti Smith Complete, 1975–2006,* and, returning to the battlefield metaphor, added, "It seemed to me that rock and roll was back on the streets, in the hands of the people. I trained, we regrouped and we joined them. And our bywords we gleaned from the scriptures, 'Fight the good fight.'"[40]

With a flare for myth making and a keen sense of when to be in the spotlight and when to bow out, Smith made a dramatic return to the stage of CBGB on Easter Sunday, 1977, playing a string of shows dubbed "Out of Traction/Back in Action" or "La Resurrection." The shows turned out to be not just a return to form, but therapy for Smith. "It's like a very ecstatic, mutual kind of vampirism that you have to have with the people. Sometimes, I need their energy, and especially after my injury, when I was first trying to learn how to be on the stage again, I was not only afraid, but my energy... I couldn't really move around so much," she told William S. Burroughs. "I hadn't been out of bed for a few months, and I was addicted to pills, or whatever, and had to be carried on to the stage.... I remember getting on the stage and I was thinking, 'This was crazy, to do this show. I can't even walk, I'll have to sit.' And I had them put a chair on the stage and I thought, 'Well, they won't mind if I sit on the chair.' Their energy, their psychic and spiritual, as well as physical energy, lifted me up."[41]

She credited the shows with her eventual recovery, and they inspired her to call her next album *Easter*.

> Everybody was a Christ figure that night...or at least Mary Magdalene, and there was just so much energy, and for the first minute....It was like being shot up by 500 people or something, it was so fantastic. We did this show and it was so great, I felt cured of something. 'Course I had to go right back to bed.... but it was like after that my...my recuperation. It was almost instantaneous. It was such a breakthrough and I was filled with so much energy and I got a lot of confidence that it got me up ten times faster. Doctors, nobody could believe it, they couldn't believe that I did it, and it was very symbolic to me. You know, Easter's a great time, so that's what [the record is] going to be called.[42]

The accident didn't appear to inhibit Smith's manic stage performances: "I thought I would be more conservative after my fall, but I think I'm crazier than ever. I have some fear, but it just doesn't outweigh my desire to be a maniac."[43]

Easter was released in March 1978. The album found her more confident and was generally well received. With Jimmy Iovine as producer, it sounded more polished and commercial, though it was a far stretch from being a sell-out, as some claimed. But the understated experiments were scrapped, and the listener could once again understand the words Smith was singing. It was straightforward rock 'n' roll, with a recognizable language—which meant you could sing along or tap your foot to it, without having to put much effort into it. Quoted on the album cover was "I have fought a good fight, I have finished my course" from the Second book of Timothy, suggesting Smith felt she had been through some divine trial and that saw her music as part of some ultimate battle of good against evil.

Easter opened with both combative and religious notes with "Till Victory," on which she begged God, "Do not seize me please, Till victory." The song also suggested, from God's point of view at least, and presumably also Smith's and that of anyone else who had been involved in the good fight, that the trials were over: "The nail. The grail. That's all behind thee." It was as though the time that Smith had dreamed about and was fighting for had finally arrived, and the world was being remade, with the people rising up to reclaim rock 'n' roll, the lost tongue.

The following song, "Space Monkey" (cowritten with Television's Tom Verlaine), is much more opaque. Is it about monkeys being blasted into space? Despite the title, its meaning is hazy. It begins by evoking images of madness and bloodshed on television news, but hope is on the way, in the form of a "space monkey" wandering up 9th Avenue, promising transcendence: "I'll never do dishes again." Is that what the good fight was all about, freedom from doing dishes? You could read this as a feminist rally against women's work or perhaps against the drudgery of any work, but it is such a small part of the song and probably was not all that carefully considered. The song also takes on elements of Revelations, with an antichrist coming to make sense of the anarchy, or perhaps Christ returning to shatter that peace and bring justice. The only clue to an interpretation comes when she drops the name of Pierre Clementi, "snot full of cocaine." The Italian actor had been arrested in 1977 on drug charges and began a hunger strike in jail. But pulling strands of meaning from the song is difficult. Overall, the song seems absurd, especially when the band starts making monkey noises toward the close. Fortunately, it has a nice melody and doesn't need to be taken all that seriously. Even the monkey noises start to sound catchy after a couple of listens. (Later live versions of the song were dedicated to Michael Stipe, who later became a good friend and who, with his band R.E.M., was legendary early in their career for his incoherent mumbling and obtuse lyrics.[44])

Much more straightforward was *Easter*'s hit single, "Because the Night," which was cowritten by Bruce Springsteen and climbed as high as number 13 on the Billboard charts, giving Smith her first taste of real rock stardom. Another darling of the American music press at the time, Springsteen had much in common with Smith: both grew up in working-class Jersey, and both were consciously searching for the heart of rock 'n' roll, for simplicity and authenticity. The two did not write the song together—Springsteen wrote the music and the song's title and passed it on to Smith, through Jimmy Iovine, telling her to do with it as she pleased.

Bruce wrote the music, and I always think of myself as the translator. He gave me the music, and it had some mumbling on it, and Bruce is a genius mumbler, like the sexiest mumbler I ever heard. I just listened to it, and the words just tumbled out of me. I wrote it alone, but it was a very direct thing. I got the tape, I immediately wrote the lyrics, he wrote the tag "Because the night belongs to lovers," which was in between the mumbling, he'd say that every once in a while. He said I didn't have to keep that bit, but I thought it was really nice—I always write the lyrics to my own songs, unless they're covers, but

I respected his lyrics, and I thought it was a very nice sentiment, so I built the rest of the lyrics, which are obviously mine, around his sentiment.[45]

Springsteen later recorded a version of the song—complete with Smith's lyrics—on his live album, *Live 1975–1985*. His version is more muscular (thanks to the beefy E-Street Band and the stadium where they performed it) and retains a sexual edge but lacks some of Smith's tenderness, the clichéd woman's touch, which was demonstrated in her single. But you can hear echoes of "Because the Night" in Springsteen's own "Candy's Room" and "Human Touch."

Others have reported that Smith wrote the lyrics while waiting for a phone call from her love interest at the time, Fred "Sonic" Smith, whom she would later marry.[46] The song is so evocative that it is easy to believe she had a real-life lover in mind when she penned it. She says she had good feelings about the song:

> I knew it was going to be a hit....Not because Bruce Springsteen wrote it, 'cos Bruce Springsteen hasn't written a hit lately. It's not that he churns hits out, it's not like Smokey Robinson or Holland-Dozier came to me with music that was formula hit music, it was just that it had something special. There was a certain heart and energy that I knew would make it a hit. And I was right— sometimes I go to horse races or greyhound races and I know a horse or a dog's going to come in. I knew this song was going to come in, and it was done by the band in that spirit—a very up, chemical, frontal, fast-action song.[47]

It's a great single, one of the greatest in rock history, and it gave you a taste for what Smith was capable of, given the right material. It begins with Bruce Brody (Sohl's replacement) playing a soft serenade on piano. Smith sings, "Take me now baby, here as I am/Pull me close try and understand." Her voice is sexy, a pleading lover's whisper in the middle of the night. The song is soon punctuated by the band joining in. Daugherty's drums thump the tune along, giving it urgency and rhythm. It's a great tune, because it is filled with the desperation that is at the heart of lust. This comes mostly from Smith's sensual yet powerful delivery; wanting her man badly, she moans, "Take me now." The song is very much an urban love song, defined as much by what is outside those bedroom walls as by what is happening inside them. Thematically, it is a whiter, raunchier (and sexier) version of the Drifters' "Up on the Roof" (which was written by another female maverick, Carole King). The implied forces that are caving in on the couple are what give the song power. The world is out there, the hard mean streets, the grind of the rat race, the pressures to survive doing backbreaking work. The world churns on, but not tonight—in my arms, dear, you're safe—until that alarm clock rings and you've got to be back at work. The song drew added punch from Smith's explicit sexual desires: she wants to be commanded and domi- nated by her lover and you can hear that in her delivery—something the more tepid cover version by Natalie Merchant never came close to. Smith is a tough rock 'n' roll chick bursting with sex and desire who uses all her ragged edginess to full effect. The song fits in the album because it is also a tribute to sacred places—the home, the bed of lovers, a refuge, a place not to be disturbed, places to be defended, places where people are reborn and rejuvenated.

The next song on the album dives further into sacred territory, aiming for a tribal feel with the prayerlike "Ghost Dance." On *Easter*'s liner notes, she explains that it was inspired by Native American dances that evoked the spirits that had passed: "the beauty of the dance was the call to convene. communication w/past and future through the sounds and rhythms of the present."[48] This is, of course, at the heart of what Smith was aiming for with her music, trying to connect to the spirits not just of rock 'n' roll's past but of art's: Hendrix, Morrison, Rimbaud, Kerouac, Picasso, and others. She aimed to find a way to continue the tradition and imbue future generations with her heroes' values and talents. The song's refrain is "We shall live again."

"We Three" is a mournful song about a lover's triangle, being wanted by someone when you want another. "You say you want me/I want another." Smith gives us both sides of desire at once, unrequited love and the spurned lover. It's depressing and you don't quite know whom to root for.

Another of Smith's torch songs is "25th Floor," written for her new lover, Fred Smith. The song is about wandering around the top of a building in Detroit, making out in the men's room, and generally getting lost. But within this love song is an ode to rock and humanity's hopeless pursuit of transforming waste. The end drifts off into a long meditation about playing guitar, the aptly titled "High on Rebellion," which also could be read as about sex: "What I feel when I'm playing guitar is completely cold and crazy...." Smith rambles on in her meditation about riding the wave of notes, and it's one of the most successful and evocative freeform rock-poetry songs she's created, no doubt in part because it was inspired by love. But it's not just a love song about Smith, it's a love song to rock 'n' roll and to the guitar noise Fred Smith was so brilliant at creating.

The album closes with the title track, which, although technically a tribute to rebirth, is a mournful lament, yet one imbued with hope. The pain and death that lead to the rebirth are obviously present: "the thorn the veil the face of grace." But the song celebrates the death that leads to the rebirth, embracing the fall for what comes afterward. It is nostalgic, but in a twisted way that remembers a long-ago funeral with fondness (and who is to say funerals cannot be remembered with fondness?). The song and album clash to a close with church bells.

Left off the original LP but included on a CD reissue was "godspeed," which had Smith singing in a frenzy. In this song, she is much more successful at her improvisational rants than in the ones she included on her records—suggesting she is not, perhaps, the best judge of her own material.

Easter was generally praised by many critics as return to form after the disappointing *Radio Ethiopia*. Nick Tosches called her the "the greatest broad poet that ever was" in *Creem* magazine.[49] In *Rolling Stone*, Dave Marsh wrote, "*Easter* makes good on Patti Smith's biggest boast—that she is one of the great figures of Seventies rock & roll.... More importantly perhaps, it focuses her mystical and musical visions in a way that makes her the most profoundly religious American popular performer since Jim Morrison."[50]

But even the favorable reviews noted that there were problems. Inspired much more by ego than love was the album's most controversial song, a landmine buried in the middle of an otherwise great rock album.

CARELESS WORDS

White Reflections on the Word *Nigger*

- In Lenny Bruce's famous routine on the word *nigger*—dramatically reenacted in Julian Barry's *Lenny*, the movie version of which starred Dustin Hoffman (which is where I first heard of Bruce and which I refer to here because it is how Bruce's sentiment lives on in pop culture)—the comedian began by asking whether there were any niggers in the audience and then pointing them out. After gratuitously throwing the word about—usually by singling out the African Americans in the audience, increasing the tension as much as possible—Bruce would then make his point: "Dig: if President Kennedy would just go on television, and say, 'I would like to introduce you to all the niggers in my cabinet,' and if he'd just say 'nigger nigger nigger nigger nigger' to every nigger he saw, 'boogie boogie boogie boogie boogie,' 'nigger nigger nigger nigger nigger' 'til nigger didn't mean anything anymore, then you could never make some 6-year-old black kid cry because somebody called him a nigger at school."

- It's summer. I'm maybe 12 or 13 years old, sitting at dinner with my family in Erie, Pennsylvania. The windows are open, letting a cool breeze through the screens. My dad, revived after work by a couple of manhattans, is telling a story and uses the word nigger. A protest or two from his kids, raised in a more polite world, prompts a mild lecture from him on how the world is. "There is a difference between 'niggers' and 'black people,'" he said. The hardworking family who lived down the block—and whose son was my friend—were black people, my dad explained. Niggers were something else, but his exact definition escapes me now.

- During the OJ Simpson trial in 1995, the word nigger suddenly found itself prominently on the front page of newspapers, as one of the police investigators was alleged to have used it—which, if true, would bias his testimony and investigation against Simpson. But many newspapers of the day squirmed about whether to use the epithet. Some, like a midsized daily where a friend of mine worked, substituted *N-word* for nigger in print. Several reporters protested this softening of it, the African Americans among them leading the charge. "Apart from the fact that 'N-word' looks unbelievably stupid in a headline, we felt that not using the actual word ended up protecting the person alleged to have said it (Mark Furman, in that case), because it wasn't really forcing people to confront the full force of what he said," my friend said. The paper's managing editor heard the reporters' concerns, but "he didn't want readers to have to sit down to breakfast in the morning and be confronted by that word. He thought it would upset them, and he didn't want to upset them....The paper printed 'N-word' in every story. But at least we got an honest answer about what was being protected: We were trying to keep readers, in some small way, from having to deal with the real world."

Smith has always declared herself free to do whatever she pleases within the realm of her art, which includes using words like nigger. While that's a fair approach to take as an artist, it has sometimes produced ridiculous results. The most controversial song of Smith's career is "Rock n Roll Nigger"—although "controversy" might be too strong an adjective, given that she was generally mocked for her choice of words and sentiment rather than attacked as a racist.

The song does rock, and "nigger" has a rhythmic ring to it as a chant. On the album, the song is preceded by "Babelogue," a fierce minute-and-a-half spoken-word piece that works as an introduction and artist's statement. Audience clapping—it's unclear whether it has been dubbed in or whether the track was recorded live—provides an intense, uneven beat that Smith plays off of. Her delivery shows just how masterful of a performer she has become—the way she accentuates lines by chuckling or stuttering, using the rhythm of the piece and moment to full advantage. "I seek pleasure," she declares. The piece builds, joined by a steady drumbeat, and as Smith yells, "I have not sold myself to God," the band erupts into "Rock n Roll Nigger."

The song is an ode to being "outside society," which, in Smith's romantic notions of outlaw artistry, is the highest place to be. She declares herself a "nigger," a notion that is clearly romantic and noble to her. Then she lists other so-called niggers: Jimi Hendrix, Jesus Christ, Jackson Pollock, and grandma (perhaps in case there was any question of why she used the word or maybe because it fit the melody or maybe she ran out of people to bestow the title on). "Outside society they're waiting for me."

It is easy to get swept away by this audacious rock anthem. Some of the best rock 'n' roll is a hammer smacking you on the head, making little sense. On *Easter*'s liner notes, Smith wrote that the word must be redefined—"any man who extends beyond the classic form is a nigger." But when you start to think about what she's really saying in "Rock n Roll Nigger," the song falls apart. It doesn't hold up to scrutiny the way great art does. You feel a little stupid for buying into such a simplistic, dopey notion—and that's what it is.

Smith's intentions might start off admirably enough. Ostensibly, she's sticking up for those who have been kicked around by history because of their skin color, yet from another perspective were the coolest ones of all, victims who created brilliant art despite being oppressed, art that continues to inspire, and who generally pushed society along a path to bettering itself. She is also engaging in some Lenny Bruce-style redefining of ugly words, trying to strip them of their negative connotations. In other words, she wants to turn an insult into a badge of honor, but an honor that anyone can earn. In her world, a nigger isn't someone who is black—it refers to someone who is a renegade, doing what they see fit, despite society's rules. Unfortunately, many people who tried living in American society were murdered, enslaved, or otherwise destroyed because of the color of their skin. Many black people weren't rebels but were law-abiding people who acquiesced but still died as niggers at the hands of cruel men. Smith dreams of joining the ranks of "niggers...outside of society," but were she to get her wish, she would find no freedom waiting for her. Nigger doesn't mean someone who lives outside of society. Instead, niggers were people enslaved and imprisoned by society. Society stripped them of their humanity. Nigger was a construct and creation of society—one of the ugliest things society was capable of: systematic and organized repression.

Smith has divorced herself from the true meaning of these words—who used them, who they applied to, the violent power the word gave some people over others. It is irresponsible for a white person to do that, given how much white America (which includes Smith) profited from slavery and racism. It is upsetting to see someone for whom words—and history—are so important savage their meanings and neglect that history. Her use of the term is especially galling, when you consider her critique of Native American culture as racist (on *Easter*'s liner-note explanation of "Ghost Dance") for excluding non–Native American souls from their spiritual rituals. "The failure of the dance was its racial aspect," she wrote. "No souls—living or transcending—were welcome if not American Indian."

Early in her career, Smith was fond of using offensive words, tossing them around not just to get a rise but also to collect a bit of contrarian cool. In early interviews, Smith often floated the word nigger around, defending it as justifiable slang. "If I wanna say pussy, I'll say pussy. If I wanna say nigger, I'll say nigger. If somebody wants to call me a cracker bitch, that's cool. It's all part of being American. But all these tight-assed movements are fucking up our slang, and that eats it."[51] But some of the people "fucking up" her slang were people who had suffered from the violence of that slang.

On the liner notes for *Radio Ethiopia*, she called Satan the "first absolute artist—the first true nigger." She also used the word in a 1974 review of a Velvet Underground live recording. The review is mostly incomprehensible. She drops the names of her heroes and experiments with language, explaining the music surrealistically but doing little to enlighten the reader as to what is happening in the music. It reflected the style of the times, a bad imitation of masters like Lester Bangs and Richard Meltzer. But this line in particular jumps out: "And I love the way Lou talks like a warm nigger or slow bastard from Philly that THING that reeks of old records like golden oldies."[52] I have no idea what a "warm nigger" is supposed to be—friendly, hot, Southern? As an adjective, it sounds like parody. She seems to use the word as a way of claiming some renegade cool, which is as distasteful a use of it as any. Despite her patronizing use of the word, it is clearly meant as a compliment. She frequently called her idol, Mick Jagger, a nigger. (At least at first, Jagger did not return Smith's admiration—however oddly expressed—and famously dissed her in an interview: "I think she's so awful.... She's full of rubbish, she's full of words and crap. I mean, she's a poseur of the worst kind, intellectual bullshit, trying to be a street girl when she doesn't seem to me to be one, I mean, everything.... A useless guitar player, a bad singer, not attractive.... I was always very attractive, much better singer, much better with words, and I wasn't an intellectual poseur. She's got her heart in the right place but she's such a POSER! She's not really together musically, she's...all right."[53])

In concert, Smith has declared herself a nigger too.[54] In an exchange with a reporter captured by *Rolling Stone* magazine, Smith said,

> Ya think black people are better than white people or sumpthin'? I was raised with black people. It's like, I can walk down the street and say to a kid, "Hey nigger." I don't have any kind of super-respect or fear of that kind of stuff. When I say statements like that, they're not supposed to be analyzed, because they're more like off-the-cuff humorous statements. I do have a sense of humor, ya know, which is sumpthin' that most people completely wash over when they deal with me. I never read anything where anybody talked about my sense of humor. It's like, a lot of the stuff I say is true, but it's supposed to be funny.[55]

But her excuse of humor is a hard sell, given how ferociously she attempted to wield her power through language.

Ultimately, any well-meaning attempt by white people to redefine nigger is doomed to fail. When white people, after using the word for centuries to dehumanize and belittle people of color, ease their guilty conscience, and justify their exploitation, suddenly declare with smug righteousness that the word now has a positive meaning, it remains dehumanizing and patronizing. A few years later, African American hip-hop artists would begin redefining the term in pop culture, giving it new nuances of meaning (both negative and positive), tossing the word back on itself. Unlike Smith, though, they could claim ownership of it without having to apologize for or acknowledge its violent legacy because they were victims of it, not perpetrators or benefactors.

Critics at the time roundly dismissed "Rock n Roll Nigger" in generally favorable reviews of the album. Lester Bangs mocked Smith, not for being racist, but for her arrogance:

She's got this song on her new album *Easter* (talk about justice! I could even accept that Jesus was a woman, but from New Jersey?), called "Rock 'n' Roll Nigger," wherein her and co-conspirator/cabalist Lenny Kaye (who used to be a real fun guy) go on about living "outside of society" (On Fifth Ave., to be precise), and cite "Jackson Pollock was a nigger, Jimi Hendrix was a nigger," etc. Well, guess I'll have to admit it: I am not a nigger. I'm a pawn of the imperialist power structure, which I guess puts me more in the line of sucker.[56]

Nick Tosches wrote that "the concept of artist as nigger is silly and trite,"[57] while Dave Marsh stated, "Though Smith's contention that Jackson Pollock was a 'nigger' (presumably in his dealings with wealthy art patrons) is amusing, her attempt to make the word respectable is foredoomed. 'Rock n Roll Nigger' is an unpalatable chant because Smith doesn't understand the word's connotation, which is not outlawry but a particularly vicious kind of subjugation and humiliation that's antithetical to her motive."[58]

In a 1978 essay for the *Village Voice* about racism and violent neo-Nazi sentiments in punk rock, which had cachet, Lester Bangs wrote,

Lenny Bruce was wrong—maybe in a better world than this such parlor games would amount to cleansing jet offtakes, and between good friends, where a certain bond of mutual trust has been firmly established, good natured racial tradeoffs can be part of the vocabulary of understood affections. But beyond that trouble begins—when you fail to realize that no matter how harmless your intentions are, there is no reason to think that any shit that comes out of your mouth is going to be understood or happily received. Took me a long time to find it out, but those words are *lethal,* man, and you shouldn't just go slinging them around for effect.[59]

Smith never seems to have grasped that her words could cause real violence, perhaps because she has always had the advantage of singing to the choir: her audience was mostly liberal and far more likely to cut her slack. Her insistence on artistic freedom comes at the expense of compassion, and she seems to have turned a blind eye to how her own words could wound or inflict pain—how art itself can be violent. It's disheartening to see someone who is clearly on the side of those who have suffered and who has spoken out so eloquently against George W. Bush's arrogant violence be so obstinate in recognizing her own arrogant missteps.

During her induction into the Rock and Roll Hall of Fame in 2007, Smith chose to play the song, perhaps as an attempt to retain some outsider status on a night when she was being accepted into the canon. In *Patti Smith Complete*, Smith writes about the controversial song, saying, "The redefining of an archaic slang term as a badge for those contributing on the fringe of society was not favorably embraced."[60] She's either stubborn or willfully ignorant: nigger was neither archaic nor mere slang in 1978 (or, for that matter, 2007) but a potent, living word that carried a heavy weight depending on who was speaking and who was listening and how it was used. Why should anyone embrace her dumb song? Equally distasteful is her view of herself as a martyr because of the song—"We took our hit and our 'Rock n Roll Nigger' stance on the road.... I packed my suitcase with my *Horses* jacket, the New Testament, and a tattered copy of *A Season in Hell*"[61]—as though she was under assault for fighting the good, sacred fight and presumed that Christ and Rimbaud would be on her side. Nobody was assaulting her (indeed, she profited from the album and went on singing the song, relishing her renegade status all the more): they just thought her song was stupid and so do I—which is all part of being an American.

Get Thee Gone

As with most rock stars—especially female ones—much has been written about whom Patti Smith was sleeping with. At times in her life, she had been lovers with Robert Mapplethorpe, Sam Shepard, Tom Verlaine, Todd Rundgren, and Allen Lanier (the unauthorized biography by Victor Bockris and Roberta Bayley dishes the salacious details on each of those relationships—a tack that can be annoying to readers sympathetic to Smith but, nevertheless, keeps them turning the pages). In 1976, a new love, Fred "Sonic" Smith, entered her life who would soon greatly affect her, inspiring her art and then a much publicized retreat from the public eye.

Born in 1949, Fred Smith had been a member of the seminal Detroit rock band MC5 (most famous for their proto-punk rave up "Kick Out the Jams" and their relationship with political provocateur John Sinclair) and later went on to form the equally influential (despite having released only one single) Sonic's Rendevouz Band, from which the more famous Sonic Youth took its name.

Smith met Fred in Detroit at a party hosted by her record company, Arista, at a small hotdog joint on March 6, 1976.[1] The chemistry between them was apparently instant. Lenny Kaye introduced the two. A dapper dresser, Fred was standing in front of a white elevator wearing a navy blue coat, the contrast adding to his attractiveness.[2] (In another account, they met in front of a white radiator[3], and in yet another, a white wall[4]—what is clear is that Fred Smith stood out from his surroundings and he was a sharp dresser.) "The communication was instantaneous," Smith said some 30 years later. "It was more than that: It was mystical, really, something I never forgot. But I didn't see him again for almost a year."[5]

Fred Smith joined Smith's band onstage that night, and she said, "I could tell by the way he played what kind of person he was—better than me, stronger than me."[6] It's easy to see why Smith—who was always drawn to the cool, strong, masculine rock stars—fell for Fred Smith. He was cool, tough, smart, and well read.

The night of their meeting found its way into Smith's *Easter,* on "25th Floor," the floor that the two partied on that night, and on "godspeed," an unreleased track from the sessions, when Smith sings, "Walking in your blue coat weeping admiral" (but the white wall/radiator/elevator doesn't make it into the song).

As her relationship with Fred Smith progressed, Smith moved to Detroit to be with him, which separated her from her band and friends.[7] Although she was working on material for a new album, it became clear that the band's days were numbered and her life was somewhere new. She confessed in an interview with William S. Burroughs that the move was difficult but that she also was excited about it. "To leave New York was a very tough thing. But I did it with great joy, too—you know, like a pioneer. It's like you have to 'Go West!' I've always been a very East Coast girl. I was raised in South Jersey—Philly, Camden, all the coolest cities. Actually, though, when I was a teenager I thought that the coolest city wasn't New York, it was Detroit—because I was from the Motown, and stuff."[8]

She also told Burroughs she had found the love of her life: "I have met the person in my life that I've been waiting to meet since I was a little girl. I feel that I have met that person. I always believed that I would meet that person. It was my greatest dream, to meet the person who I recognized as my person. And it came late in my life, I mean later than I thought. I thought it would be the person I met when I was sixteen, you know."[9]

On the resulting album, her fourth, *Wave,* Smith expanded her palette once again. The religious references and calls for rock 'n' roll rebirth remained, but this time she consciously showed a more feminine side of herself. But there are also meditations on America and democracy, as Smith came to grips with being an American and the responsibilities that entailed. The album brought Richard Sohl back on keyboards, and his playing is strong throughout.

The cover showed her dressed in white and holding two doves—her trademark stringy black hair the same, but swapping her bad-boy image for something more akin to hippie femininity. She quoted Rilke on the cover: "For one human being to love another: that is perhaps the most difficult of all our tasks; the ultimate, the last test and proof, the work for which all other work is but preparation." The album suggested a transition to a new phase in her life, which indeed it was. Just in case there was any doubt as to who the love interest might be, Smith dedicated the record "to my clarinet teacher Fred Sonic Smith."

Produced by Todd Rundgren, *Wave* has a much more polished sound than her previous albums and begins with three pop gems in a row. It is one of her most accessible albums and infectious from the start. It kicks off with a great song, "Frederick," written for her new love. It begins with a "hi hello" that has Smith sounding as innocent as she has ever sounded. It's a long-distance love song that takes the form of a bedtime prayer, perhaps a late-night phone call before sleep, beseeching the one who is in her heart over the miles. But she prays to her lover, not God, declaring, "Frederick, you're the one." In Fred Smith, she saw her dreams being realized and herself becoming complete—God realized through a union, which is how marriage is considered in most religions.

The second song on the album was a favorite among her fans and one of the best she has ever recorded—"Dancing Barefoot." In it, she switches back and forth from first to third person, a narrative device Dylan used in "Tangled Up in Blue." It is simultaneously a declaration of independence and a celebration of submission to a lover or God. She feels confident and drawn to act but isn't sure what, specifically, she is responding to; she is compelled to surrender completely. The song ends with an ode to childbirth and the circle of life. But there are also allusions to Christianity, the Virgin Mary, which is followed up with "Oh, God, I fell for you." In Smith's mind, love, lust, and God are all entwined, and each points to the other. On the liner notes, Smith dedicates the song to Jeanne Hébuterne, an artist who was the mistress and model for Amedeo Modigliani. After her lover died in 1920, Hébuterne committed suicide, jumping from a window of her family's fifth-floor apartment. She was pregnant with the couple's second child at the time. As someone who had once wanted to be an artist's muse and mistress, it is easy to see why Hébuterne's story attracted Smith. In a way, the model-mistress completely surrenders her identity to the artists, but there can an attraction in such submission and, if your artist-lover is talented enough, as was Modigliania, a certain kind of immortality.

The third song on the album is a cover of the Byrds' "So You Want to Be (a Rock and Roll Star)." The original is a bittersweet paean to rock stardom, or rather the fantasy of rock stardom. In Roger McGuinn's version, the song ends with the would-be stars getting torn apart by chicks and struggling with their sanity because of the riches and fame (despite the Byrds' warning about the "vicious game," they still make rock 'n' roll—both as a song and a goal—sound quite attractive).

Smith wrote on the liner notes to *Wave* that when she first heard the song, although it "filled [her] with a vague sense of future memory," she really didn't like it. "It seemed to say that in this field of honor, sooner or later, everybody gets hurts and I just didn't believe it." Her recording of it suggests that, finally a star herself, she did believe it. It is also interesting that she calls rock 'n' roll stardom a "field of honor," as honor is not generally associated with rock stars.

The song is an appropriate choice, given Smith's desire to return the music to "the people." She wanted to inspire other kids to action, pushing them to create and take back the culture. To drive the point home, she adds her own lines: "Hey you, come here, get up, ah, this is the era where everybody creates." If you want to be alive, you need to partake. Passive consumption is a dead end. The song's bitter warnings make it a perfect punk anthem as well: there's a cynicism that doesn't trust the institution of stardom, and the only antidote is for everyone to become a star, destroying the institution.

"Hymn," in turn, is about being comforted in the dark, lonely night, although it is unclear what the source of comfort is, a lover, the Spirit of God, or art. Ultimately, that's unimportant. The song is a tribute to being comforted and "filled up."

"Revenge" is a song about regaining power over a lover who hurt you. But as a song, it is an unsatisfactory comeuppance: it's no "Time Is on My Side" or "Don't Think Twice, It's All Right." Perhaps it's unfair to measure Smith's songs against those classics, but the songs themselves appeal to common experience and shared language—most know or can imagine a jilted lover's wrath—and so the song fails or succeeds on those terms. She fails in "Revenge" because she appeals to shared experience rather than trying to recreate her own experiences, a task that she is capable of elsewhere (as on "Frederick" or "Because the Night"). There's simply no emotional payoff, because Smith doesn't do a very good job creating a world within her music. The music on "Revenge" doesn't help—it's listless and droning so that you just want the thing to end almost as soon as it has begun. After the album's first three songs, it's a letdown.

But "Citizen Ship," a song written about and with guitarist Ivan Kral, picks up the tempo again. Kral grew up behind the Iron Curtain in Prague, Czechoslovakia, where playing rock 'n' roll was literally a subversive political act. He had a band there called Soot.[10] When Kral's father denounced the Russian invasion of Czechoslovakia in the spring of 1968, the 17-year-old Kral found asylum in the United States.[11] He became one of Smith's main songwriting collaborators throughout her career.

"Citizen Ship" is a tribute to Kral's earlier life. It opens with an image from the Prague Spring, with children throwing rocks at invading Soviet tanks. Parallels are drawn to the Chicago and Los Angeles riots of the 1960s, but mostly the song is about the search for a home and place to be a citizen—and how much those things establish identity—especially sans passport. "Lady liberty lend a hand to me I've been cast adrift," Smith sings. As the song progresses, Smith yells out Kral's name, in order to firmly establish his identity, then repeats the slogan scrawled on the Statue of Liberty. Oddly enough, the song ends with the dismissive "Ahh, it's all mythology."

"Seven Ways of Going" is a speculative prayer about choice and which direction Smith should choose: "Seven...seven ways of serving Thee." She thanks the Lord for waking her up and then giving her purpose, but adds an eighth possibility: "seeking love without exception," an apparent break from all the ways that God has shown her.

"Broken Flag" is dedicated to Barbara Frietchie, a U.S. patriot most notable for taking a stand against the Rebel army during the Civil War. When Stonewall Jackson's troops were marching through her town of Frederick, Maryland, Frietchie—then 95 years old—is said to have waved a Union flag outside her window. Her act was mythologized in art. John Greenleaf Whittier wrote a poem for her in 1864, in which he described Jackson being touched by the old lady's defiance: "The nobler nature within him stirred/ To life at that woman's deed and word;/'Who touches a hair of yon gray head/Dies like a dog! March on!' he said." Her life was later fictionalized in a play by Clyde Fitch, called *Barbara Frietchie, The Frederick Girl.*

Smith's "Broken Flag" is hymnlike. The organs make it sound like church music. But it is no anthem. Patriotism is found in the small defiant acts done in service of an ideal, not in some mob. Patriotism is standing up to the mob, as Frietchie did, going against your culture or an invading army, on principle. In Smith's song, there is a continual reference to Algiers—"we're still marching for Algiers"—where another civil war had been raging for years, but there are no obvious connections between the two conflicts in this song.

But Frietchie's allure for Smith is understandable, because Frietchie is a prototypical Smith hero. Rather than mythologize the collective will or ideals, Smith's patriotism centers on the individual who takes a bold stand against a country, society, or government gone wrong—which makes the collective will and values stronger. A culture or society draws its strength from its rebels and provocateurs. But Smith's song is not just a tribute to those who stand up against tyranny and for ideals but is also about how fragile a society can become when it ignores its artists.

Wave ends with the album's title track, a weird but tender portrait of an obsessive fan's vulnerability. In it, we get one side of a random conversation between two people—the narrator is a woman desperate for some connection with a person she's been seeing around and whom she believes she knows. But this is their first conversation. The person she is talking to is presumably a star (or some other human deity—included on the album cover is a picture of Pope John Paul I wearing a malevolent grin and waving), who was waving from his balcony at several fans, including the singer, who found a personal connection in the wave: "it's not that you were just waving to me, but that we were we were waving to each other." For someone who spent so much of her life trying to connect with her idols and then suddenly found herself an overwhelmed idol, it's a provocative song. For if anyone understood the fan-star dynamic, it was Patti Smith. Smith later said that in the song she imagined running into the pope walking down the beach.[12] But the object of the adoration is ultimately unimportant—it could be anyone—for this is a song about a fan's obsessions.

It's the desperate craving of a fan wanting so badly to connect with one of her heroes, and it's painful to listen to, because you can hear the insanity and desperation of the woman. Smith doesn't judge. She understands that even though these encounters may seem one sided, both parties feed off of them and connections can be made, desire and revolution sparked. However fragile the desperate fan might seem, the connections she seeks are real and the potential is great. Of course, that desire to connect can be terrifying if the subject of it is unwilling.

Recorded for the session but not released until the CD remaster in 1996 was "Fire of Unknown Origin," which is a fan's lament to her fallen idol. It's supposedly a tribute to Jim Morrison, but in the song, he becomes feminine: "Swallowed her up like the ocean in a fire thick and gray." But she realizes that "there must be something that remains."

Critical reception of the album was again mixed. On the whole, critics were sympathetic to her music and her mission but annoyed by her myth making. In a generally positive review of the album in *Melody Maker,* Simon Frith theorized about where Smith went wrong:

> Patti Smith's problem is that what was touching in a rock fan is obnoxious in a rock star. Her desperate faith in the cleansing spiritual power of rock 'n' roll was inspiring as long as she was on the outside.... Unfortunately, inevitably, once Patti had made it—long term contract, rave reviews—she became, given her belief in rock stars as shamans, her own myth. Her music became self-indulgent, bombastic, arrogant.... *Wave,* thank the Lord (the Pope features here, rather than Haile Selassie), restores to the Patti Smith Group some sense of perspective. This is because Patti herself is in love and subordinates her spiritual and bohemian conceits to a new account of her muse.[13]

In other words, falling in love seems to have grounded Smith and made it possible for her to relate to real people once again. But, as Tom Carson noted in *Rolling Stone,* her self-mythologizing remained problematic.

> Patti Smith possesses some qualities that are fast disappearing from most American rock 'n' roll: passion, flamboyance, a sense of the epic, a belief in the music itself as a revolutionary force. As a moony high priestess of art, forever building altars to herself, she's a bore—as pretentious as a college sophomore who's just discovered decadence, as ingenuously egotistic as a spoiled 5-year-old. But as a demagogic purveyor of barbed, gutbucket rock 'n' roll, she ranks above most performers today. At her best, she makes rock seem dangerous again.... Success has encouraged all of this artist's worst vices—her self-indulgence and overweening preciousness—and the new record tries to have it both ways: to retain her big, newfound audience, while allowing her taste for arch, artsy self-glorification and highfalutin' poetic nonsense full reign.[14]

In fact, Smith was increasingly becoming overwhelmed by the demands and meaning her fans were imposing on her. So her love was an understandable elixir. The tour supporting *Wave* was particularly grueling, with its final stop in Florence, Italy, a tumultuous event that sealed her retirement. The band was greeted at the airport by a mob of fans and a press corps. "I thought somebody really cool must be there. I had no idea that they were there for me. There were thousands of people camping all over the streets."[15] She found herself mobbed by fans everywhere in the city and hid out in a hotel drinking espresso.[16]

The band played at a soccer stadium before 70,000 people on September 10, 1979 (another account lists it as 80,000[17]), and as the concert drew to a close, with the band's usual encore of "My Generation," audience members stormed the stage. Smith wrote in *Patti Smith Complete* that she felt the band had come full circle in its purpose. "We did our work. We finished our course. It was our last 'My Generation.'" "I remembered the first time we performed it in Cleveland, Ohio, crying out, 'We created it, let's take it over!' I solicited them to do the same." The crowd took her up on it. "The cries through my microphone and the discordant music was their own. I turned all the amps up to ten, saluted my brother, and said goodbye." In an interview, she said, "It was anarchistic, but it wasn't destructive. We gave them our instruments. They yelled in the microphones."[18] Feeling that she had inspired a new generation, Smith decided she wasn't needed anymore. At the hotel room after the show, she told the band she had had enough. [19]

Smith later told an interviewer that she no longer felt direction in her work. "I felt that I didn't know where my work was going. I was in Italy and people were expecting me to help them with their charities, with their revolutions. I thought, If I'm going to be a leader, where am I leading people to?"[20]

"I...felt that as a band we had accomplished our mission," she told the *New York Times* years later. "I had said everything that I could say at that point. We did what we set out to do. There was a new guard; rock and roll wasn't going to die. I felt like it was a discreet time to leave. I never regretted that, ever, not for a moment."[21]

But, at its heart, the decision was a personal one. "Basically, I had fallen in love with Fred and I didn't like being parted from him. When I had the band and we started performing, I really gave everything to it. I gave my time, my energy, my love. But my feelings for Fred were so strong that when I was on tour and away from him it didn't mean anything, and I felt extremely false being on stage."[22] In a 2007 interview, she reiterated this sentiment:

> I stopped everything because I loved my husband, and he wanted a family. We changed our life, lived a really simple life, and that was my priority. I was still an artist. I still studied and drew and wrote; it's just that the public didn't know about it. And I think that's another thing that people have to be aware of: this whole culture of celebrity. It's an unhealthy thing in a way, because it makes people think "if the public doesn't see you in a magazine, you don't exist." That's total bullshit. That's total consumerism. You have to feel good about yourself. You have to know who you are. The magazines can't tell you who you are.[23]

There's truth in that sentiment, but also a hint that she missed being the spotlight and resented that it had moved on from her.

In her last interview before quitting the business—a conversation with William S. Burroughs—Smith confessed that the music business had turned out to be different than she expected and that she was worn out. "I'm very exhausted, because I've just spent two months in almost a psychic kind of war, between myself and the people who are helping to perpetuate my records. And I actually have respect for these people, even though I fight them. A lot of people would call me naive because I respect these people that I have to fight, but I still respect the fact that these people are my investors. But they try to get aesthetically involved with what I do, and it holds up my work."[24]

Smith also told Burroughs that she felt she had achieved what she had set out to do. "Our credo was, 'Wake up!'...I wanted to be like Paul Revere. That was my whole thing I wanted to be like Paul Revere. I didn't want to be a giant big hero, I didn't want to die for the cause. I didn't want to be a martyr. All that I wanted was for the people to fuckin' wake up. That's all I wanted them to do, and I feel that that's what happened." Burroughs then asked her if she thought she'd helped inspire the punk generation's anti-heroes, but Smith refused to take credit: "I don't agree with these kids. I believe in heroes. See, I love these kids, but I think that I've spawned a lot of little monsters, though, sometimes. Because I don't feel the same way they do. I don't think it's cool to shoot yourself up with heroin at 21 years old and die."[25]

Of the things that Patti Smith has added to the rock star model, this is one of the most unique: how to bow out gracefully and survive success. She had spent much of her life worshipping brilliant, self-destructive artists, but she was too smart to fall into the same trap. "There's a way to find balance, to sometimes go overboard or sometimes experiment without ruining your life," she said in 2007. "That's important in everything we do, whether it's using a cell phone, smoking pot, staying out all night. You have to find balance. You have to not be a slave to this stuff. You have to be the master of everything."[26]

After quitting the music scene, Smith retreated to Detroit and settled down with Fred. The couple was married on March 1, 1980, in a private ceremony. At first, they lived in Book Cadillac Hotel before buying a home in Detroit's working-class neighborhood of Lake St. Clair in 1982.[27] As she disappeared from public view, rumors began spreading that her marriage with Fred was less than ideal—that Fred abused her and was controlling.[28] Smith has always denied this, and, barring any evidence to the contrary, her word will remain the last on the subject. Any speculation here would be pointless and insulting. For whatever Smith's life was like in Detroit, it was one that she chose.

"In 1979, when I moved to Detroit to live with Fred, my life changed drastically....We had children. We had house. We faced financial struggles. We lived very simply. We did everything ourselves, whether it was clearing out

little piece of land or—because we lived on a canal that often flooded—
sandbagging in the middle of the night. I had to wash diapers and clean
toilet bowls and nurse sick children and find time to do art."[29]

The rumors circulated perhaps in part because Smith had come to mean so
much to so many people and they did not let go of her easily. Years later in
2002, Smith told the *New Yorker* that her fans had mistaken her persona and
myth for reality—that she wasn't quite the radical she appeared in her music.
"I had brief periods of youthful experimentation and frivolity and promiscu-
ity. But I wasn't a sixties person. I didn't want free love and free drugs. In
my work, I've raped, murdered, ingested drugs that never existed. But in my
life I've been pretty straitlaced on the whole."[30] In other words, she did not
express her radicalism, so evident in her art, through her personal life or in
her relationships.

But she was a icon of feminism, and it was hard to imagine such a fiercely
independent artist and groundbreaking rock 'n' roller, who paved the way
for others to extend the boundaries of what is acceptable, submitting herself
to the traditional, seemingly banal (to those who haven't lived it, at least)
role of housewife and mother. For Smith, the reality was far from banal,
however: "I don't mind being called a housewife, though I didn't disappear
to be a housewife. I disappeared to be by the side of the man that I loved. It
was a sometimes difficult but always honorable position, and I think nothing
greater could have happened to me at that time. I learned a lot of things in
that process: humility, respect for others. We had two beautiful children, and
I developed my skills and hopefully developed into the clean human being
that I was as a child."[31]

In a rare interview almost 10 years after she left the public eye, Smith said
she had no regrets:

> It's not the easiest thing to do, but I never thought of it as walking away
> from success. To me, the most difficult thing was leaving New York City. I
> always loved New York, and I did miss the light of the city and how good it
> had been to me and my friends. But I never for a moment had any regrets,
> or thought that "I could have been a contender," or any of that stuff. That
> doesn't mean that certain aspects of adjusting weren't difficult, but for me the
> most important things are the people that I care about and my work. We'd be
> somewhere performing, in Europe, where there might be 30,000 or 40,000
> people there to see me, and really, all I felt was that I wanted to be where Fred
> was, sharing my life with him. . . . It was the best decision I ever made. It gave
> me a chance to develop as a person and also, to get healthy.[32]

Smith had two children with Fred, a son, Jackson, in 1982 and a daughter,
Jesse, in 1987.[33] A clear account of her daily life hasn't been written, and this
period will probably forever be shrouded in mystery. But after she came out
of her retirement, Smith spoke of it with almost a sense of longing as a time
of domestic bliss and a spiritual and intellectual retreat. "I did all the usual

things, laundry and tending to children. But I also did a lot of studying, which I have always really loved. I'm completely happy just immersing myself in something. I studied 16th-century Japanese literature, I studied painting again. And I wrote diligently through the 1980s, novels. There are about five books that I haven't published yet."[34]

Having children also greatly changed her perspective and forced her to struggle for her art in a new way.

> They immediately take you out of yourself. Overnight, you cease to be self-involved. All the million little things you were concerned with in terms of life or work—you know, I had to work a special way, I needed silence, I needed this kind of music—all that's gone immediately. You have to relearn everything you do. If I wanted to write, I had to learn to write in the morning, whereas I used to write all night and sleep all day. Now I come downstairs at eight o'clock in the morning when Jesse is having her bottle, sit there in the morning light, and have a cup of coffee, and I have to teach myself to write at that time. Everything shifts. . . . Perhaps the hardest thing to give up was the mobility, but we travel with the kids as much as we can.[35]

She spent a lot of time watching movies on the VCR, especially old art-house classics by Kurosawa, Godard, Bertolucci, and Woody Allen, and got hooked on kung fu movies and reruns of *Route 66* on cable television. She also found inspiration reading about people who were doing charity or activist work—Mother Theresa's work with the poor in India and Elizabeth Taylor's efforts to raise awareness and money to fight AIDS.[36]

The family didn't listen to a great deal of contemporary music, but music was very much a part of their lives. "Certain nights [Fred would] play piano and I'd play clarinet, and we spent many nights improvising. All through the years, he kept me very much involved with music. Basically, I was studying and writing, and Fred was helping me develop a sense of myself as a singer. I still have trouble thinking of myself as a singer, but he encouraged me to sing again, and wrote songs especially for my voice."[37]

Indeed, although her art was largely private during this period, she did not stop creating. "I had to get up at five in the morning and write before the baby woke up. My art didn't suffer. My work actually flourished in that period because I learned new disciplines. I had to become much more focused in those time periods when I could work."[38] She later described their life like this: "I wanted to study, write and raise my children. My husband spent his time learning mathematics. He became a pilot. We just decided to broaden our abilities. We lived very simply and took care of everything. It was no hardship to me to spend long hours reading and writing."[39]

Of course, her fans never got to hear any of this private music. But she was not forgotten.

Dream of Life

During their marriage, Patti and Fred Smith collaborated on just one album. But it is one of Smith's best, the 1988 *Dream of Life*. Produced by Jimmy Iovine and Fred Smith, the album reunited several Patti Smith Group alumni. But guitarists Lenny Kaye and Ivan Kral were conspicuously absent, their roles now filled on the record by Fred. Patti Smith wrote that making the record was at times difficult because both she and Fred were very "self-critical people trying to please themselves as well as each other."[1] She added, "We were aided by the patient and supportive Richard Sohl, who came to work with us for some months prior to recording. His sense of humor, his classical knowledge, and our long history enabled us to realize our efforts, bringing them out of exile into the world."[2]

The album opens with perhaps her most poppy song, "People Have the Power." It is one of her few anthems—her art has always focused heavily on individuals, making anthems of collective action difficult to pull off—and it remains popular on the activist circuit. Maybe "People Have the Power" works because it picks up the strands of many individuals to offer hope in shared experience. Smith said the original idea for the song was her husband's:

> I was sitting in the kitchen, literally peeling potatoes, and Fred came into the kitchen and said, "Tricia, people have the power—write it." And I said, "All right." I had been reading the Bible, as I often do, and I had just reread the section about how the meek shall inherit the Earth. I was thinking a lot about all this and he and I spent several days talking about what we were going to try to communicate through this song—we often did that, he'd have an idea and a philosophy but he'd ask me to write the lyrics. "People Have the Power"

was the perfect song for the two of us to write. He had protested the Vietnam War he had supported the Civil Rights movement. His band, the MC5, was a very political band. I also had addressed these things I did it in my way, which was more biblical. He was more politically articulate. So we just merged all of our ideas.[3]

But the song was also inspired by signs of the times. "A lot of different things were on my mind. The first verse abstractly addressed the state of the environment. The second verse was actually about Afghanistan—Russia had invaded Afghanistan—and I was imagining these Afghani shepherds and the Russian soldiers just lying together on a hill at night and looking at the stars and talking about things, instead of fighting. It was a vision."[4]

U.S. politics also worked their way into the song: "That song came out in an election year, in 1988, and I saw Jesse Jackson delivering speeches and I felt like, if I knew his phone number, I'd call him and say, 'I have a song for you.' His speeches, the concepts he was addressing, were very similar to the lyrics in the song."[5]

Just as Dylan's subtler "Blowing in the Wind" (a song that is essentially just a moralistic riddle, not a judgment with fingers pointed, and more powerful because of it) was used a generation earlier, "People Have the Power" is still often played at political rallies and protests (Smith herself has often performed the song at rallies for Ralph Nader, the ultimate grassroots political outsider). "People Have the Power" is a great song and performance, in no small part thanks to Daugherty's drums and Gary Rasmussen's thumping bass, which almost steal the show (but Smith's growl wrestles control back). As a political anthem, it does its job well: firing you up, giving you hope, making you want to take back control from the bastards in power. A key lyric is "people have the power to wrestle the earth from fools"—Smith drawling out "foo-ahls" in Dylanesque style.

Aesthetically, the sentiments on "People Have the Power" are in keeping with Smith's view of rock 'n' roll. In the 1970s, she hoped to breathe new life back into the art form, which to her was always a kind of pure folk art. "To me, rock 'n' roll is a totally people-oriented, grassroots music. It came up from the people, from the blues. The roots are deep. It came from the earth. It's our thing. Rock 'n' roll is great because it's the people's art. It's not an intellectual art. It's totally accessible. The chords are totally accessible. The format is totally accessible. But it's not ours anymore. Right now, rock 'n' roll belongs to business. We don't even own it. The people have got to wake up and reclaim what belongs to them."[6]

Smith is right, and that has always been part of the music's attraction for the masses. Marrying rock 'n' roll to grassroots politics makes perfect sense, as it did with the folk generation in the 1950s. And it is why the song continues to be powerful and moving. Smith has frequently weaved contemporary political statements into her more recent work.

The song shows the heights Smith was capable of reaching, given the right collaborator. It's a pity that Fred Smith didn't collaborate with his wife more, because on *Dream of Life,* he seems to have pushed her outside her comfort zone by forcing her to work within narrow boundaries. Equal to the task, Smith pushed back against those boundaries and created some of her best work. The songs didn't start out with the idea of "let's go crazy and see what happens," as seems to have been the case with "Radio Ethiopia." Instead, by working within a simple framework, magic was created; rather than limiting Smith's power or energy, it seems to have energized her. Her singing on this album was as strong as it had ever been up until this point in her career. On "People Have the Power," she seems to have discovered a new way of delivering a song: her voice quakes with righteousness, wisdom, and strength.

Dream of Life started out with a bang, but there are many other highlights. "Looking for You (I Was)" offers another great pop hook. Thematically, it could be a sequel to "Redondo Beach," a woman searching for some loved one. It could be read as a love song or a prayer to the heroes who guided Smith early in her life. In it, she talks about her spiritual quest to find "love true."

"The Jackson Song" is no mystery—it was written for the Smiths' son, Jackson. It's a touching song, in the form of a nursery rhyme and in the mold of Dylan's "Forever Young," which was written for his children. It's not simply a wish for the child to go to sleep, but a wish for life and a pledge of support: "May your path be your own" The song is also about the inevitability of loss, about the child leaving the nest and the parents' wish to be remembered and thought of.

Aside from "People Have the Power," Smith forged into more overtly political songs on *Dream of Life,* most notably with "Where Duty Calls." The song is for the soldiers who were killed in the suicide bombing of the U.S. barracks in Beirut, Lebanon.[7] In a trademark of her political songs, Smith imagines the lives of others caught up in extraordinary circumstances, struggling to cope and often failing. But there is also, ultimately, a strong sense of good and bad: evil committed, innocence violated. So it is in "Where Duty Calls," as Smith imagines both the sleeping soldiers and their assassin and the dreams of all of them. "Their breath for his breath/All to his end." The last line of that verse lays the judgment on heavy, decrying an unspeakably selfish violation. The next verse quickly tempers that, however, with a call for forgiveness, telling God to forgive them and noting that they are all "calling to you" in their own twisted ways. She hopes he answers them and stops the bloodshed.

Smith also recorded a song about Somalia—called "Somalia"—that was dedicated to Audrey Hepburn's efforts to battle famine there. But it wasn't released on the original record.

A sadness hangs over *Dream of Life* that is hard to pinpoint precisely from listening to it, and I don't hazard to guess at what the personal reasons might be. But even the up-tempo, pop numbers like "Looking for You (I Was)" and the touching song for Smith's son are weighed down by some sense of foreboding and a feeling of something lost. Speculation would be cheap and easy and would say more about the speculator than Smith. Most likely, Smith was simply evoking the bittersweet nature of life, which passes too quickly in a kind of dream and is filled with loss and pain, along with its many joys. You cannot have one without the other. She tells her son as much in "The Jackson Song."

Some of the songs on *Dream of Life* dealt with actual mourning: "Paths That Cross" is written for Samuel Wagstaff, the photo archivist who was a friend of Smith's (and who helped pay for her rehabilitation after her stage fall) and who died in 1987. The song asserts that "paths will cross again" and that death isn't really the end.

The album's title track is also tinged with sadness. She sings to some loved one—presumably Fred or her old friends or maybe her children (ultimately it's unimportant). The song begins with Smith softly moaning before the band kicks in, and she declares, "I'm with you always." It's a heartfelt pledge but sad, perhaps because you realize her pledges cannot stand up to time: death will come and steal a loved one away. The tune's heaviness clashes ironically with the notion of a "dream of life," suggesting the dream is actually quite sad and painful.

Throughout *Dream of Life* there is a focus on natural wonders and forces (particularly the sun) that cannot be controlled in either their violence or benevolence. The power of the people, too, becomes like a natural force, capable of moving mountains. For example, "Up There Down There" is a rocking meditation on the origins of inspiration and inspired people. The sun and heavens give energy and strength, but their "energies are not for hire." The song also focuses on life on earth and how "days are numbered." She ends, however, by adding that "all communion is not holy." Some other-worldly inspiration is evil.

In "Going Under" the sun also makes an appearance, giving happy dreams to the people it shines on. But Smith craves the sea, on which the sunlight dances, and sweet surrender. Sohl's playing on "Going Under" gives the song the perfect touch of melancholy. The song is about wanting to seize control of the beauty and happiness, rather than letting them be dictated. "Let's go under," she sings.

The cover of *Dream of Life* was shot once again by Robert Mapplethorpe, who was at the height of his celebrity but was dying of AIDS. He captured a simple black-and-white photograph of Smith, her hair in braids, holding her hands lightly in front of her. In contrast to her androgynous look on *Horses,* Smith looked like an earthy, hippie mama—a look that matched sentiments on the album, especially "People Have the Power." Her gaze is penetrating, as though she is focusing hard on something and trying to understand it. But you are also drawn to her skin, how smooth and sensual it seems. Her look also displays sympathy.

The Smiths never toured for the album, which didn't sell particularly well. They never played live much, except for occasional benefits and gigs at Ann Arbor's Second Chance bar, not far from Detroit. Reviews of *Dream of Life* were mixed, with some critics disappointed. Some reviewers expressed baffling feelings about the record, which they nevertheless ended up liking. This is due to the fact that *Dream of Life* more or less came out of nowhere, with little precedent for it at that time in rock. Vin Scelsa expressed this befuddlement well in *Penthouse:*

> At first listen, I felt slightly embarrassed. Can she really believe all that raised-fist, "power to the people" sloganizing? Has time stood still in domestic Detroit? Does she continue to think that wearing her poetic heart on her sleeve will change the world? But as the record took hold, I realized that I was embarrassed for myself—not Patti; embarrassed because I'd allowed some of these dreams we once shared to get lost in the yuppie shuffle; embarrassed the way we are by something that strikes hidden chords. Once again Patti is venturing down paths virtually untraveled. How refreshing it is to witness an artist creating, without regard for fashion or formula. A friend said, "I didn't realize how much I missed her." And how much we need her nurturing vision and spirit.[8]

Old fans expressed similar sentiments, including Robert Christgau, who wrote, "At first I took this for that most painful of embarrassments, a failed sellout. Was she unwilling to waste her hard-won politics on weirdos? Proving herself a fit mother by going AOR, only she hadn't heard any AOR in about five years? Sad, sad. But soon I was humming, then I was paying attention, and now I think of this as the latest Patti Smith record. If she doesn't sound as unhinged as last time, she probably isn't, but as matrons go she's still out there."[9]

It's a shame the album didn't get more attention, but its impact lingers, especially in her great anthem, which gets some of the best response in concert and has continued to inspire people.

Smith's own dream of life was about to endure several crushing blows. The first came not long after *Dream of Life* was released. Her old dear friend, Robert Mapplethorpe, succumbed to AIDS on March 9, 1989, at age 42. "I was sitting up all night in vigil because I knew he was dying. His brother called me at 7:30 in the morning to tell me that he had finally passed away. I wept for him so much while he was still alive that I found when he died I was unable to weep. And so I wrote. Which I think he would have preferred anyway."[10] She began working on the poem that would eventually become her book, *The Coral Sea.*

Just over a year later, Smith lost Sohl, another dear friend and bandmate, on June 3, 1990, from a heart ailment.[11]

Fred Smith had long been suffering from liver and kidney problems, aggravated by years of alcohol abuse. He died on November 4, 1994. "Fred was sick for a long time at home. He had liver and kidney problems. It seemed for a while that he was getting better, and then he relapsed. He was part Indian, and he wasn't born in a hospital. He told me long ago that if he ever went into a hospital he would never get out. But then he had to be hospitalized on an emergency basis. He was there for a week. I thought he would pull through but he didn't make it."[12]

One more blow was delivered about a month later, when Smith's brother, Todd, died of a stroke. He had suffered from high blood pressure for years and often neglected to take his medication.[13] Todd's death was made all the more painful by the fact that he had been consoling Smith after the loss of her husband and friends, encouraging her to work. She had spent that Thanksgiving with him and their family. "It was a dark time for me and it was good to be with them. Saturday morning my brother Todd wrapped his coat around me and took me for a drive. He rolled the windows down, started up a tape of 'Rock n Roll Nigger' full volume and sang along, cajoling me to join him.... 'You're gonna make it,' he said, 'and I'll be there. You'll do new work and take it to the people and I'll be right by your side.'"[14]

Although her brother in fact wouldn't be there, Smith didn't want his enthusiasm and dreams to go to waste. "When my brother passed away, all of the energy that he put into me, all of that encouragement, all of that love, I didn't want it to go in vain. And so I picked myself up and began to work really hard after my brother passed away."[15]

Having been visited so frequently by death in a span of just a few years, Smith looked hard for comfort and ways in which all of her lost loved ones could endure and live on through her.

> I felt like after Fred died I was a better singer. Fred was a master musician, while I've always been a glorified amateur. When he died—I've never written so many songs, my voice was strong, I really felt like I was magnified by his spirit. When Robert Mapplethorpe died, my work got better because Robert and I always had a very intense working relationship. And when my brother died, who was so joyful and so happy and so supportive, when he died, after the shock passed, I felt really happy. It's just like his happiness was in me.[16]

Where I Have Yet to Roam

7

Before Fred's death, the Smiths were in the process of returning to public performance. Patti had given a poetry reading in Central Park the summer before, and she and Fred were working on material for another album. "Fred wanted to do another rock album. He wanted to do a very globally-concerned album. And we also, it was time for us to, do some work, to prepare for our children's future, you know, their formal education and things like that. So we had pretty much planned to record and do some minimal touring. So what I have done is just continue on our mutual battle plan," she said a couple of years after Fred's death.[1]

As Smith was grieving her losses, hope and inspiration came from many corners. In the early 1990s, the music industry had been discovering a new crop of bands, as college radio and so-called alternative rock cracked the top 40, reinvigorating rock 'n' roll. Many of these artists began giving attention to their spiritual ancestors. Nirvana, for instance, pointed to the Meat Puppets and the Raincoats as influences. Also, various female artists—Courtney Love, PJ Harvey, Liz Phair, Kirsten Hersh of Throwing Muses (for whom Kaye produced a record), Garbage, and Helium, to name just a few—were earning critical and popular praise, drawing attention, of course, to Patti Smith. Many critics viewed PJ Harvey, in particular, as a direct descendant of Smith. They had much in common: Harvey's manic music, her dark brown scraggly hair, and the way she turned gender upside-down. The Asian music magazine *Big O* named *Horses* the best album of the past 20 years.

These comparisons only increased the demand for Smith to return. In February 1995, Allen Ginsberg called Smith and told her, "Let go of the spirit of the departed and continue your life's celebration."[2] Ginsberg was scheduled to read at a benefit for Tibetan Buddhists and he encouraged her to join him. She accepted, and on February 16, 1995, she read poetry at the benefit in Ann Arbor. Here she met the poet Oliver Ray. She saw Ray a few weeks later in Detroit, and they began writing songs together.[3]

Smith also began reconnecting with members of the Patti Smith Group. Lenny Kaye helped put together a new band and "pieced together the songs Fred had left behind."[4] Ray helped Smith create some new material and encouraged her. "He was unjudgmental, and he encouraged me to write about what had happened. I wanted to write some songs for Fred. And I needed to record to support the kids."[5]

The new Patti Smith Group began playing club dates in New York City and other select cities, performing some of this new material for the first time. The shows had the air of a remarkable comeback and must have been good therapy for Smith, as she returned to the loving arms of her fans after so much tragedy. At a show at Toronto's Phoenix club on July 5, 1995, Smith told the crowd, "I was never gone. I was with you always. When I was cleaning my toilet, I thought of you. When I was changing my children's diapers, I thought of you. Do you believe that? You may."[6]

The band began recording in the summer of 1995, returning once again to Electric Ladyland, where they had recorded their first records.

> I didn't want to record uptown in New York where my husband and I had recorded *Dream of Life* because I thought it might be a little too difficult and sad. So I mentioned to Lenny, "We should record downtown somewhere," and he said, "Well, we can go back to Electric Ladyland." And I thought that was a great idea. I didn't really realize, I hadn't thought about how long it had been or anything. It's an inspirational thing. Everybody's been so great here. It's wonderful to walk in because the room we're in has huge murals of Jimi Hendrix and all of Jimi Hendrix's gold records, and it has a really great spirit. You know, it's right off 8th Street in the Village. I go out, people say hello to me, it's got a good feeling.[7]

The resulting album, *Gone Again,* is much more conventional than her experimental 1970s work, but it is also one of her best. Aside from reuniting the old Patti Smith Group—sans Sohl and Kral—the album brought together some old friends, such as Tom Verlaine and John Cale, and new collaborators, like guitarist Jeff Buckley and Ray; it also included an appearance by Smith's sister, Kimberly, on mandolin. Luis Resto replaced Sohl on keyboards, and Tony Shanahan was added on bass. Malcolm Burn produced the album. It is extremely melodic, with several great hooks, yet also a very somber album, at times even spooky. But it's not quite the rock album Fred Smith wanted his wife to make. Throughout there is a sense of resignation—not apathy per se, but rather a sense of accepting the cards you're dealt and not questioning or complaining, but instead celebrating the beauty and joy, however ephemeral they might be, sentiments that are both understandable and even admirable. From that acceptance comes hope and a feeling of connection and love.

The album demonstrates how strong her collaborative writing with Fred Smith was, but also Smith's abilities in realizing that vision. Fred had written many of the songs, but when the record was made, it was thoroughly her show. She triumphs.

The cover image is a stark contrast to her *Horses* cover. On *Gone Again* there is no look of defiance. Instead, Smith holds her right hand to her face as she looks down, a tuft of hair dropping over her forehead and eyes. A leather coat is draped over her left shoulder—as if to symbolize her rock 'n' roll past or perhaps Fred. Whereas *Horses* projected defiance, the cover of *Gone Again* suggests defeat, sorrow, and a woman recoiling against the horrors of the world—or perhaps pondering life's painful lessons. Although the title and cover image were ominous, they directly reflected the period of mourning Smith had just survived. The image captures the mood of the music.

The album begins with a rocking note with "Gone Again"—declaring Smith's return to rock 'n' roll. It was a strong return, not necessarily "to form" since the album presented shades of Smith not yet seen. The lyrics to "Gone Again" suggest that we are all already dead, belonging to the wind and the earth: it's a celebration of the moments we have together that death cannot take. There's an irony here, for if Smith was returning to the rock world, she was, in fact, "Gone Again," moving beyond the state of the world to some other realm, where spirits rise and art is made.

The title track was cowritten by Fred. Patti wrote in *Patti Smith Complete* that in their method of work Fred came up with subjects and titles for Patti to flesh out lyrically.[8] Part Native American, Fred took the opportunity of working on a song to express something of his heritage. In "Gone Again," "he saw the song from the point of view of a tribe's shaman. An old woman comes down the hills to account to her people their history, reaffirming to them, in time of strife, the cycle of life and the changing seasons."[9]

The sha-woman image is one that Smith had already toyed with in her performances. She would increasingly play it up. It fit her career, personality, and this stage of her life. She could play the wise, old (yet still quite sexy and youthful) woman, bestowing wisdom and channeling spirits (renegades, one and all). Even her body seemed perfect for the part—still rail-thin and gaunt, her frame suggested more third-world matriarch than the roundness and lumps that so often visit Westerners in their later years. Smith was leathery and tough with a shimmering intensity that seemed always ready to burst—all of which fits neatly into the popular imagination of Native Americans. Even as she merely stared blankly at the camera, she seemed to have vast energy stored within, energy that she carefully and meticulously controlled, as through breathing.

Smith had always tried to channel energy from beyond the grave—that of Rimbaud, Genet, Hendrix, and Morrison. But having been so recently touched by death, it was an easy role for her to fit into. It's understandable that she would try to connect with her husband, Mapplethorpe, Sohl, and her brother through her music and performance, as specific songs conjured up memories of each or as she tried to reach them. The beauty of Smith's art is that it never feels obviously exploitive, the way, perhaps, Eric Clapton's "Will I See You in Heaven" does (but, to be fair, Clapton's song wouldn't feel exploitive if it hadn't become a hit single, a problem Smith has yet to encounter).

Shortly after the album's release, Smith admitted to feeling connected and "elevated," but downplayed having any innate or psychic abilities.

> I am definitely on another plane, but I don't know how much of that can be attributed to mysticism, or even intelligence. A lot of it's to do with grief. So part of my elevation, if it is an elevation, is to do with that. I think of my new songs as gifts from Fred—his last gifts to me. When he died, my abilities magnified through him. At this point in my life, I'm trying to rediscover who I might be. I'd been a wife for 15 years, and my husband and I were very entwined; a lot of who I perceived myself to be was an extension of him.[10]

On her own again, Smith was quickly rediscovering her voice and her identity alone, however. Her singing—perhaps helped by years of encouragement from Fred in their home—was as strong as it had ever been, as she displayed on the album's second song, "Beneath the Southern Cross." Her trademark screams and growls give way to moans and singing (not that she forgot how to growl or scream). "Oh, to be not anyone—Gone," she sings at the opening, over acoustic guitars, drawing out the "ohhhh" and the "gone." The song was cowritten with Oliver Ray and is about his near-death experience in Guatemala. "I had abandoned life and was bumming around Guatemala.... I was getting pretty far out. Then I fell off a cliff and had a compound fracture of my femur. I crawled through a jungle for twelve hours." But in true Bohemian spirit, Ray found strength in the ordeal. "Falling off the cliff was the greatest thing that ever happened to me. I felt like God slammed me."[11] It could also be a metaphor for Smith's own experience, being overcome with grief but crawling back to the world of the living, where her family and friends needed her.

Contrasting with this experience of walking back from the edge (or going over the edge and living to tell about it), the next song is the foreboding "About a Boy." The topic is Kurt Cobain, leader of the band Nirvana, who jumped off a metaphorical edge with his suicide on April 8, 1994. Smith's connections to her idols have often been bittersweet, as she finds hope and guidance in them, only to see them destroy themselves. But Cobain was the first she had written about who was younger than she was, dying after she had already become a star. In Cobain, she saw a bright young talent taking up the torch she had passed but soon finding himself engulfed in it. The song references Nirvana's own "About a Girl." The Nirvana song about the mutual exploitation of teenage sexuality was presented with a great pop hook and masked with adolescent punk fury. "I take advantage while you hang me out to dry," Cobain sings. The way that men take advantage of women (and how that ends up damaging men as well) was a regular theme in Cobain's work. In this way he was a male version of Smith, channeling sensitivity into the male rock star myth, opening up new dimensions for rock performers and fans to follow—writing from the perspective of rape victims and declaring that "everyone is gay." He wasn't the first sensitive male rock star, and he never engaged in gender bending the way David Bowie or the New York Dolls had, but in his own calloused, raggedy punk way, he showed a softer side of masculinity (perhaps made acceptable and safe by his ferocious music), which, absent any cross-dressing theatricality, felt genuine. He was also married to a tough, strong woman, Courtney Love. But Cobain collapsed under the weight of that sensitivity and the pressures of being human, losing himself to drugs and depression.

"When Kurt Cobain took his life, Fred and I were extremely disturbed about that. Both of us liked his work. We thought it was good for young people. I was happy that there was a new band I could relate to, and looked forward to watching them grow," she told *Mojo* magazine. "He had a future. As parents, we were deeply disturbed to see this young boy take his own life. The waste, and the emotional debris he left for others to clean up. I was also concerned how it would affect young people who looked up to him, or looked to him for answers. I guess that's the danger of looking to anyone else for answers, but I perceived that he had a responsibility. To himself, to the origin of his gifts, to his family, to the younger generation."[12]

The opening guitars on "About a Boy" are chilling, and the song is quite spooky. Smith has been good at imagining other artists' endings and has usually found some glimmer of hope within them, a spirit that endured and triumphed. But this is no happy ending. It is overwhelmed by a sense of waste and destruction, swept away with the jagged guitar playing, moving to a place of emptiness, not light—"toward a dream that dreams itself." It's a place of solipsism, except the self offers no comfort, only agonizing ridicule and defeat, turning its back on itself, a reminder of its loneliness and weaknesses. Cobain is now beyond anyone who could help comfort him or ease his pain—he's beyond connection, in a way that perhaps those who accidentally killed themselves (Morrison, Hendrix) are not. The song, however, is as much a warning to others who would follow Cobain's path—just as her tributes to Morrison and Hendrix were meant to comfort his fans and herself, as much as they were an attempt to comfort her lost idols.

Smith's worry about the effect Cobain's suicide might have on fans is in part a mother's concern for her figurative children. But it's borne of someone who knew the power rock stars hold over their fans: rock stars were capable of inspiring the desire to live and to create great art and revolution, as she herself had been inspired to create. Smith also knew the devastation and terrible pain they could sow, the desperate longing of "Wave." The emptiness and negativity those stars could spread were real to her.

> So I wrote the song for two reasons. One was as a well wish, even after what he did, that his continuing journey be beautiful. But it was also written with a certain amount of bitterness. The chorus says "About a boy/beyond it all"—One way of looking at it is that he's beyond this particular plane of existence. But it's also a wry statement, a frustrated refrain. It relates to my sorrow for the various boys we've lost. Whether it be Jim Morrison or Brian Jones; any of these young, gifted, driven people who do feel they're beyond it all, that they can completely ravage and ruin their bodies or have no sense of responsibility to their position and their gifts. We all were pioneering some kind of freedom, but I don't think what's been done with it is all that constructive.[13]

Smith's comment is revealing, for it suggests she feels some responsibility in championing a freedom that was so horribly misused. At the very least, she feels a need to clarify her intentions, just as she disavowed an earlier generation of nihilists to William S. Burroughs. But Smith and punk rockers always went their separate ways at this point. She could never see anything sexy or meaningful in nihilism, whereas they mocked and derided her for believing in 1960s ideals and the beat generation. Patti Smith was determined to fight the good fight, whereas punk rock found comfort in believing the game was hopeless, because that belief made walking away a viable option.

Her low growl on "About a Boy" is devastating, an angry condemnation of adolescent selfishness. In her lyrics, God tells Cobain, "Boy, I knew thee not" but adds, with a note of compassion and hope that he finds peace somewhere: "Now that I have you in my face, I embrace you, I welcome you." The implication is that Cobain had yet to realize the strength and power of his talent, which would have enabled him to know God during his life. Instead, he would never realize the full power of his talent.

The suicide is tragic for countless reasons—a widow and child left behind, all the music that wouldn't get made, the devastation it wreaked on his devoted fans. Another tragedy is that, in Smith, Cobain had a perfect example of how one could walk away from the torment and pressures of the music industry with dignity, preserving a sense of the self, your life intact, your gifts reserved for another day while you build something just as beautiful: a family. In his final years, Cobain turned to other rock stars—such as R.E.M.'s Michael Stipe—for help in trying to cope with his anguish. It's a shame Smith never got the chance to help him manage.

"About a Boy" also gives listeners a chance to share Smith's grief. Most of her losses have been private: listeners can empathize with what it's like to lose a partner, a sibling, or a friend, as many of them no doubt had. In contrast, Cobain's death was a public one that most fans of rock 'n' roll experienced in some way. If fans live out their fantasies through pop figures, their worst nightmares are also sometimes confirmed by them. If you related to the intense emotions in Cobain's music—which is a very real personal connection—it was hard not to be cut by his suicide, the severing of that connection.

Smith follows "About a Boy" with the heartbreaking "My Madrigal," a song obviously for her husband. It's achingly beautiful, with Smith at her best as a singer (which was fitting because Fred encouraged her singing). The lyrics evoke private, tender moments shared with her husband—moments lost now but not forgotten: "We waltzed beneath motionless skies." She sings "My Madrigal" accompanied by piano and cello, which add both tenderness and chill. A madrigal is a song that has roots in Italian music and is generally written for two or more singers to sing in harmony. Now Smith sings alone—her partner is gone and she has only the instruments left to sing with.

"Summer Cannibals," another song that germinated with Fred Smith, "address[es] the darker side of being a rock musician. Vampiristic energies, which provide no energy at all."[14] The song is filled with irony. One of the few rocking numbers on the record, it condemns the relationship between fans and stars that has always been a source of inspiration for Smith. But it's not entirely clear who is eating whom or if it's a mutual feast between fans and stars that leaves everyone hungry. The fans definitely take a bite, as girls surround Smith, "saying grace." But on the chorus—"Eat, Eat, Eat"—it as though Smith is cheering the feast on, at times sounding like some maniacal cookie monster. There are oblique references to her retirement in the song. "And it all got too damn much for me."

It's a far darker—and consequently more one-sided—take on the rock profession than the Byrds' "So You Want to Be (a Rock and Roll Star)," which at least offered some justification for being in the game: chicks and money. But Smith's song is also more heartfelt, and there's an earned righteousness in that Smith defiantly walked away from the game that leaves so many feeling empty and sporadically leads some to suicide. She refused to compromise or sell herself at the height of her popularity, and thus has the right to judge those who would sell or buy.

"Dead to the World" is another ironic song—the bleakest title on the record, it is, at the same time, one of the most hopeful tunes. About an awakening of the senses after a period of sleep, both literal and figurative, the song could be read as an ode to wonder. A spirit or presence has periodically moved Smith, but she never fully comprehends it and always longs for it, because it brings her to life, inspiring her art. "I was feeling sensations in no dictionary."

If Bruce Springsteen, as Smith once claimed, was one of the sexiest mumblers in the business, she establishes herself as one of its sexiest groaners on "Wing." It's an ode to being free, but to a freedom found in surrender and powerlessness. "I was a pawn . . . But I was free." It's the dilemma of freedom that those who are truly free have nothing left to lose, as Kris Kristofferson and Janis Joplin both sang. The song is a wish for a "wing" to fly away on, one that Smith had found in her life. She wanted others to know the joy, but it's a pleasure they would have to take for themselves by establishing their own freedom.

The best part of the song—maybe the whole point—comes two-thirds into it, when Smith groans. It's a groan filled with mortality and authority but most of all with sorrow and pain: raw feeling expressed through her voice. It's cathartic. It seems disconnected from the lyrics and expresses emotions that cannot be articulated in words, which is the true power of music and a fitting ode to mysterious inspiration. The tension of it is relieved when she sings, "You'd be a wing/In heaven blue." It's a wish for the departed, her children, her fans, and herself—in short, a wish for everyone.

"Ravens" is one of the brightest songs on the record, despite its embrace of death. It's an ode to death and how time will "make ravens of us all." There's no point in fighting tonight. It's a somber, more heartfelt "We All Make the Little Flowers Grow." But at heart, it's a drinking dirge played with acoustic guitar, accordion, and mandolin. In it, she sings about how mighty her lover was, but he could not cheat death. But it's more than a song of mortal defeat. Smith recognizes her own impending death, but declares that she is not done living: "Oh there are places I agree/Where I have yet to roam." She is not afraid of death, but neither is she afraid to live—and it is still her time to live. She will keep fighting for life.

The album includes one cover, Dylan's "Wicked Messenger," which becomes a much different song in Smith's hands. Dylan recorded his version on his 1968 album, *John Wesley Harding*, which was a comeback of his own after his legendary motorcycle accident took him out of the public eye for a couple of years at the height of the 1960s counterculture (and inspired a different set of rumors). Dylan's version included only acoustic guitar, drums, and a harmonica. Smith's band gives the song a much more rousing performance. The electric guitar intro sounds like an evil wind blowing through the land. It's one of the few songs on *Gone Again* where we hear Smith's former fury as she yells and yowls. Both versions are dark. But whereas Dylan's version sounds like a parable, Smith's sounds like a personal vendetta, as she screams the lyrics. There's a special context at the end of the song, however, as she scowls, "If you cannot bring good news, then don't bring any." It's one of the few places on the record where you feel Smith's cold-blooded rage at the loss she's suffered.

For all the anguish and mourning on *Gone Again*, it's ultimately an album about persevering, remembering lost loved ones but carrying on. "Fireflies," a song cowritten with Ray, speaks to the journey of life. On it, Smith recognizes that her journey isn't finished, but that she is moving toward something or someone, and the end is inevitable. "Eleven steps till I'm blessed by you." It's an acknowledgment and acceptance of whatever trials are yet to come and the cost of being alive.

The album's coda, "Farewell Reel," is one of the few places where she indulges her self-pity. But it is hard-earned self-pity, and only the heartless would begrudge her for it. Another stark acoustic number, Smith sings, "It rains on me / The sky just opens." The song is also a goodbye to Fred, wishing him well and reassuring him that the kids will be fine. Even here, Smith sees a sign of hope: a rainbow smiling down at her, which Smith imagines is Fred. After the album was released, Smith described the song this way: "I think, when I listen to it now, it seems like a sort of a painful but successful journey of one who didn't want to get out of bed or didn't want to rise, to feel life again and to keep, and to keep going. And, and I suppose y'know it's also in some ways a love song for Fred."[15] It's an apt description for the album as a whole, too.

While recording the album, Smith played several high-profile shows in New York, including a show in New York's Central Park in August and a surprise appearance there again the next night on the Lollapalooza tour, at the invitation of its organizer, Perry Farrell. Other bands on the tour were awed by the legend, who played an energetic hour-long set, wowing not just the audience but also the many alternative rock bands that had been influenced by her.[16]

Her shows during this period were often rocking and full of energy—as her shows have always been—but they were also at times fragile and tearful, especially during songs she had written for or with Fred. During her performance of "Farewell Reel" in Central Park, she had to stop twice to collect herself, the *New York Times* reported.[17] In Toronto, she struggled to get through "The Jackson Song."[18] But overall, Smith was thrilled to be performing again, seeming to feed off the energy and affection of the crowd.

That fall, Smith got a surprise invitation from one of her dearest idols: Bob Dylan asked her to open on the East Coast leg of his U.S. tour in the fall of 1995. Dylan also invited her to sing with him during his set on a song of her choosing. She picked "Dark Eyes," a standout track from one of his otherwise forgettable albums, the 1985 *Empire Burlesque*. "The atmosphere was happy at our first show," Smith told the *New York Times* about her show with Dylan. "I thought the audience was basically Bob's people, but they seemed real happy to see us because they know that I'm one of Bob's people, too. They couldn't lose, and neither could I. I feel nothing but joy. If I had to spar with a hostile audience every night, I'd still be happy."[19]

Michael Stipe also tagged along on the tour, offering Smith encouragement and taking pictures, which he would later publish in a book, *Two Times Intro*.[20] Stipe said he was swept away with excitement on the tour, remembering what it is like to be a fan. "The air was just bristling with excitement the whole time—it was so exciting every night. And it was great for me to be in the audience and be such a fan. Nobody knew I was there, nobody expected to see me there, so I just pulled my cap down and went out and stood in the

12th or 13th row and rocked and cried and beat my chest and all the stuff that you do when you love music."[21]

When *Gone Again* was released in 1996, the album got several good reviews. Critics were thrilled to see Smith return; there was little of the old derision, and much was written about Smith's place in the canon and her influence on contemporary artists, especially the new crop of female musicians. No doubt the rave reviews also had something to do with the grief Smith had just endured—it would have been difficult to trash a record so full of personal and painful images—and that she came roaring back like a champion. But the album is one of her best and was deservedly praised.

"Retooling three-chord rock to fit her meditative mood, Smith has created a song cycle with universal resonance," Tom Moon wrote in the *Philadelphia Enquirer.* "The compositions on *Gone Again* can all be viewed as part of Smith's healing process, but none feels insular or closed. Instead, Smith claws through her loss to discover unexpected inspiration."[22]

Entertainment Weekly wrote, "Viscerally, it's hard to connect this woman with the wave of feminist rockers she inspired. Smith's impact was, and is, deeper. Now, as then, she doesn't make a grand statement about being a woman, or a 'woman in rock.' Simply, she's a pushing-50 widow with two children who has decided to reinvest in the healing power of music and career."[23]

Robert Christgau called it simply "pure as death and taxes," a witty but apt pun.

However, a few did question her updated persona, as she engaged in self-mythologizing as always. James Wolcott wrote in the *New Yorker,* "At the risk of being offensive, I think she's overdoing her widowhood.... When she sings 'Our love came from above,' I want to say, Stop the romanticizing."[24]

In interviews, it was apparent that Smith was full of hope for the future and glad to be back performing. Whatever her life had been like in Detroit, she had clearly suffered from the ending of that life. At the same time, she had things to look forward to. "As long as I think that I have something worthwhile to impart on the people, I'll do work. I think right now if all I can do is be a small reminder to people that in the face of all of our difficulties, all of our sorrow, all of our personal tragedies and disappointments, we can still be all right.... Basically what I'm trying to say is, 'Well, it's good to be alive.'"[25]

As a Citizen

Having reestablished herself in the music scene, Smith did not let the moment fade away. She played her newfound sha-woman persona for all it was worth, often using it as an opportunity to pay tribute to recently departed figures of the counterculture scene. Smith was able to play live shows only sporadically, because her children were still young,[1] but she was quickly reestablishing herself as a phenomenal live performer.

"In concert Ms. Smith marries charismatic showmanship to self-indulgence, collapsing the distance between herself and her audience," Ann Powers wrote in the *New York Times*. "Her aim is a sweeping self-transformation; it is the goal of the shaman, and of Ms. Smith's role models, who range from James Brown to Allen Ginsberg."[2]

It is hard to pinpoint specifically where the idea of Smith as a shaman came from: whether it originated in Fred Smith's idea for the song "Gone Again," or whether the critics somehow saw it and latched onto it. But the persona stuck, and Smith tended to play the role in concerts. There were, of course, traces of it from the very beginning in Smith's ecstatic, frenzied performances in which she'd bang her head against the stage or get so lost in the moment that she'd tumble from the stage. In concert, she often seemed possessed—whether by divinity, rock 'n' roll, or the ghosts of her heroes.

While making her 1997 album, *peace and noise*, Smith lost two of her friends and mentors, Allen Ginsberg and William S. Burroughs. Both naturally found their way into Smith's work. She consciously tried to foster her connection to them and other spirits she held dear. "The dead speak, but we as a people have forgotten how to listen. We hold them in our hands, they course through our blood. They are found in the leaves of the Koran, the Psalms, the Torah, the Constitution, the New Testament. All revelations, all poetry, all the sacred books," she wrote in her nearly indecipherable scrawl in the liner notes for *peace and noise,* which were reprinted in more legible text in *Patti Smith Complete.* Then she added, "They send words of love and woe. And we entwine their ideas with our own, forming a new body."[3]

Arrogance is at work here, in her belief of connection to old countercul-ture writers, daring to speak for them, assuming that she is part of that tradi-tion. But at the same time, if Smith couldn't speak for them, who could? It's not a stretch to see her in that tradition, though a bit presumptuous that she would place herself there. Smith also saw a duty to continue the tradition of the beats, her renegade heroes calling her to arms. So in this sense, she wasn't trying to self-mythologize or immortalize herself with the connection but rather to carry on the work of her friends in whatever way she could.

But as she struggled to retain a connection with the past, she also used her platform to speak out about the current state of the world, infusing the values of her heroes into rock 'n' roll. From this point onward in her career, politics would play an important role. Today, she is one of the few musicians who regularly takes a stand on political issues and comments on them in her songs. It is hard not to imagine that having been away from the music scene—and largely forgotten by the media—she was determined not to squander her second act in the public eye.

PEACE AND NOISE

In 1997, she began work on *peace and noise,* which would become a politi-cally charged rock album, similar to the one she and Fred Smith had wanted to make before he died—but she has said that Fred's album would have rocked much harder.[4] "After I got stronger, I really did want to do the type of record we had talked about," she said. "I really wanted *peace and noise* to, one, completely reflect the band I was playing with and, two, address some of the things I'm thinking about. The landscape was really exciting to work on."[5]

She told the *Progressive* that this shift in her ambitions had come from her quiet years in Detroit with Fred. She developed a more heightened aware-ness of environmental issues and took the trouble to use—and clean—cloth diapers, for instance, instead of using the more convenient but wasteful dis-posable ones. It might seem a simple gesture, but Smith knew such actions can be enduring and have meaning.

When I was younger, the last thing I wanted to be was a citizen. I wanted to be an artist and a bum—what Genet would call one of "the sacred bums of art." That's pretty much all I wanted to be. I was concerned about certain things—about censorship, about nuclear power, about the Tibetan situation, and the famine in Ethiopia. I did have concerns, but still, as an artist and a human being and an American, I was basically self-centered. I didn't really have an understanding of what it was like to be a citizen. In 1979, when I moved to Detroit to live with Fred, my life changed drastically. I came to understand George Washington's quote after he left the Presidency, when he said, "I have resumed my life as a citizen." I took comfort from that, because I actually became "as a citizen."[6]

Her newfound political stance was strikingly similar to her stance in the mid-1970s, when she was trying to rescue rock 'n' roll and return it to the people. This time, however, her approach was much more political, with specific ideas she was pushing. But her ideas were tempered, perhaps, by an understanding of what it is like to be a regular person raising children, cleaning toilets, changing diapers, worrying about bills.

Peace and noise opened with "Waiting Underground," a tribute to being a disenfranchised outsider, not unlike "Rock n Roll Nigger." But rather than a declaration of outsider status, "Waiting Underground" was a song of hope for anyone who felt excluded. The song is both a call to arms and hymn of encouragement. Underground is not just a figurative place, however—Smith is also referring to the dead literally buried in the ground, who have become part of the earth, part of the rhythm of life, and who haven't left us, but are a source of power and comfort the living can draw on, if only they believe and listen. "If you seek the kingdom," she later sings, "there will be a gathering."

That line was significant enough for Smith to include it in the CD booklet, although rephrased from prophecy to advice: "Be a gathering." In other words, you find hope in forming communities and movements, just as Smith had in the mid-1970s by forming a scene surrounding CBGB, a community of artists and musicians. The song is a tribute to untapped potential and innocence that waits in "snow white shrouds...Underground." It's underground—outside society—where Smith has always found the most interesting gatherings and ideas percolating, from Christ to Genet. The song also includes a sample of Folkways recording of an African American prayer meeting—a reference to an earlier underground music that offered solace to an oppressed people and eventually erupted into the civil rights movement in the 1950s. Unfortunately, the sample is buried too deep in the mix to be noticed, let alone recognized, and does not become an integral part of the melody. (Smith could have learned a thing or two from Moby, who has used archival sample to rousing effect.)

"Whirl Away" is about a world spiraling out of control and a loss of world community, with a sense of shared history and a common plight: "who stands guard for each other/why must we guard anything at all," she wonders.

The song "1959" is about the Chinese invasion of Tibet in 1959. The song is about parallel worlds, how a sovereign nation could be overrun by its neighbor, while the world was more or less oblivious to it: "Best of times" for America; "worst of times" for the Dalai Lama and the Tibetan people "in

1959," she sings. The song is thus as much about the United States turning away from another country's plight as it is about Tibet.

Growing up in the Cold War boom times of the 1950s (in *Patti Smith Complete* she remembers running to the bomb shelter in regular school drills[7]), Smith was stunned by the invasion. As mentioned earlier, she was assigned to pick a country to follow in the news in school that year and selected Tibet. Her teacher was skeptical that she'd find much on it in the news, but China invaded, and, at the time, Smith was devastated with guilt, feeling somehow responsible because she had prayed it would be in the news. The muted reaction to the invasion she saw from other Americans upended her sense of propriety, she said in 1997. "I was devastated by this. My father [had] fought in World War II. I was pretty much raised with the idea that the great wars were settled and the world was free. I just couldn't understand how this could happen in Tibet. And what I really couldn't understand was how no one seemed to mind. I've been baffled by the Tibet situation since 1959," she said.[8]

Having met the Dalai Lama just a few years before at the World Peace Conference in Berlin in 1995, Smith's attention was focused again on the injustice. Meeting the Dalai Lama greatly affected her. "I learned quite a bit from that man. He had to be constantly putting things in balance, constantly adjusting. He would stand in front of a large body of people and project and magnify his joys and hopes so that all those people would be smiling. But he had to protect himself and do what he must do."[9] A picture of Smith and the band with the Dalai Lama appears on the CD jacket.

Smith tackles several other topical songs on the album. "Death Singing" is about the musician Benjamin Smoke, who led the Atlanta-based band Smoke. Smoke reportedly began cross-dressing at an early age. Inspired by the punk rock movement and Patti Smith, Smoke moved to New York City in the late 1970s, where he got a job cleaning up at CBGB. In the 1980s, he returned to Atlanta, where he became active in a number of experimental projects. His best-known band was Smoke. Onstage, he talked openly about his sexual orientation. Smoke was the focus of the documentary *Benjamin Smoke* by Jem Cohen and Peter Sillen, which featured an interview with Smith.

Smith was inspired to write "Death Singing" during Smoke's farewell show in New York, impressed with how he was handling his battle with AIDS.[10] Smoke died in January 1999 at the age of 39. In the song, she sings of his activism: "He sings of youth enraged." Nevertheless, the song fails because it sounds neither sad nor angry at Smoke's death. Its vagueness forces the listener to supply the character and narrative at the core of the song. The song is too plodding and rote, and you cannot hear much emotion in Smith's voice. Her manic energy seems confused and wasted, which is a pity, since Smoke was certainly worthy of a tribute and his story sad enough to jerk some tears.

"Last Call" was thrown together for the album at the last minute. The band had taken a break from recording for Easter in 1997, heading to Provincetown and camping near the sea. Smith wrote that she intended to meditate on Christ during the weekend, but then she heard about the mass suicide of the Heaven's Gate cult. Thirty-eight of the cult's members and their leader Marshall Applewhite committed suicide on March 26, 1997, in San Diego, California, believing that Jesus was riding on the Hale-Bopp comet, which was passing near earth at the time. They believed that by killing themselves— by drinking phenobarbital and putting plastic bags over their heads—their souls would hitch a ride with Jesus on the spaceship. They also believed that the earth was about to be cleansed or recycled—an apocalypse born of New Age philosophy, the Old Testament, and science fiction. When their bodies were discovered, news photographs showed the covered corpses, their soon-to-be-iconic uniform black-and-white Nike tennis shoes poking out from under the sheets on their bunks.

The contrast of a violent cult ritual occurring on Easter, a twisted reading of Christ, struck Smith. She and Ray worked all night writing a song about it. She said it was a wish for people to think for themselves and to respect all life. "And if we should desire to believe in something, it should be a beacon within. This beacon being the sun, sea and sky, our children, our work, our companions and, most simply put, the embodiment of love."[11]

Using what had by now become a stock approach for Smith—imagining people in their death throes—her lyrics imagine one of the cult members taking part in the suicide ritual that day, putting on his shoes as clouds floated overhead and draining his cup. As the song winds down, Smith sings about Christ." But the song is a warning about following false gods and idols. "Don't be led away."

In other words, it would be better to question and challenge Christ as Smith had done in her youth than to follow false prophets. The real gods and heroes will hold up to scrutiny, and your questioning will only aid your spiritual search.

Michael Stipe, whose voice is generally warmer than Smith's, adds nice background vocals to the track. As the last song written for the album and the last one on it, about a cult's last wish to reach their god, the title comes off almost as a pun. But it's a fitting ending to the album.

"Dead City" is about a different kind of suicide—an urban treasure, Detroit, laid waste by its inhabitants, the culture that built it ironically destroying it. She sings that Detroit "longs to be." But all the schemes of the city's officials are bound to fail. Her disgust is easy to understand if you have ever visited Detroit, a city with gorgeous architecture and treasures like Diego Rivera's mural in the museum of art depicting an assembly line in finely detailed panorama. The city has some of the best Middle Eastern cuisine in America. Beautiful old mansions (constructed by auto executives during the American auto industry's heyday) lie in ruin, boarded up and decaying. It's also a city of alarming and disturbing contrasts. Smith told the *Progressive*: "I would drive through Detroit on this road called Jefferson. You drive through downtown Detroit, a once-proud city that's trying to build up, and then you drive through deeper downtown—which is pretty much boarded up. Then, a block away, there is one of the richest communities in America, Grosse Point. It's flabbergasting."[12]

"Well I built my dreams on your empty scenes," she sings. She never specifies what those dreams are; they could be her dreams of family or perhaps American dreams. She's not just singing about Detroit. Her song—just like the Pretenders' song about Cleveland on the much more catchy, heartfelt, and angry "Ohio"—could be about almost any U.S. city destroyed by suburbanization, automobiles, shopping malls, highways, parking lots, and, in a sad twist, desegregation, which helped obliterate mixed-income black neighborhoods, further hastening urban blight.

For all the political anger that supposedly fueled *peace and noise,* it is a disappointingly tepid rock album, however. There are no anthems, no rousing "People Have the Power" hooks to rile up the masses. The righteous anger is hard to embrace or share, because it's hard to hear, even for sympathetic listeners. Smith's lyrics are simply too hard to understand: you almost have to be an insider to embrace and enjoy the anger.

Much more effective and moving were the songs in which Smith remembered her old friends. On "Spell" she puts Allen Ginsberg's footnote to his poem "Howl" to music written by Ray, giving a rendition that is as much Smith's work as it is Ginsberg's or Ray's, as she chants all the things that Ginsberg saw as holy, which was pretty much everything: the world, the soul, the skin, the cock and asshole, everybody, everyday, the typewriter, and the ecstasy. The words are Ginsberg's, but the emotion in the song is Smith's. It works because, unlike Smith's own compositions here, Ginsberg stated his thoughts clearly and lucidly. Smith delivers the lines from his signature poem in a crisp and believable voice.

"Memento Mori" is an improvisational piece that built off of a Bo Didley beat.[13] Recorded in an old airplane propeller factory, Smith said the song evolved during live performances into a song about the Vietnam War, as she imagined a helicopter pilot extinguished in a crash. She names the hero of her song, Johnny, who could be the Johnny (in some alternate world) of *Horses* or perhaps the Johnny of William S. Burroughs' novel (to whom the album is dedicated) or maybe an anonymous Dear John, one of Smith's generation who vanished without much trace in the Southeast Asian war. One of the more effective improvisational pieces Smith has done, in part because it works so well as a hallucination and also because the scenes she paints are vivid and gruesome, the narrative is strung along with a series of nightmare visions, as Johnny's copter crashes. His name is carved on a slab of marble, but "Johnny's comrades stood speechless." They know memorials are pointless and don't convey what their fallen friend meant to them, all the potential that burned away, the life that cannot be measured by marble slabs. Smith then imagines a movie being made about the fallen hero, but the movie only further robs his life of meaning, "some mad apocalypse." Kaye's and Ray's guitar playing spice the tune with the right amount of chaos and anarchy, while Smith's frantic singing drives it all along—it's her nightmare, after all.

"Memento Mori" works as a political statement, because at its heart is the loss of a life, but rather than try to make a point about what the life did or did not mean, she gives us concrete images of its loss, which makes that loss sink in. The song is about what any life means and how it is remembered, forgotten, misrepresented, or used for political gain. You don't have to know precisely where the narrative is going or what specifically Smith is singing about—her images convey that this is a nightmare; in it, you feel a brooding sense of loss that makes you ponder the delicateness of life.

"Blue Poles" shares a title with a Jackson Pollock artwork, but as a narrative it is set as a letter written by a young woman to her mother about her Depression-era flight westward from the Midwestern Dustbowl, searching for better times and more fruitful land. In it Smith, conveys the landscape the way a painter might: "Hope streaking the canvas sky." But as the song ends, the narrator expresses sorrow for what was left behind.

In a review for the *New York Times,* critic Ben Ratliff wrote, "Patti Smith is obsessed with the idea of impermanence, and the lyrics on *Peace and Noise,* her seventh album, portray her in a constant state of mourning for everything that's finite, whether it's Allen Ginsberg, the Heaven's Gate cult or an anonymous soldier."[14]

There's some truth to Ratliff's claim, although, to me, Smith seems more obsessed by the passing on from life to death, what gets left behind, what is lost forever, what connections can still be made, and what pushes us through that void. Also, Smith is fascinated with the Christlike sacrifices people make, dying for their art or their country (whether intentionally or as a consequence of their devotion), in order to enlighten or protect. Sometimes, these deaths are misguided and wasteful, as with the Heaven's Gate cult, Kurt Cobain, or some anonymous helicopter pilot in Vietnam, but that doesn't make the sacrifice less real, less meaningful, less painful, or less significant. It is as if, for Smith, dying crystallizes all that a life is worth and is the pivotal moment when sacred truths are revealed. By putting herself, metaphorically, in the state of mind of someone dying, she hopes to discover those secrets.

If the album is obsessed with death, it's not as engaging about it as her last one. *Gone Again* was captivating and touching in its mournfulness, a mournfulness most could relate to, whereas *peace and noise* is stiff and rigid, plodding along without much tunefulness or drive. It's noise but not nearly as noisy as you'd hope for or expect, given the title (and without the noise, the peaceful moments offer little consolation as a contrast). It's a noise that doesn't scare the parents or piss off the neighbors, but it might just bore fans. It's a rock album that doesn't have much bite. And you miss the bite—essential for art that aims to stir up consciousness or wake people up. *Horses* burst with so much of it that it became a classic; *peace and noise* was quickly forgotten.

The album simply falls short on listening pleasure: no pop hooks, no angry rock 'n' roll rave ups, nothing you could dance to. These are qualities that have marked most of Smith's failures, and it points to the trouble with trying to marry literary pretensions to rock music. Rock may indeed be the "people's music," as Smith has said, but her poetic ramblings are something else, especially when she has tried to intellectualize the noise. Her lyrics sometimes come off as academic, self-indulgent nonsense. Listening to them, you feel as if you're being schooled. Plenty of fans have enjoyed interpreting lyrics—discerning the metaphors of Don McLean's "American Pie," trying to decipher "Paul Is Dead" clues in the Beatles music, guessing who Carly Simon's "You're So Vain" might be about, or figuring out the political and literary references of a Mekons' album. Unlike poetry, however, Smith's worst lyrics don't give you enough information, and there's little payoff in studying them. She also seems to miss the natural cadences of the best rock lyrics—it's just too hard to hum along to these songs, which for me has always been essential to even the noisiest rock. There's very little pleasure in *peace and noise*. As Emma Goldman famously said, "If I can't dance, I want no part of your revolution."

Still, *peace and noise* was consistent with Smith's artistic development and saw her venture into more overtly political territory, groundwork that would prove fruitful on later compositions, as she regained her confidence on the stage and in the studio.

GUNG HO

If *peace and noise* was missing something, *Gung Ho*, Smith's 2000 effort, opened with a gorgeous guitar riff that felt like a breath of fresh air and that immediately gets your foot tapping. The song, "One Voice," is a call for compassion, love, and charity: "And you will hear the call." For *Gung Ho*, Smith continued writing political material, but this time you could hum along and tap your foot. Reportedly about Mother Theresa, there are no obvious references to the Calcutta patron, other than the notion that one person could hear a calling and make a difference. "Give of your voice/one voice," she sings at the end—making that voice sound paradoxically both gigantic and small, highlighting both the power and preciousness of an individual.

Overall, there's a tunefulness on *Gung Ho* that was missing from *peace and noise*—although *Gung Ho* is at times reminiscent of 1980s stadium rock, and more than a few guitar riffs sound like Mark Knopfler from Dire Straits (which certainly isn't a bad thing). Recorded with her old collaborators Kaye, Daugherty, Shanahan, and Verlaine, as well as Ray, the album was produced by Gil Norton and also included guest appearances by Michael Stipe and Grant Hart from the college rock band Hüsker Dü.

There are a number of poppy songs that in some alternate universe would have been hit singles. Most notable is "Glitter in Their Eyes," a song against commercialization. The song is a rant against commodifiying sacred things—

whether it be CBGB or Angkor Wat. Smith says the endless quest to commercialize and sell has tainted everything and everyone. She sees children selling trinkets to tourists and says they've been sold out for "chunks of Angkor Vat"—the Vat a pun: a vat used to melt down gold souvenirs and the like, only perhaps this time people are being melted down. The song ends with help from Michael Stipe, who sings the moral: "All that glitters is not all that glitters," meaning that there is a sparkle and value in things that do not sell.

In a similar vein, "Persuasion" is about the many types of seduction or ways that people sell themselves. Desire is intoxicating, but "true love is so complicated." At the end, she warns a boy or girl scout against formulas.

On an album filled with obviously political songs, "New Party" is perhaps the most obvious of them all (and also the least interesting). It's a straightforward call to create a new political movement in the United States. A vocal supporter of Ralph Nader's bids for president and the Green Party, Smith seems to have tailored the song for them. (In *Patti Smith Complete, 1975–2006*, the lyrics to the song are printed across from a flier for a "Bring the Troops Home" rally featuring Smith, Ralph Nader, and Howard Zinn—as if to dispel any confusion as to which party she was talking about and supporting.) There's plenty of humor in the song, as she asks politicians to fertilize her lawn "with what's running from your mouth" and makes a plea for clean drinking water. But it's not much of a rabble-rousing anthem, unlike "People Have the Power."

Some of her political commentaries falter on *Gung Ho*. Probably the hardest to swallow is "Strange Messengers," a song about the slave trade. On the surface, it's a respectable song that wrestles with America's legacy of slavery. It gives an account of the auction block "men knew it was wrong but they looked away." Smith hears the pleas of the enslaved people.

Smith says—correctly—that America is not free from these cries, these ghosts and "strange messengers." But to drive the point home, Smith makes a connection to contemporary African Americans, as she imagines these strange messengers yelling at their descendants, modern-day African Americans. I'm not sure whom Smith is singing to. Does she imagine herself as a medium for dead African slaves, passing messages on to their descendants? Has she forgotten that outside society is a good place to be? Did she hope this song would be an R&B hit and reach a black audience? More likely, she just had something she felt she needed to say. But it's one of the most patronizing songs she has ever written. Her audience is mostly white people, mainly in their thirties or older. Pity is another way of dehumanizing people, and Smith smartly avoids falling into that trap. Nonetheless, her judgment feels a bit harsh and misplaced—her energy might have been more fruitfully spent trying to put herself in the shoes of one of those crack addicts. It's not hard to imagine her white, affluent fans feeling smugly self-righteous when listening to the song, as they feel pity for the poor, misguided black crackheads. Besides, there are plenty of white crackheads she could be lecturing,

perhaps channeling messages from their Polish, Irish, and German ancestors. The song rings false because Smith has assumed a moral authority she
doesn't have (especially as someone who has admitted to smoking marijuana,
which may less destructive than crack but is still an escape). A more effective
approach would have been to have the messengers confront the descendants
of the slave owners over a debt unpaid.

In contrast, the title track is much stronger, imagining the life of Ho Chi
Minh. Rather than judge nameless anonymous poor people—such as the
black American drug addicts on "Strange Messengers"—Smith imagines the
life of a historical figure, Ho Chi Minh, seeing the difficulties he transcended,
and asks a basic yet complicated question about him: Was he a good man?
She leaves the question open rather than attempt to answer it. The image
she paints isn't simplistic. Smith sees Ho Chi Minh escape a death penalty
to fight colonialism and imperialism as he wrote eloquently of his people's
struggle. But Smith also recognizes the horrors that he wrought in the form
of a bloody civil war.

As the song ends, Smith longs for "one more turn of the wheel," for the
revolution to turn completely, freeing Vietnam at last, giving it totally to the
people. The song and album fade out with the band softly chanting—with
little passion—"gung ho." It's the two-edged sword of rebellion, how it can
go terribly wrong, enslaving people, albeit with the noblest of intentions. A
mob's enthusiasm mutated into the forced chant of an army, forced conscrip-
tion. It's what could happen when "People Have the Power" movements are
co-opted or perverted. Smith has said the phrase originally meant "working
together" but was adapted by the U.S. Marines, its meaning twisted. The
song was written after a trip to Vietnam with Ray, during which they visited
a cave where Ho Chi Minh hid out in the 1940s.[15] But Smith was seeing
connections between cultures as well. The cover shows a photograph of her
grandfather, Grant Harrison Smith, dressed in his army fatigues.

The album is filled diverse voices that almost counterbalance each other,
demonstrating the depth with which Smith has pondered the album's
themes. "Libbie's Song," an infectious folk ditty complete with banjo, fiddle, and flute, is about Custer's wife, who longs for her husband to return
home. After "Strange Messengers," a ballad about one of America's most
notorious killers is a reminder that American history is multidimensonal and
hard to comprehend in its whole. Her approach is sweet, not judgmental—
one wishes she could have mustered some of that compassion for the crackheads.

It's not all politics and historical melodrama, of course. "Grateful" was
written for Jerry Garcia, the late Grateful Dead guitar player. Smith wrote in
Patti Smith Complete that not long after recording *Gone Again,* she was back
home in Michigan, feeling depressed one afternoon, feeling that everything
had gone wrong—even her gray hair was making her sad. She closed her eyes
and saw an image of Garcia smiling and winking at her, pulling on one of
his beard's gray hairs. "I opened my eyes and this little song came to me,"

she said.[16] But the song isn't an obvious tribute. It's a song of hope, as Patti imagines Jerry giving her a pep talk to persevere. He tells her life is easily transcended. It's a wish that dreams won't die, that desire and hope will live on in the world.

Describing the album to *Rolling Stone* magazine, Smith returned to the Paul Revere metaphor once again, saying she thought his work waking people up had never been finished.

> I look at what's happening in our culture and I think that it's important for people to voice their concerns. I'm seeing things happen now that I've never seen before at such a huge extent: people's concepts of themselves in terms of their material things, their lifestyle, what they own, what they look like. We've become a very external society. And young people [are being] targeted as a demographic mode. When people think of 12- to 25-[year-olds], I think more emphasis is placed on their consumer possibilities; how they can be fed all kinds of ideas about their body language, their hair, their clothing, and their music. A lot less time is put into how they're feeling about themselves as human beings, their spiritual content, their education.[17]

Overall, the album was welcomed warmly by critics. *Entertainment Weekly* wrote, "*Gung Ho* is simply a collection of hypnotic, human rock & roll that extols such seemingly antiquated virtues as moral fiber, history, and love as spirituality. What's even more remarkable is that at least for its duration, *Gung Ho* makes the idea of such rock uprightness feel timeless and not a bygone notion from the days of vinyl LPs."[18]

"Smith's *Gung Ho*...is a wild burst of adrenalin and beauty," *Salon* declared. "And with a sharper, more focused band than she has had since her heady CBGB days in the mid- and late-1970s, Smith's musical vision matches her poetics."[19]

Not everybody gushed. Robert Christgau dismissed the album, saying that Smith "always took herself too seriously, still touched with the divine."[20]

After the album was released in March 2000, Smith took her band on an extensive tour of the United States, including a stop in Knoxville, Tennessee, where I saw her. The next few years were relatively quiet for her, in the music industry at least. In March 2002, Smith released a two-CD greatest-hits retrospective of her career called *Land (1975–2002)*, which included some rarities and outtakes, such as "Piss Factory" (available on CD for the first time) and a cover of Prince's "When Doves Cry."

In 2002, she debuted an exhibit of photographs, drawings, and silk screens, *Strange Messengers*, which opened at the Warhol Museum in Pittsburgh, Pennsylvania, and then traveled to three other museums. It opened less than two weeks after her mother, Beverly, died on September 19, 2002.[21] Smith's father, Grant, had died a few years earlier in 1999.

In 2002, Smith also signed with a new record label, leaving Arista Records after 25 years for Columbia Records (home of Bob Dylan, among many others). She symbolically signed her new contract on the birth date of Arthur Rimbaud.[22]

TRAMPIN'

In April 2004, Smith released her first record with Columbia, *Trampin'*. Just as she urged her listeners to "be a gathering" on *peace and noise*, *Trampin'* opened with her urging them to be a "Jubilee." A jubilee is a celebration of an anniversary, a happy occasion to mark a milestone. It also has religious significance. In the Roman Catholic Church, jubilee is a time of forgiveness and acts of repentance; in Judaism, it's a year of restitution. On "Jubilee," Smith sings "we are love and the future." She saw the people in the midst of their suffering, dreaming of happy times. The song suggests that, for Smith, this was a moment of carpe diem, a time to shed sorrows and make a new world. It's also a tribute to communal experience and ritual.

On *Trampin'* Smith may have found the right mix of solemnity and rock. Many of the songs offered reflections on motherhood—about her late mother, Beverly, and about her children. The politics became less abstract and more topical.

"Mother Rose" is the most obvious song for her mother. In it, Smith remembers being cared for by her mother "every little morn'" and pledges to care for her in return. But her mother is gone. So Smith pledges to nurture her love for her, seeing her essence in roses growing by the door.

"Cartwheels" is for Smith's daughter. Smith looks at her with wonder but cannot comprehend what could make such a lovely, vibrant young girl, with so much to live for, sad. She wants to ease her daughter's burden but doesn't know how. She implores her to "open up those eyes of brown." Smith knows the only cure for her daughter's blues is to experience the world and gain perspective. Cartwheels are an activity that young girls do but also a metaphor for their rapidly changing world—turning and tumbling into uncertainty, their bodies changing in awkward bursts. It's an apt comparison.

"Trespasses" is written for her son, Jackson but is also haunted by the ghost of Fred Smith. The "trespasses"—such as they are—refer to the father role Smith was forced to assume when her husband died but also to Jackson's taking up his father's trade of guitar playing. The song is not an apology for trespassing, however; in the opening lines, Smith recognizes that people are compelled to assume roles that once belonged to others, and we carry on as best we can: "Life is designed/With unfinished lines," she sings. The song expresses a hope that all these disparate strands will connect back to the whole. For Jackson isn't simply continuing his father's work, but building his own ideas. May the ideas of the father and son connect in some beautiful piece of music or guitar riff or in a life lived with meaning.

"Stride of the Mind" could be for Oliver Ray (the lyrics appear opposite his picture in *Patti Smith Complete*). The song is a tribute to the quest for knowledge, to not being afraid of where it might take you, just as Smith had done two decades earlier and continued to do. "Come on move where dreams increase." It could also be read as Smith's goodbye to Ray, urging him to follow his dreams and continue on his journey without her. It's a fitting wish for a mentor to have for a student as well.

In a similar vein is "In My Blakean Year," which is a rededication to the innocence of one of Smith's youthful dreams. In it Smith admits that the journey is not what she expected when she began it, years ago. Even so, she wouldn't have traded any of the journey. "Embrace all that you fear."

She did not abandon topical or political material on *Trampin'*. "Cash" is a tribute to not selling out and an indictment against accepting laurels. "It's only life that you're cashing in," she sings at the end.

On the fierce "Radio Baghdad," Smith directly addressed the U.S. invasion of Iraq as part of U.S. President George W. Bush's war on terror. She frequently switches voices in the song—sometimes assuming the voice of a mother in the city, sometimes the voice of the city itself. She begins the song's narration as though she were the city talking to the world, proudly bragging of its achievements: great mosques, the mathematical zero, the cradle of civilization. Smith draws connections between Baghdad (Mesopotamia) and the rest of the world. She sees the invasion as the arrogant West turning back on its ancestors, its history: "But we mean nothing to you," she whispers.

The song is filled with tension, as the band gets quiet, trailing off like ghosts in some dark Arabian night, and Smith's voice drops reverently as though she's walking through a sacred place. Then she urges some anonymous child to sleep, "a lullaby of Baghdad," both a literal child sleeping in the city and the city itself, a child of humanity. But she quickly breaks into a scream, "Run, run, run," as the band erupts into skronking noise, and in her desperate cries you hear her genuine wish for reprieve for Baghdad and its residents.

It's an intense moment. Having sung so many songs that imagine people in their final moments, this time Smith imagines the moment when bombs erupt upon a city, in a violent spasm of light and noise. It's powerful, because she puts the listener in Baghdad, feeling some nihilistic, incomprehensible wrath rain down. The song ends as it began, with hope for compassion, that people will extend a hand of help.

Even though most of Smith's fans were no doubt firmly rooted on the left side of the political spectrum, this song was still politically daring. It was one of the first musical critiques of the war in Iraq—and a bold statement from a committed artist, who felt a duty to speak out in whatever way she could.

Smith has said that she related strongly to the point of view of a mother in Baghdad and was trying to humanize Iraqis with the song. "It's from the point of view of a mother. A mother in Baghdad, trying to sing her children to sleep the night of Shock and Awe. I wanted to speak out against the strike, but in a way that no one could really criticize," she told *Pitchfork*, an online music magazine. "Because no one can criticize the point of view of a mother going through that kind of horror. All the rage and love—all the things a mother would feel. And you know, if more of us looked at these things, took everything personally, we wouldn't allow the things that happen to happen."[23]

While "Radio Baghdad" is a triumph of force, "Gandhi" is muddled and at times gets lost in the band's improvisations. It begins with an apology to Martin Luther King—Smith's apology for having a dream. The absurdity of the beginning almost tanks the song; it's as though she's sarcastically lashing out at or mocking King's historic speech, but then she quickly adds that she was trespassing in this place of holy men. Her tone simply strikes an odd note. Smith follows this with her dreamlike biography of Gandhi's life, but mostly mentions just the surreal details: he was afraid of the dark when he was a boy; then he gets lost in a dreamlike state, while his mother dies and he sees the people falling; but Gandhi eventually awakens, to "get 'em with the numbers." It's a touching sentiment that also portrays Gandhi as the brilliant revolutionary tactician that he was, instead of a saint.

The song gathers speed and force, as the group recreates the Indian independence movement, collecting people and becoming an immutable force: "People, people, people . . . ," she chants. It's a bit frightening, for you could imagine Chairman Mao or Stalin expressing similar sentiments, sacrificing their citizens to the cause. That's not the point she's making, but it's an easy leap from where she sits. The song then becomes a tribute to all revolutions and urges people to rise up. She keeps bringing King back into the song, which slowly makes more sense and sounds less hostile.

Politics are always personal. But on the sweet "Peaceable Kingdom," Smith marries the political and personal in a direct way. She has dreamed of some lost loved one, perhaps Fred Smith, or Ginsberg, or all of her lost loved ones, and she wants to tell them their "tears were not in vain." The song is a wish for the strength to create peace.

The album ends with the soothing, "Trampin,'" which is a traditional folk tune made popular by Marian Anderson. "I'm trampin', trampin', trying to make heaven my home," the song goes. The sentiment is the same as on Dylan's "Highlands," which appeared on his 1997 LP, *Time Out of Mind* (the Dylan comparison is perhaps unnecessary, but hard not to make, since they are kindred spirits and had both found critical acclaim in late-career rebirths of sorts). In both songs, the singers declare that they're striving to rise above earthly attachment, sin, and weakness: they want to be worthy of heaven. But it's not just a literal heaven; they want a connection to it while they're on earth. They're struggling through the trials and tribulations of the world with a clear goal.

Trampin' was released on April 27, 2004, and Smith took the band on the road again, touring both the United States and Europe. *Trampin'* found Smith feeling more confident in her music, in part because this incarnation of her band had been playing together for so long. "This band has given me more confidence than I ever had before," Smith told *Rolling Stone*. "I know that I have more experience now, but it's not just that. There is something about the way we all work together."[24]

Kaye told the same magazine that he thought Smith had simply hit a peak as a vocalist. "I feel that on this record, Patti's confidence and maturity as a performer are at the forefront. There are vocal performances here—and this is coming from somebody who has watched her sing for three decades—that she's never come close to having on record before. Maybe she'd get them on the odd night in some Midwestern town, far from any tape machine. But there are things that happened on this record that raised the hairs on my arm."[25]

Of all the things that tie these three albums—*peace and noise, Gung Ho,* and *Trampin'*—together, Smith's reemerging and increasing confidence in her voice and work is one of the most important. One of the biggest results was her increasingly political stance. As she gained strength and confidence, she became more and more outspoken about the world, her country, and politics. In part, she simply saw it as her duty, "as a citizen" (both of her country and of the world) and as an artist, to stand up for principles and fight for the soul of her country and the kind of world she wanted to live in.

In a 2007 performance in Montreal, she told the crowd, "I once said, 'I am an American artist, and I have no guilt.' Now, I must say, 'I am an American artist, and I feel guilt. I feel guilt every day.'"[26]

Smith was part of a very small group of pop artists willing to speak out on political matters. Aside from hip-hop artists, few other pop stars dared to speak out about the political situation in the United States. (Bruce Springsteen, Steve Earle, Neil Young, Yo La Tengo, the Fiery Furnaces, and the Dixie Chicks are a few notable exceptions, as artists who spoke out about current affairs in either overt or oblique ways.)

As the Iraq War dragged on, Smith became particularly outspoken against it, and against the abuses of the war on terror in the United States, as well as the political situation in the Middle East. In September 2006, Smith released two songs—"Without Chains" and "Qana"—as free downloads on her Web site. Both were strong and bold political statements—fully realized songs of protest and social commentary.

"Without Chains" is about Murat Kurnaz, a German resident of Turkish descent who was arrested in Pakistan in 2001 and spent four years in the U.S. military prison in Guantanamo Bay, Cuba. "He is the same age as my son, Jackson. When I read the story, I realized how I would feel as a mother if my son had been taken away at the age of 20, put into chains, without any hope of leaving, without any direct charge."[27] It was horrifying for her to imagine losing someone she loves for five years.

Kurnaz was released in August 2006 (reportedly flown home in shackles, muzzle, goggles, and earmuffs and denied food during the 17-hour flight). Kurnaz claims he was tortured while in U.S. custody. The song is a rough biographical sketch of Kurnaz: he worked as an apprentice building ships, got married, felt a spiritual call to study Islam in Pakistan, was taken into custody without reason (U.S. agents mistook him for another man), and then sent to prison as an "enemy combatant." The chorus is about Kurnaz's struggle to adjust to being free again, or to literally "walk without chains." "They say I walk strange." Smith adds that he also must learn how to talk, vote, and dance without chains. Smith played the song during her show when CBGB closed.

Recorded with My Bloody Valentine's Kevin Shields on guitar, "Qana" is about the southern Lebanese city of Qana. In July 2006, Israel bombed the village in its efforts to rout the Hezbollah political or terrorist group (depending on your perspective). At least 22 people were killed, including 16 children.

In "Qana," Smith again uses the perspective of motherhood to make her point, as she did with "Radio Baghdad." In this song, however, the mother is trying to rock herself to sleep—her baby didn't make it, buried under the debris from the bombings. The mother is trying to escape her despair at the sight of the dead "wrapped in plastic in the street" through unconsciousness. Unable to endure the pain, she craves the easiest escape she can find—sleep. Smith contrasts these images with a sarcastic telling of the news reports on Israel's justifications for the military assault.

U.S. support of Israel perhaps outraged Smith the most and inspired her to write "Qana" and "Without Chains." "These are injustices against children and the young men and women who are being incarcerated. I'm an American, I pay taxes in my name and they are giving millions and millions of dollars to a country such as Israel and cluster bombs and defense technology and those bombs were dropped on common citizens in Qana. It's terrible. It's a human rights violation," she said after the songs were released.[28]

The songs are a bit simplistic in their politics—the situation is not solely the U.S. and Israel's responsibility (Hezbollah is far from innocent and has lobbed its own bombs on civilians in Israel), but there is definitely blood on both countries' hands. Both songs are powerful because they highlight the innocent victims and senseless murder and abuse in conflicts that have been exacerbated by misguided and self-serving foreign policies (which are, in themselves, very simplistic). In some ways, the songs are reminiscent of street busking songs, which were often adapted to traditional melodies in order to tell stories that were in the news of the day—such as the sinking of the Titanic ("When That Great Ship Went Down") or a famous murder ("Stagger Lee"). Only instead of being performed on city streets and slowly digested into the culture, the songs are unleashed on the Internet, a kind of global street corner.

Smith's bold musical commentaries have not gone unnoticed by other musicians. Bruce Springsteen began playing her song "People Have the Power" at political rallies—high praise from someone who is no slouch in the anthem-writing department. And at least in one case, Smith inspired younger musicians—albeit not an American band, but Japan's Soul Flower Union. The group's guitarist and vocalist, Hideko Itami, told the *Japan Times*, "Do you know of any American musician who speaks out about all the unbelievable events that have been happening in the world? I can name one: Patti Smith. Who else?"[29]

But Smith has said her political stance hasn't come without a price.

> My patriotism is constantly questioned. We spoke out a lot against the impending strike on Iraq, and my so-called patriotism was questioned by even my peers." It's always being questioned, because people don't even know what patriotism is. Patriotism is really having knowledge and a love of our organic law.... Patriotism isn't about backing your government; it's about understanding and abiding by our organic law, and that's often two different things. Especially within the Bush administration; they've done so many illegal things, and so many things in opposition to our organic law. So my people were angry because I spoke out for John Walker Lindh, and still do; angry because I backed Ralph Nader, and continue to be his friend and champion. So I'm no stranger to people questioning my integrity, but that doesn't bother me.[30]

Although she spoke about troubled times and corrupt governments, Smith remained hopeful about the future, her country, people, and art.

> Things are really bad. They're bad in our country. Our morale is down, our economic situation is bad, our health care situation is bad, what happened in New Orleans is terrible. There's what's going on in Iraq, what's going on with our soldiers, what's going on with our soldiers that returned. There are a lot of bad things everywhere, but also, simultaneously, there are always great things. There are beautiful things. There's new children being born, you know? The sky is beautiful.... That makes things hopeful. People sometimes criticize me for being an incurable optimist, but you know? I've seen a lot of bad stuff in my life. A lot of it. And I still feel really happy and alive and excited about stuff, and interested in new things.[31]

Smith understood her part in the ongoing rock 'n' roll experiment (if it could still be called that—"institution" might be a better word); acting as a citizen, she spoke out about things that moved her and worked to communicate ideas. She has endured for so many years as an artist, because she has a sense of purpose that keeps her going. A craving for fame may have been a strong motivator early in her career, but she found other motivations as she grew and aged. Into the twenty-first century, one of the primary motivations was to try to wake people up: in part to shake up the culture (as she had in the 1970s) but also to shake them up politically, to wake them up to the horrors of the world and inspire action.

"Art has always traditionally inspired and rallied people, but it's the numbers that make change. I think it's a beautiful thing to have strong leaders, whether artists or clerical leaders or spiritual leaders. But still—especially in these times, more than ever—the numbers are what we need. Numbers. Millions. Millions of people out on the streets, taking charge. Taking their planet back again."[32]

Rock 'n' Roll Icon

In the past several years, Patti Smith has reaped the accolades that come with being recognized as a bona fide rock icon. The music press, industry, and fans have begun to treat her as an elder spokeswoman, a treatment well deserved for someone whose work is as pioneering as hers. She was asked to perform the final show at the legendary CBGB on October 15, 2006. She was a fitting choice, as one of the few performers from the club's original scene who was still active in the music business and continued to embody the club's do-it-yourself, populist spirit.

Her three-and-a-half-hour set was both mournful and hopeful. At one point during the night, she demythologized the grungy punk club's aura. "Kids, they'll find some other club," she told the crowd. "You just got a place, just some crappy place, that nobody wants, and you got one guy who believes in you, and you just do your thing. And anybody can do that, anywhere in the world, any time."[1] After performing the Who's "My Generation," she barked, "This is not a fucking temple. It is what it is."[2]

At the end of the night, she played "Elegie," reading a long list of the departed who were once part of the scene or had inspired it or mythologized it: Bryan Gregory of the Cramps, Lester Bangs, Helen Wheels, Robert Quine, Johnny, Joey, and Dee Dee Ramone, and Richard Sohl. She then added the club itself, pointing out that it was closing at the same age Jesus died, 33 years.[3]

The following year, Patti Smith was formally recognized as a pioneering and influential rock artist by the industry and her peers with induction into the Rock and Roll Hall of Fame in 2007. She had been eligible since 1999, 25 years after her first recording was released. She was inducted along with

Van Halen, Grandmaster Flash and the Furious Five, the Ronettes, and her friends, R.E.M.

The Hall of Fame's biography on Smith singles out *Horses* as a ground-breaking album in rock history. "*Horses* arrived at a time when rock and roll needed a jolt from its unadventurous rut and upwardly mobile arena-rock pretensions," it reads. "*Horses* contained vivid, disturbing imagery that poured from Smith in impassioned torrents ('Land,' 'Birdland'). The musicians proudly flaunted a garage-rock aesthetic, while Smith sang with the delirious release of an inspired amateur who knew her voice conveyed more honest passion than any note-perfect rock professional."[4]

Smith, however, was somewhat conflicted about the institutionalized honor, which seemed to go against the grain of everything rock stood for. The Sex Pistols famously snubbed their noses at the honor, in punk rock defiance, just the year before, with a terse handwritten statement posted on the group's Web site: "Next to the Sex Pistols, rock and roll and that hall of fame is a piss stain. Your museum. Urine in wine. We're not coming. We're not your monkeys. If you voted for us, hope you noted your reasons. Your anonymous as judges but your still music industry people. We're not coming. Your not paying attention. Outside the shit-stream is a real Sex Pistol."[5] It was a gesture not unlike some Patti Smith had made over the years, and many half-expected a similar response from her.

Smith had expressed similar sentiments about the Rock and Roll Hall of Fame in interviews. "I think we've gotten way too cute with all these tons of awards we're giving to each other. Too much bullshit, too much cute stuff. The Rock and Roll Hall of Fame. It's another money machine. I did appear at one of those to induct the Velvet Underground. I did that out of respect to the Velvets, and because that recognition meant something to them. But I feel about the Rock and Roll Hall of Fame pretty much the way Fred did: that we should be ashamed. The spirit should be the museum."[6] Her song "Cash" from *Trampin'* explicitly condemns the idea of selling out and could be read as a critique of such honors.

Nonetheless, Smith would end up accepting the laurels with grace, merely noting her ambivalence, which in turn heightened the power of the moment. In March 2007, as she prepared for her induction into the Hall of Fame, Smith wrote about her ambiguous feelings in the *New York Times*. She wrote that she was torn about becoming institutionalized for an art form that she felt was most powerful outside of society. "Should an artist working within the revolutionary landscape of rock accept laurels from an institution? Should laurels be offered? Am I a worthy recipient?"[7]

She came to a populist—and quite touching—answer to her conundrum. She wrote about how so many of her loved ones (her late parents and husband) had wanted her to be recognized and about how so many other people were thrilled by and proud of her induction, even the postman and the sanitation man driving down her street, who said, " 'Hey, Patti, Hall of Fame. One for Us.' I just smiled and I noticed I was proud. One for the neighborhood. My parents, My band. One for Fred. And anybody else who wants to come along."[8] If rock 'n' roll was really the people's music, as Smith had said many times in her career, than the award truly did not belong just to her, but to all her fans as well, to anyone who had been moved by the spirit in some smoky club, to anyone who felt that Smith spoke for them. To turn down the honor would, in a way, be a snub to her fans and a slap in the face to too many people who cared about her.

On the night of the formal induction ceremony, March 12, 2007, Smith told the crowd that the people she loved—her parents, husband, friends— were there but "seated a little higher," as she pointed to the heavens.[9] According to the *New York Times,* she also told the crowd about an argument she had had with her husband, Fred, shortly before he died. Fred, convinced that Patti would eventually be named to the Rock and Roll Hall of Fame, asked her "to accept it like a lady and not say any curse words and to make certain to salute new generations. Because it is the new generations that will redefine the landscape of rock 'n' roll."[10] Perhaps he feared she would make a defiant spectacle in the style of the Sex Pistols.

Nevertheless, the *Times* noted that the curse words did arrive during Smith's performance of "Rock n Roll Nigger" (although the *Times* didn't print the name of the song, calling it simply "a punk anthem" about being "outside of society"). Smith dedicated the song to her mother, who liked to vacuum to it. Smith was joined onstage during the performance by her usual band, with her son, Jackson, on bass. The group also played the Stones' "Gimmie Shelter" and her own "Because the Night." Later Smith joined R.E.M. to play the Stooges' "I Wanna Be Your Dog," a pointed reminder that this other pioneering band has yet to be inducted. (In these gestures, Smith found a delicate way to walk the line between defiance and grace in accepting the award, retaining some of the piss and vinegar of her rock 'n' roll roots without being overtly disrespectful to the institution or the people who were honoring her.) For the traditional closing all-star jam, Smith was further honored when they played "People Have the Power."[11]

TWELVE

Having been formally accepted into the rock canon, Smith turned her attention to that canon and paid tribute to the parts of it that have moved her. In the spring of 2007, Smith released *twelve,* an album of cover songs (containing 12 tracks, it was also her 12th album). Although it was generally trashed in the music press, the album fit nicely in Smith's career, bringing her full circle. Her early work was built off of traditional rock 'n' roll songs, and now, enshrined alongside many of her idols, she tipped her hat to them and to the simple joy of a great rock tune. Produced by Smith and the band, the album is a love song to the art of rock and rock stars, picking gems of wisdom she's found on the airwaves, vinyl, and CD.

The cover is a photograph of a tambourine Robert Mapplethorpe made for Smith for her 21st birthday in 1967—a year, she says, in which many of the songs she covers were first released. The tambourine is tattooed with Smith's astrological sign. Created when the two were unknown to the art and pop worlds, it could be seen as a tribute to being a nobody, working in obscurity for the love of art or hungering for recognition. It is a state of being that many great rock songs emerged from. She recorded the album around the time of her 60th birthday, on December 30, 2006. It was released on April 16, 2006, about a month after her Hall of Fame induction.

The album opens with a song by one of Smith's oldest idols, Jimi Hendrix's "Are You Experienced." Also included on the album were other obvious choices: the Rolling Stones' "Gimmie Shelter," Bob Dylan's "Changing of the Guards," and Nirvana's "Smells Like Teen Spirit." Knowing Smith, her selection of these artists was not surprising, but some of the songs chosen were a bit unusual.

Smith told one interviewer she had always wanted to do a covers album, which makes sense, given her fascination with rock 'n' roll and its stars. However, it wasn't until 2007 that she finally had the confidence to tackle the project. "I always wanted to do a covers album, but I didn't really feel I had the range to do the kind of album I wanted to do. I didn't know enough about singing. But now it seemed like the right time. As the project evolved, a lot of the songs on the list I made in the beginning didn't make the final cut, and a lot of songs that I didn't plan on doing wound up being the ones I chose. They're all special to me for different reasons."[12]

However, Smith said picking the songs was not easy and joked that she could probably fill "100 box sets" with covers, given her love of rock 'n' roll. "I had to really explore all different songs and different keys, see what kind of range I have. It's a lot different. If you're writing your own songs, you're always writing in your range of comfort. And you write songs that are natural to your voice. And when you're covering songs, well, sometimes I wanted to do songs that I just couldn't sing. I didn't serve the song well with my vocal range. It was a learning process to do these songs, and these songs have greatly evolved live, far beyond the recorded versions."[13]

But all of the songs make sense in the context of Smith's work and life. Each represents a kindred spirit or sentiment, in some way. "Some of them were great moments I wanted to be part of, to share with people," she told the *Scotsman*. "I wanted to remind [people] of the lyrical power of all these artists. Some were newly discovered, like Tears for Fears—I didn't even know that song, but it's such a great line [Everybody Wants to Rule the World], I felt the political resonance of it was important."[14]

As you would expect in such a project, a few wild cards were thrown in, most notably, "Everybody Wants to Rule the World," by the 1980s new wave act Tears for Fears. The original is a polished pop tune that seems far from the frenzied emotional performances Smith had built a career on. But the song expresses a fascination with power and passes a moral judgment on those who crave it—all of us—that was not alien to Smith's work. On *twelve*'s liner notes, Smith says that she had never heard the song when it was a radio hit. Writing at her favorite coffee shop one day, the song came on and the chorus immediately struck her.

> I was sitting there and I was thinking about everything in our world...and I just got so depressed about it. I thought "what is wrong with everybody? What is wrong with our world? Why can't we just get it together?" And just as I was thinking that, this Tears for Fears song came on. It was like, "Hey Patti! You asked the question, here's the answer." And "Everybody Wants to Rule the World" came on, and I was like, "Whoa. This is a genius of a good pop song." It's a great pop song because in one sentence, they say it all. That's what's the matter: everybody wants to rule the world. We're in a time of imperialism, corporate rule, greed.[15]

Smith's version is rawer, more haggard, and more overtly political than the original, which focused more on our attempts to conquer our own nature; it suggests that the urges of early cave men, who sought to conquer and control nature and mortality, haven't left us. And in our failure to conquer these urges lies the root of our own depression and melancholy. These urges could certainly lead to imperialism and corporate rule. But if that is true, then imperialism and corporate rule are merely extensions of human nature.

Smith heard another of the album's political tracks, Paul Simon's "Boy in the Bubble," at the same café. At the suggestion of another patron at the coffee shop, she recorded it with a dulcimer. Simon's songs—especially from *Graceland*—are political in a subtle sense. His meaning is often couched in irony and mystery. On Simon's version, he refers to details and wonders of the "modern world"—"the way the camera follows us in slow motion,"—and contrasts them with the refrain "don't cry." You wonder, what would anyone be crying about during an age of miracle and wonder? Simon's protest songs work by capturing a general feeling of social malaise: things just aren't right but he gives you no clear sense of what is wrong, which is a potent device, because his songs sit with you as you ponder their meanings. The song describes how, despite all human progress, our basic cravings—the baby crying in the middle of the night—remain the same and must be met in the same old ways. It is the only song on *twelve* where Smith manages the same tone as the original artist: contrasting sarcasm with earnest yearnings.

It's not surprising that Smith chose to cover a Nirvana song, given her love for the band. But her choice of the group's anthem of teenage alienation was perhaps somewhat unexpected, given Smith's age. She chose to cover it in an unorthodox manner, with a bluegrass arrangement, or "porch style," as she explains on the liner notes. The song was recorded at Electric Ladyland, with guests Sam Shepard and his son, Walker, on banjos, Peter Stampfel on fiddle (both Stampfel and Shepard had played in the Holy Modal Rounders in the 1960s), and Duncan Webster. "Smells Like Teen Spirit" is such an iconic song—it was a breath of fresh air on the radio at a time when commercial rock had seemed completely hopeless. The song opened the floodgates to countless other bands, as rock radio discovered new voices and new heroes, coining the new genre "grunge" and bringing profits to "alternative" and "college" rock, something Cobain would later regret. In the wake of Cobain's suicide and all that followed, the song has also become an icon of the 1990s, a time that has already become mythologized. But the song endures. It perfectly captures and crystallizes a moment of teenage confusion, angst, and yearning—perhaps in part because the lyrics are largely incoherent, and Cobain mumbles them. The song isn't just about those confused teenage years, however, but also how those emotions are commodified and represented in the pop culture. Cobain sounds as though he has forgotten how to feel anything and depends on the radio to feel something: "Here we are now, entertain us"—just another part of the freak show. Cobain's song works, not in a literal way, but because it captured a feeling of emptiness in a five-minute burst of pop delight. It captured a moment of youth rebellion and angst just as well as "Satisfaction" and "Like a Rolling Stone" did a generation earlier.

"Smells Like Teen Spirit" is the kind of song that absorbs whatever the listener brings to it. For Smith, the song was about the divide between artists and fans. "The song really articulates the schism of being an artist and a performer. On one hand, you feel this special power, but on the other, you don't want to be isolated from other people. I think the schism of both being dogged as an artist and wanting to just be a human being was very difficult for him. But I wanted to do the song in a genre he embraced. He loved bluegrass music."[16]

Smith's version was not the first radical translation of the song. Tori Amos famously covered it as a down-tempo number with her piano just a year after it had been released, except that in her version you could understand the lyrics. But Amos retained the song's barely contained seething rage. Smith's version has rage too but found a more specific target for that rage; none of it was self-directed, as it was in Cobain's and Amos's versions.

Smith's version is a minute and a half longer than the Nirvana original, in part because she slows it down, but also because she adds a beat poem in the middle, sung with a mother's concern for the world's orphaned, desperate, lonely children: "haunted beat, sniffing, stoned out of their shaved heads. . . ." Cobain could be the patron saint of all those wayward children. You can almost picture little Kurt Cobains, little musical prodigies, in your head, running through garbage dumps, sniffing glue on the streets of the world's urban wastelands. But in these desperate faces, Smith sees hope for the future, for art, for life, because they will create the next spark, the next cultural and political rebellions.

It's one of the better songs on the album, because of the lines that Smith added. Most of the songs are okay, but you end up craving the original when you listen to Smith's versions—she doesn't push the songs far enough to reinvent them and make them her own. This is especially true with the Rolling Stones' "Gimmie Shelter." The Patti Smith Group does an admirable job recreating the chilling guitar line that introduces the song; they understand that what makes it work is a brooding feeling, as though a cold wind is blowing through the land. They use the entire band to create this feeling, with Daugherty's cymbal work played to good effect. As good a singer as Smith has become, her vocals are outmatched compared to Mick Jagger. She cannot power her way through the song the way she did with Van Morrison's "Gloria."

In covering some of her old heroes, a few odd choices emerged. Smith admits that she did not want to record the Doors' "Soul Kitchen":

> I had this dream that I should do "Soul Kitchen," and I woke up and thought, "I don't really want to do 'Soul Kitchen.' It's not like one of my favorite Doors' songs. And then I went out on the street, and this big sanitation truck almost ran me down and the guy was blaring the radio, and "Soul Kitchen" was on. And I thought, "All right, okay. I'll do it, I'll do it." I don't know why. And that's all. I mean that's the strangest scenario on the record, but all of the songs had some element like that.[17]

Smith's "Soul Kitchen," like most songs on the record, is fairly faithful to the original. She does an admirable job with the vocals, but the song misses the guitar playing of Robbie Kreiger, one of rock's underrated guitarists, and the churning organ of Ray Manzarek.

On "White Rabbit," the Jefferson Airplane song written and sung by Grace Slick, the band does a good job creating a psychedelic landscape (complete with *Sketches of Spain* flourishes) for Smith to traipse through. Smith has said Slick was a big influence on her singing. "Her voice defied gender," she writes on *twelve*'s liner notes, calling her "the maverick queen of rock and roll." Slick's vocals on "White Rabbit" are seductive, drawing you into this dark vision that sounds so enticing. You want to swallow the mushrooms and get lost with her in this world, which is why it was seductive in the late 1960s and continues to be a drug anthem. Smith's version is much more forceful and scary. But the danger isn't sexy, the way Slick's version was. It works better as an ominous warning. Slick's version was a warning too, but one you didn't particularly care to heed.

On other songs Smith delivers competent renditions. Dylan's "Changing of the Guards," from *Street Legal,* an album she says she listened to a lot when she first moved to Detroit, made her cry, and she covered it in an attempt to find the source of its power over her. Her daughter harmonizes on it. She also covers Neil Young's delicate "Helpless," an anthem of fragility in the modern world. Smith had performed the song with Young at a benefit concert in 1996. The band recorded it after a frustrating recording session.

Smith's singing on it is vulnerable. She pulls off these two covers because her ragged voice matches the earthy wisdom of Dylan and Young.

Also covered are the Beatles' "Within You Without You," the Alman Brothers' "Midnight Rider," and Stevie Wonder's "Pastime Paradise." None of them stand out all that much.

The best covers by any performer upend the original, almost creating a new song, discovering new depths of meaning and nuance in the original. Hendrix did this with Dylan's "All Along the Watchtower," turning a spooky song into something laced with foreboding danger. Kurt Cobain may have recorded the definitive version of Leadbelly's "Where Did You Sleep Last Night," with his ferocious scream, which is one of the greatest ever recorded.

Smith herself did this on *Horses*, careening off in new directions with old rock standards "Gloria" and "Land of a Thousand Dances." Overall, on *twelve*, Smith simply doesn't put a sufficiently distinctive stamp on the songs to make them hers, the way she did on *Horses*. Part of the trouble is that most of these songs are so well known, so iconic, and Smith deserves some credit for taking up the challenge. But she cannot wrestle them away from their originals, let alone top them. She doesn't have the audacity and inventiveness she possessed in 1975.

Although she is capable of being an emotive singer, she is not good enough to carry the songs on her vocal chops alone. As a result, the songs on *twelve* are not much different than hearing a cover band at the corner bar or a well-practiced karaoke singer. Nevertheless, the cover band truly loves these songs and they would no doubt have you tapping your foot in that bar. But there's a muted, generic quality to them: innocuous tracks that would melt into the background of a coffee shop, just like the location where Smith selected many of them. Her songs just don't have the danger or excitement the originals did.

Most critics were unimpressed and trashed the album. "There truly is no justification for the existence of this album. Smith doesn't add anything to any of these songs. It's sad, but Patti, it's over," Patrick Daugherty wrote on themaneater.com.[18] Others were more sympathetic. Robert Christgau wrote, "Many interpretive singers have superior pipes, and some equal brains, but few match her quality of belief."[19] As usual, his take is dead on. While *twelve* certainly didn't reinvent rock or the covers album, it was an understandable indulgence, one Smith had earned. It's also an album many of her long-time fans enjoyed.

Smith continued to work hard, touring for *twelve*, with a band that now included her son, Jackson. Performed live, the covers made much more sense to people, who were swept away with the ferocity of Smith's performances. Smith has always shined brightest live, which is why she has maintained such a devoted following. Smith is simply one of the all-time great live rock performers, because of the energy she brings to each show—sustained because she loves and is devoted to rock 'n' roll as an art form. She rivals Bruce Springsteen, James Brown, Prince, and the Grateful Dead as a live performer.

"Patti Smith has always been better live than on record," wrote one fan on his Web blog, after a show in Dublin. "She's got that thing.... *It*...whatever *It* is...and It can't be captured on a record. You have to be there to experience It. So it matters little what the critics are saying about her version of 'Smells Like Teen Spirit;' because if you're lucky enough to be in the same room as Patti Smith when she's singing, you get taken to a place where the words of critics don't mean shit."[20]

"Veteran concert-goers hear Hendrix covered quite frequently, but very few acts can pull it off convincingly," wrote another blogger on the Concert Blog about a show in August 2007 at the Fillmore in San Francisco. "That's where Smith's pedigree and her authenticity come into play. When she roars out the lyrics—'Have you ever been experienced? Well, I have'—there's simply no doubting her qualifications to walk in Jimi's shoes."[21]

Live settings fostered her improvised tangents, which sometimes turned into rants against or related to George W. Bush's foreign policy, the Middle East, war, and other social issues.

And Smith continues to look forward. She remains hopeful about rock 'n' roll, pop music, and art in general, excited to see what younger generations will produce. If she feels any competitiveness toward these younger generations, she doesn't show it.

Asked about the current state of rock 'n' roll, she told one interviewer in 2007: "I think it's a powerful cultural voice. It has its periods of exploration, some more political than others. Right now, people are regrouping and a lot of new things are in store for us, and I look forward to what new generations are doing. I've always believed rock 'n' roll is the people's art. It's a way all people at any age can voice their opinions, their sexuality, their spirit, their political ideals. It's there as a format, as a uniting principle, it's really up to the people how they use it."[22]

But rock 'n' roll was also, for Smith, a community. Through it, and despite all her weaknesses, she connected to people, the world, culture, God. For her, connecting was the whole point. "I know technically I have a lot of shortcomings: I'm not a great singer, I make a lot of mistakes, I meander. I know all of my shortcomings. But one thing I also know about myself is my whole reason for being on a stage, in front of people, is to communicate—is to take this somewhere. Or to figure out something, or to be transformed. Or to detox. Whatever. But to do it together. Or else, what's the point?"[23]

Conclusion

Had Smith never written another word or performed again after leaving the music business in the late 1970s, she would still have retained icon status. Her early career alone was of such significance that she deserves accolades and a place in rock's canon.

But her return to the music business made her career and life all the more exceptional and noteworthy. The remarkable music she continued to make into the twenty-first century, together with her inspiring live performances, demonstrated how rock stars could remain vital and engaging even in old age. Smith was aging, but far more gracefully than Mick Jagger. Even into her sixties, she was still a bona fide rock 'n' roller, retaining much of her original boyish charm, sex appeal, fire, and outrageousness.

She had almost achieved instant icon status with *Horses,* and the rest of her career—while perhaps not quite as spectacular—only reinforced and built on that achievement. For proof of how iconic Smith has become in pop culture, one need only read a 2007 issue of fashion magazine like *Women's Wear Daily*—which certainly wasn't paying much attention to punk rock back in 1976—that described a contemporary designer's line as "the Jazz Age meets Patti Smith."[1] Being raised to the level of a descriptor (such as Dylanesque) or an era (the Jazz Age) is a sign of how deeply embedded a person's art has become in the culture. Most people in America would get an idea of what clothes look like from the above description. Smith had once had a premonition of working for *Vogue* magazine—she probably never imagined her name would be used to describe a line of clothing in the far more mainstream and conservative *Women's Wear Daily*. Her name was used in mainstream culture to invoke something edgy, a woman's transgression into masculinity. In fashion terms, it meant to be daring and original, while still fashionable and sexy—taking something boyish and tough and making it feminine and alluring, which epitomizes what fashion is all about.

Measuring Smith's effect on rock music and pop culture is difficult, because most of what you can say about influence is anecdotal or a matter of opinion. It's easy to limit that discussion to her impact on women, since she was, after all, a female pioneer, and her influence on women musicians is omnipresent.

Smith's impact on rock 'n' roll and pop culture has manifested in concrete, artistic ways. In 2005, the Scottish singer-songwriter KT Tunstall had a minor hit with her single "Suddenly I See," from her 2004 debut album *Eyes to the Telescope*. The song was about Tunstall's reaction to the cover of *Horses*. The lyrics are about being entranced by a woman whose face is a "map of the world" and filled with mystery. The image makes Tunstall want to see the world and be "a tower," a line that evokes Smith's reference to building the tower of Babel in "Land."

In that picture on the cover of *Horses*, Tunstall saw a defiant, sexy, confident woman, and a world of possibilities opened up. "I aspired to what this image was about—which was a woman dressed in man's clothes with such mystery, but such confidence and attitude and character," she told the BBC. "I just thought, 'that's so what I want to be when I grow up.'"[2] It is these magical moments of inspiration, affirming possibilities, that make pop music so powerful, and it was a power that Smith has always intuitively understood and tried to harness.

"Suddenly I See" was later used as the theme song for the TV show, *Ugly Betty*, about a frumpy, slightly plump woman with braces who gets a job at a stylish fashion magazine. She boldly looks terrible yet ends up with a coveted job, in large part because she's unattractive. The Betty character is a far cry from Patti Smith's scrawny, scruffy beatnik image, but the sentiment—defying social conventions and creating your own image—is similar, albeit distilled through a mass-market TV show and made somewhat "safe" (which is no slight to television—some of the most subversive moments in pop culture arrive in the safest, most mainstream venues, such as the *Tonight Show* or *The Simpsons*). But while Smith has steadfastly resisted commercialization, those she inspired were more pliant. Aside from being used as a TV theme song, "Suddenly I See" was also used in a British Telecom advertisement.[3]

But Tunstall's song is a testament to the power of Smith's music and the confidence Smith projected. Smith's image and music spoke truths—the world is yours, you are free, you can be whatever you want, you don't have to follow conventional notions of beauty to be pretty or sexy—that Tunstall had yet to hear in any convincing way. Prior to that, Tunstall's world contained limitations that *Horses* somehow obliterated, helping her discover her own art—an epiphany she never forgot and later paid tribute to.

Smith has influenced countless musicians, both female and male. There are many anecdotes from other artists who were overcome when they first listened to or saw Smith. Female punk group The Slits met at a Patti Smith show, when she toured England in the late 1970s (though they later dissed her music and pointed to another of the era's trailblazers, the guitar-wielding Chrissie Hynde of the Pretenders as an even bigger influence). Shirley Manson, of the rock band Garbage, remembered the first time she heard Patti Smith's music.

> I was about nineteen when I first heard a Patti Smith record. It was *Horses*. I remember sitting there, very taken by the sound of her voice, this ferocious delivery. Later I was struck by how literate her lyrics were, how intellectual and political. I loved how, in her songs, she talked about anything other than the love in her heart for a man. And I loved her image: this non-glam look with the chopped-off hair, looking like a skinny boy. She was the complete opposite of the images that were pumped into me as a child, of what I was supposed to aspire to in a woman.[4]

Kirsten Hersh, of the group Throwing Muses, wrote that when she was a little girl, her father was a big Patti Smith fan. But Hersh was initially repulsed by the loud music and by a woman who—in Hersh's little-girl mind—tried to co-opt Easter from the chocolate bunnies. When she got older and started to make her own music, Hersh would listen to *Horses* and *Easter* while walking to and from the recording studio, a three-hour trek. "While I was listening to it, it was this whole planet. It's her planet. She made a whole world. She can bring you into her bubble of sound, but nobody else can, not even your own brain can. It's not your bubble, you can't grasp it and carry it around. Yet I remember that she said the word 'fingers,' because she made it sound so beautiful and sleazy at the same time, and I couldn't figure out how you could just take a digit and do that with it."[5]

The message that these younger female musicians took away was more than that it was okay to look and act like a man, but that they could do anything a male musician could do—they didn't have to fear appearing unfeminine. There was no rule book you had to follow as a woman in the music business. The palette of rock's history belonged to everyone, men and women, black and white. It was yours to pick and choose from and build on, and you could be whatever you wanted, if you simply dared.

Smith's influence extends well beyond mere "female rock," if such a thing even exists. She has inspired plenty of men, both rock artists and fans, like myself. R.E.M.'s Michael Stipe was profoundly touched by her music. In 1996, Stipe reminisced to *Mojo* magazine about discovering *Horses*:

> *Horses*...pretty much tore my limbs off and put them back on in a different way. I was 15 when I heard it, and that's pretty strong stuff for a 15-year-old American middle-class white boy, sitting in his parents' living room with the headphones on so they wouldn't hear it. It was like the first time you went into the ocean and got knocked down by a wave. It killed. It was so completely liberating. I had my parents' crappy headphones and I sat up all night with a huge bowl of cherries listening to Patti Smith, eating those cherries and going, "Oh, my God!...Holy shit!...Fuck!..." Then I was sick.[6]

When Smith burst onto the scene in the mid-1970s, she was an anomaly, filled with mystery. Her music and lyrics felt—and continue to feel—completely unique, their own thing. At a time when women's liberation was an issue for debate, Smith defiantly claimed the right to be whatever she wanted—not as some blow for women's lib, but as a declaration of freedom as an artist. She liberated herself, making it seem remarkably simple and easy.

She could not be contained by dogma, theory, or a political agenda—she was her own person, free to imagine herself as a man, even raping and killing, if she felt like it. Her rights, as a person and an artist, derived from her being a human being who dared to take risks. The distinction of gender, in Smith's eyes, was more or less immaterial, as she played with and subverted notions of gender roles. Just as she had moved with confidence in the scene surrounding the Chelsea Hotel in the mid-1970s, she placed herself on equal terms with her heroes: Rimbaud, Burroughs, Morrison, and Jagger.

Smith continues to have similar effects on people when they discover her work. *Horses* in particular is an earth-shattering record for people, because it crystallizes a moment of artistic rebellion or realization, a fan becoming a bona fide artist, using the world and history as a palette to create a new world. When you listen to *Horses,* rock 'n' roll sounds paradoxically less mystifying and more mystical.

I've always puzzled over many issues regarding pop culture and the relationship that icons and stars have with their fans. How do artists affect the culture? How do fans determine which performers to accept, which to reject? Why were women musicians—to me so enticing—rejected for so long, and why was the culture suddenly receptive to them in the '90s and beyond? These questions are central to Smith's career and art, because she helped bring about an enormous shift in the culture. She pushed a do-it-yourself aesthetic that had always been present in rock 'n' roll but was becoming forgotten, as polished session men and studio tricks conquered the garage rock bands.

In wondering about the gulf between performers and fans, it at some point occurred to me that throughout most of the past 50 years of pop music and beyond, women had generally been on the fan side of the dichotomy. But because I was especially drawn to female performers—Sally Timms, PJ Harvey, Throwing Muses, Liz Phair, Sleater-Kinney, Bikini Kill, Gillian Welch, the Raincoats, Liliput, Neko Case, Björk, Kat Brock and Angela Santos (of the Knoxville band, Dixie Dirt), and, of course, Patti Smith—it felt at times as if I had come along as a fan during some seismic shift in cultural dynamics. Had there been some gender-role reversal, with me as the stereotypical giddy teenage girl and PJ Harvey in the role of übercool Keith Richards? Seeing PJ Harvey for the first time in Toronto in 1992, I felt absolutely giddy—was this how Smith felt when she first saw the Stones live? I had a similar feeling seeing Sleater-Kinney in Atlanta a few years later. Was the way I related to music the same way that women had been approaching the pop culture for decades, as adoring fans, craving transcendence and fighting unbearable, impossible crushes? Or was it just that women—working outside the accepted mainstream norms—had the most to rebel against in the 1980s and 1990s and, therefore, struck me as the most engaging, in-your-face artists?

This feeling of being on the other side somehow comforted me, made me feel more aligned and empathetic with the women I idolized, whom I had, in the feminist courses I had taken in college, perhaps been taught to invariably see as the victims of male tyranny. It also felt revolutionary and subversive. Of course, the sex appeal was undeniably part of the thrill, but then, what is good rock 'n' roll without sex appeal? Another part of the draw for me was the chance to try to understand women through the music some of them made. It was one of the first ways I related to and connected with women as people—not some abstract fantasy, but human beings, with desires, needs, hang-ups, fears, and problems.

In addition, it felt good to root for the sex that had been traditionally oppressed and marginalized. Because women had plenty to rebel against (first and foremost, a sexist patriarchy), they seemed rightful heirs to rock 'n' roll's revolutionary fervor. Growing up after the feminist movement, this might seem a kind of victory. However, the institution of rock and roll was still (and continues to be) extremely sexist and limiting. In today's world, female performers are often valued primarily for their sex appeal with short shelf lives. (The maverick Smith is a notable exception.) But progress has certainly been made. Women are taken seriously as both artists and musicians (ala PJ Harvey, Sleater-Kinney, Björk, Missy Elliott, Lucinda Williams, Gillian Welch, M.I.A., Lady Sovereign, Kelis, and others) and are commercially viable on many levels (witness Madonna, the Spice Girls, Amy Winehouse, among others)—often both at the same time.

If the tide had shifted and the tables turned, Smith somehow seemed an integral and indelible part of the change. But it was also true that if she changed the perception of female musicians and broadened the opportunities available to women, it was partly because fans were ready for opportunities to explore new possibilities, models, and ideas.

In *Air Guitar*, Dave Hickey described the divide between performers and watchers but expanded it, realizing that some watchers are not merely passive. According to Hickey, in any art scene, there are spectators (his father called them "looky-loos") and there are participants, who actively seek out obscure and unknown art to support and nurture.

> The distinction is critical to the practice of art in a democracy, however, because spectators invariably align themselves with authority. They have neither the time nor the inclination to make decisions. They just love the winning side—the side with the chic building, the gaudy doctorates, and the star-studded cast. They seek out spectacles whose value is confirmed by the normative blessing of institutions and corporations.... Participants, on the other hand, do not like this feeling. They lose interest at the moment of accreditation, always

assuming there is something better out there, something brighter and more desirable, something more in tune with their own agendas.[7]

Thus, a remarkable woman named Patti Smith sought to be a star and people—bandmates, critics, record producers, but mostly fans who supported shows in dank clubs like CBGB and bought records—invested in her, making her a star. With the encouragement of their friends, several bands formed in the mid-1970s in New York's Lower East Side. They were inspired by legendary bands, such as the Velvet Underground, as well as classic garage bands and the British invasion groups. Most of them couldn't even play their instruments well, but they decided that the music they heard on the radio wasn't very good and they could do better. They found a platform and audience when Hilly Kristal opened his club, CBGB, to them. The people who went to the shows nurtured and fostered the scene, making it grow as it attracted attention from music critics, then more fans. And then yet more bands were inspired to pick up their instruments.

What started out as a scene accumulated social value through commerce—people paid for it (investing in it), so it became more valued and its commercial potential grew. What started as a scruffy group of misfit artists became legendary and institutionalized.

This process seems so rudimentary that it seems a little silly to spell it out. But as a scene, CBGB was consciously about looking for something new—something more personal (and thus "real" or "genuine"—although I dislike the implications those words hold—Michael Jackson and Brittney Spears are no less "real"), less "commercial" or polished, and more exciting. As an exercise in scene building, there were certainly precedents or roadmaps that could be followed. (The San Francisco music scene of the mid-1960s, the British invasion, the musicians who created Bebop, as well as literary and art scenes like the beatniks or the modernists, to name just a few.) But it was also a scene consciously looking for something new and different, as most scenes invariably form. It is a key reason that Smith, an eccentric, aspiring poet with ambitious ideas, could find a following in the New York rock scene and why her following would spiral into a national and international audience. She felt the culture needed waking up, but so did lots of other people, so that they were receptive to her. (The model also explains why critics later turned on Smith—at the moment of accreditation, they lost interest and went looking for something better and fresher.)

On some level, Smith understood this process. It's why she talked about rock 'n' roll being "the people's music" and called herself the "field marshal of rock 'n' roll." It was why she wrote in the *New York Times*, shortly before her induction into the Rock and Roll Hall of Fame, calling herself, "one who has loved rock 'n' roll and crawled from the ranks to the stage, to salute history and plant seeds for the erratic magic landscape of the new guard."[8] Large corporations might help spread the word by bestowing record contracts and sponsoring international stadium tours, but Smith saw rock as something that had to be nourished and maintained and propagated by people, by scenes, in dank, dark clubs, and on underground radio stations. New sounds and new excitement could only be generated in these places. On the stage during the final show at CBGB, Smith told the crowd: "Kids, they'll find some other club. You just got a place, just some crappy place, that nobody wants, and you got one guy who believes in you, and you just do your thing. And anybody can do that, anywhere in the world, any time."[9]

She later expanded on this in an interview, saying: "What makes [CBGBs] is the people and their collective energy. The people make CBGB. You can all start your own."[10] This is, of course, what Knoxville's Pilot Light was for me. Jason Boardman is the city's Hilly Kristal, giving the city's weird collection of artists and musicians a platform to make some noise, express themselves, take chances, reflect their culture, share ideas, conspire, fall in love, and create.

Even when she indulged in elitism and pretension, Smith has always kept this notion of people creating and nurturing art, music, and culture (a notion that is at times elitist and pretentious). It is perhaps why she could write an incredible song like "People Have the Power" (kind of corny, but also utterly righteous and true)—because she knew she gained her power from the people. If they made her a star, they could elect a better president. And maybe that's why she always had mercurial relationships with critics, because she sensed they hated her for her power and might try to divide her from the people. Or perhaps she hated critics because they aren't "of the people," but came representing individual tastes and authoritative opinions of art theory.

When I think back to when I first discovered Smith's music on *Horses* (after *Rolling Stone* magazine named it one of the greatest rock albums of all time) and began peeling back its layers, one of the things that struck me most was the violence of it. A switchblade slicing open Johnny's throat, dipping into the possibilities…of what? Suicide, murder? Masturbation? Rape? The privilege to rape either a man or a woman? I wasn't sure. It was extremely violent and very graphic in the way it visualized that violence, romanticized it, in a way that male musicians didn't. But at the same time, that violence didn't seem real—it struck me as make believe and role playing. (Today, I'm not sure if that's due to my own sexism: perhaps I just believed that coming from a woman, it had to be make believe. But then other women musicians have conveyed violent urges much more convincingly—as PJ Harvey did on her album *Rid of Me*.) On *Horses* there was a disconnect between the literal meanings of the lyrics and what they actually seemed to be suggesting—a distinction that was both powerful and vital (powerful because of the freedom it offered, vital because I needed to stay on the right side of righteousness and wanted my heroes to be good). But it seemed dangerous, and I guess that was the point, what Smith was driving at, getting off on the thrill of breaking a taboo: masturbating on record, if you will. What's more, the homoeroticism inherent in it—a man raping another man—was shocking. It's hard for me to remember now what was more shocking about it: the violence or the homosexuality. Unlike, say a Led Zeppelin or AC/DC song (which seem tepid compared to Smith), the lust on "Land" was directed from a guy to a guy, but it all came wrapped up in the voice of a woman, which made it all seem safe. It is a very phallic and violent image, that knife dipping into Johnny's smooth (virgin-like) throat. In someone else's hands, it would have sounded like parody, but Smith played it straight and with deadly seriousness. It liberated listeners much the way Little Richard did 20 years earlier,

Smith was not acting on behalf of women, however. She was out to liberate herself and anyone who cared to listen, but her messages weren't aimed at other women or against men. Smith—like many female musicians—has resisted feminist labels. Early in her career, she complained to Nick Tosches—in *Penthouse* magazine of all places, defiantly refusing to be cast as a feminist hero—about the popularity of the courtesy title, Ms. "It sounds like a sick bumblebee, it sounds frigid. I mean, who the hell would ever want to stick his hand up the dress of somebody who goes around calling herself something like Ms.? It's all so stupid."[11]

She resisted more than just the cosmetic aspects of feminism, though. For her, being lumped into a group defined by her gender—no matter how equal it might be—was simply distasteful.

> I don't like answering to other people's philosophies. I don't have any phi-
> losophy, I just believe in stuff. Either I believe in something or I don't. Like,
> I believe in the Rolling Stones but not in the Dave Clark Five. There's nothing
> philosophic about it. Whenever I'm linked with a movement, it pisses me off.
> I like who I am. I always liked who I was and I always loved men. The only
> time I ever feel fucked around by men is when I fight with a guy or when a
> guy ditches me. And that's got nothing to do with women's lib. That has to
> do with being ditched. I don't feel exploited by pictures of naked broads. I like
> that stuff. It's a bad photograph or the girl's ugly, then that pisses me off. Shit,
> I think bodies are great.[12]

Nevertheless, Smith did see her band and her music as presenting a more feminine aspect to rock 'n' roll—a broadening of the landscape to include new perspectives. She went so far as to contrast her music to male rock, using the metaphor of gender differences in orgasms. "We're not like a male band either, in that the male process of ecstasy in performance is starting here," she told one interviewer, as she mimed jerking off—"and building and building until the big spurt at the end. We're a feminine band, we'll go so far and peak and then we'll start again and peak, over and over. It's like ocean. We leave ourselves wide open for failure, but we also leave ourselves open to achieving a moment more magical."[13]

Smith certainly belongs in a long line of renegade women who have advanced feminism, pushing the boundaries and shattering stereotypes of what women could do or were allowed to do: how they could act, what they could wear, and what they could sing about.

Many engaging women performers had risen to prominence before Smith, bursting out of these constraints, but they largely continued to follow isolated gender roles, or to be marketed and perceived within those roles, no matter how original they were and how much they spoke to both female and male fans. Generally, women were pushed into two different categories as performers: the ultrafeminine diva and the brainy, granola folk singer. Both were extremely limiting. Female artists such as Fanny, Suzi Quatro, or the Runaways that tried to create straight-ahead rock 'n' roll were seen as novelties, women playing at being men, almost a form of dress up. They continued to be dogged and haunted by sexual stereotypes.

Another of rock's great mavericks, Joan Jett, once complained that the Runaways were always asked the same question in interviews. "The first question would be, 'I heard you girls are all sluts, right?' It was torture."[14]

Even some enormous female talents were limited by the way they were portrayed in the music press and by their record labels. Janis Joplin was an obvious groundbreaker, fronting various rock bands with a performance as powerful as any male rock star. But underneath her ferocious delivery, was a fragility. Her image was one of a brokenhearted, jilted lover—never mind that this was a persona she created. Of course, she was a phenomenal, over-the-top performer, but she never let it overwhelm her femininity.

The shadow of Janis Joplin loomed large over any female rock musician of the day. Without question, Joplin was a groundbreaking performer. Unlike the girl groups and soul singers before her—who were viewed as teen novelties—Joplin was the first to be a bona fide rock star, idolized on the stage in the same way that men were. She performed with an abandon—suggesting hedonism and rock 'n' roll excess—that was similar to male rock stars. Rosanne Cash wrote of her: "Janis Joplin was absolutely a barnstormer and a complete groundbreaker. She wasn't just a great woman in rock—at the time she was the woman in rock. Janis really created this whole world of possibility for women in music: Without Janis Joplin, there would be no Melissa Etheridge. Without Janis, there would be no Chrissie Hynde, no Gwen Stefani. There would be no one."[15]

Smith also played with a spirit of decadence and abandon, but she managed to stay in control. Her ability to not be consumed by her mania and her art is one of the biggest characteristics distinguishing Smith from rock stars who treaded similar territory. The others lost control and often died; Smith never did. She survived and continued to make engaging art, to be a cultural force and an icon. "You don't have to be devoid of fun; you don't have to be a square," she told *Pitchfork*. "There's a way to find balance, to sometimes go overboard or sometimes experiment without ruining your life. That's important in everything we do, whether it's using a cell phone, smoking pot, staying out all night. You have to find balance. You have to not be a slave to this stuff. You have to be the master of everything."[16]

One of Joplin's contemporaries, Grace Slick of Jefferson Airplane, also helped pave the way for other female musicians, but unlike Joplin, Slick was a survivor. Smith had credited Slick with pioneering a gender-neutral singing voice. Smith said of all the artists she covered on *twelve* in 2007, only Slick's "White Rabbit" scared her: "It was the heavy song to do, it was most difficult to hit the notes, it was most difficult to try and keep step with her. I tried to make it more of an atmosphere piece, because I couldn't possibly match the height of Grace Slick. So it's really like a salute to her. Even though there's only one woman on the record, she rules."[17]

But as part of an ensemble, Slick did not dominate the attention of Jefferson Airplane. Although she wrote the group's biggest hits, her accomplishment was often overshadowed by her male colleagues. Slick used to downplay her own talent. "I'm nothing except possibly more aggressive than most females my age," she told one interviewer. [18] At any rate, Jefferson Airplane—despite Slick's iconic anthems—did not have the cultural impact of other 1960s bands and soon faded from the scene. (They reemerged as Jefferson Starship in the 1980s for the MTV generation, later called simply Starship—but the group's second act was a tepid one: its banal, self-congratulatory anthems such as "We Built This City" may have made money but were a far cry from the group's earlier, edgier work.)

Joni Mitchell and Carole King both displayed independence, intelligence, and toughness in their songs. But these traits were often overshadowed by the sensitive, singer-songwriter genre they worked in—you had to listen for the payoff. However great and, at times, ferocious Mitchell's guitar playing was, she didn't quite rock. Both Mitchell and King were seen as gifted, smart songwriters, but they were never rock stars the way that many male rock stars were.

Another pioneer was the often-maligned Yoko Ono, to whom Gillian Gaar attributes the roots of punk rock: "*Yoko Ono/Plastic Ono Band* did not merely define the roots of what punk rock would become, it *was* punk rock, a harsh, confrontational barrage of noise in which the instrumentation and vocals were just barely restrained from tumbling over into complete chaos."[19] But unfairly blamed by many in the music press for breaking up the Beatles, Ono never got much credit for her talent during her heyday. Gaar makes a direct connection from Ono to Smith by pointing out that Ono and Lennon were making music together at the time when Smith was establishing herself on the New York scene, suggesting that Smith—subconsciously, at least—absorbed much of Ono's influence. But despite her considerable talent and vision, Ono was never able to make much of a favorable impression with the public. She never wrote anything that could have been radio friendly, the way Smith did with dozens of songs. Ono could never escape the radical notion of art rock, whereas Smith's music was favorably received in many different scenes.

Another art rock favorite was Nico, a German model who later became an actress and then connected with the Warhol crowd, dating a number of rock stars, before joining her own band, the Velvet Underground, which also included the amazing Moe Tucker, one of rock's all-time greatest drummers. Nico was much more of a chanteuse, performing other people's songs.

The Patti Smith Group found its first audience among the same art-house, urban rock crowd. At the same time, as a tough girl from New Jersey, Smith also understood the working-class appeal of rock 'n' roll. Although she was never quite a working-class hero the way Bruce Springsteen has been, she was—and is—capable of appealing to a more grassroots rock crowd.

There are many predecessors to Smith—far too many to name here. But most of these predecessors remained in obscurity or found success only by reflecting the dominant gender roles, playing the part of diva or sexpot or earthy, brainy intellectual. There were few models for what Smith wanted to achieve in the music business. As such, she was inspired mostly by men. "When you saw females in, in the music business, they were all either like, lot of square white girls, who were good singers and stuff but, like, Lesley Gore or Sandra Dee or people like that, or you saw some really great singers like Darlene Love and people like that, but they were singers," she said during an interview on National Public Radio's *Fresh Air*. "I was raised that all the great rock performers were guys, y'know, y'know, from, I mean I loved, y'know, Jimi Hendrix, I liked the Rolling Stones, and Jim Morrison, and, and Bob Dylan, and people like that. I mean even somebody like Elvis Presley. I mean, I just like a committed performer."[20]

There were a few obscure female musicians—such as Lotte Lenya—who did catch her attention and influence her. But in the field of rock 'n' roll, Smith was largely working with a blank slate.

Critics Simon Reynolds and Joy Press, in their book *The Sex Revolts: Gender, Rebellion, and Rock 'n' Roll,* posit that women have traditionally rebelled in one of two ways in rock music: either by trying to forge a distinctly female model or focusing on the confusion that arises in trying to determine sexual identity. "Some of the most powerful music by women originates in confusion rather than certainty. These artists have worked from within the problematic of (female) identity....Identity is seen as open space rather than structure, full of the clamor and turmoil of divided impulses and contradictory desires. So this torn subjectivity is expressed through language that's fractured and frayed, that oscillates between incoherence and visionary lucidity."[21]

Reynolds and Press describe Patti Smith as epitomizing the latter approach, fighting an internal sexual identity war that is laid bare in her music, which made for compelling art. They also argue that Smith's heroes—Morrison, Rimbaud, the Romantic poets—felt connected to their own feminine side. "By identifying with these male avant-gardists and Romantics, Smith found a way to reclaim women's own wildness."[22] In their view, this wildness—and the musical attempt at feminine orgasm—characterizes "Land" and "Radio

Ethiopia," which subvert rock 'n' roll structure and format. "Patti Smith's double bind was that she admired the psychic surfers (the male rebels who could 'play with madness,' skimming its turbulent surface without drowning in it); at the same time, she worshipped 'the infinite sea.' And because she lacked a prototype for a female Dionysian spirit, she was out there on her own."[23]

It was that Dionysian spirit that gave Smith her spark—that was so confounding and captivating to me when I first heard *Horses* as a teenager. By sheer force of will, Smith claimed authority, demanding attention and claiming for herself an independence that was contagious to anyone who heard it.

Many other female—and male—musicians have examined, toyed with, and used gender confusion artistically, but Smith was one of the pioneers of this approach. As such, it's hard not to see her figure towering behind anyone else who treads similar territory.

Although Smith's music has certainly been inspiring, in some ways it is almost overshadowed by her image, which looms larger than life. Critics have written almost as much about the cover of *Horses* as they have about its music. Camille Paglia, herself a renegade in the field of feminist theory, has written how the album's cover touched her profoundly, just as she was working on her landmark *Sexual Personae*. She hung the album on her wall.

> Smith's persona was brand-new. She was the first to claim both vision and authority, in the dangerously Dionysian style of another poet, Jim Morrison, lead singer of the Doors....No female rocker had ever dominated an image in this aggressive, uncompromising way....Smith defies the rules of femininity. Soulful, haggard and emaciated yet raffish, swaggering and seductive, she is mad saint, ephebe, dandy and troubador, a complex woman alone and outward bound for culture war.[24]

In recent years, Smith has acknowledged the difficulties women performers face and continue to face, but has said her main crusade has been for liberation, not just of women, but of all people. "It was a lot harder back [in the 1970s] for women to do things than it is now, and I'm certain that it's still more of a challenge, but I think that we've come a long way. I never think in terms of gender-specificity, but I'm certainly a woman and a mother. Somebody said to me that they were disappointed that I wasn't more involved in women's rights. I said, 'Well, I'm a mother. I have a son and a daughter. Who do you think I should fight for?' I fight for both of them."[25]

It might be true that all female musicians working today owe some debt to Patti Smith—it's hard to imagine Courtney Love, PJ Harvey, KT Tunstall, or Sleater-Kinney without Patti Smith. But it would be insulting to suggest that Smith's impact on rock music was primarily on women. Male musicians owe plenty to Smith too—and it's hard to imagine Kurt Cobain, the Sex Pistols, the Clash, and Marilyn Manson without her. Smith broadened the landscape of what rock music could do and what it meant to be a star.

She helped reinvent the genre during its most bloated and pompous period. Unlike the punk rockers she inspired, she did so without being overwhelmed by irony—an approach that can certainly be used with purpose but eventually turns on itself. Smith held fast to the ideals rock musicians expounded in the sixties, which ultimately affirmed life and the possibilities to create. There were times when she indulged in pretentious notions but also moments when she stripped pretension from the form, humanizing it.

Throughout her career, Smith has toyed with several different personas and images, which are sometimes hard to separate. But some specific identities emerge. There is the gender-bending artist who mixed and matched from the various pop personas of her day, picking and choosing what she liked best, in order to create something new. There is the sha-woman who works to channel the dead—or simply remind the living of the dead—in intense, emotional performances. There is also the elder statesperson who speaks out against evil in the world. There is the motherly figure who worries about her children, both her literal children and the figurative ones whom she helped inspire in the rock 'n' roll world.

But perhaps Smith's most enduring achievement in the past 30 years has been her steadfast belief in rock 'n' roll. Although Smith utilized and toyed with myth making throughout her career, her belief in rock 'n' roll is not rooted in the power of myth (although there is plenty of power to be found there, to be sure). Instead, it is a belief in the power of communication, of people talking to each other, and in the idea that everyone has something to say and that, in the expression of these desires, magic can happen: new voices are heard, people inspired, movements created, love and culture remembered and nurtured. Walking to Sunday School with her mother in 1955, Smith heard a song—Little Richard's "Tutti Frutti"—that mystified her with a power that transfixed her for the rest of her life, a power she continuously tried to reconnect with and feed off of.

Smith wanted to mystify people with her own arresting visions and rants, and she did. But she remained open to others' ideas, influence, and music. In the *New York Times,* Smith wrote about how the Internet is the global CBGB, a space for creating new sounds and new ideas; in it she saw great potential for what kids—young and old—could do with it. "They will dictate how they want to create and disseminate their work. They will, in time, make breathless changes in our political process.... Their potential power to form and reform is unprecedented."[26]

In other words, as she sang on "Land" more than 30 years ago, *there is a sea seize the possibility.* Smith's art—whatever missteps or false notes it might include—has always been a testament to seizing possibilities: harnessing your passions, your society, culture, and art. In her music, Smith liberated herself and showed the rest of us how it's done.

Discography

ALBUMS

Horses (Arista, December 1975). Producer, John Cale. Side one: "Gloria (in Excelsis Deo)" (P. Smith, Van Morrison), "Redondo Beach" (Smith, Richard Sohl, Lenny Kaye), "Birdland" (Smith, Sohl, Kaye, Ivan Kral), "Free Money" (Smith, Kaye). Side two: "Kimberly" (Smith, Allen Lanier, Kral), "Break It Up" (Smith, Tom Verlaine), "Land: Horses" (Smith), "Land of a Thousand Dances" (Chris Kenner), "La Mer (de)" (Smith), "Elegie" (Smith, Allen Lanier). Bonus track on 1996 CD reissue: "My Generation" (Pete Townshend).

Radio Ethiopia (Arista, October 1976). Producer, Jack Douglas. Side one: "Ask the Angels" (Smith, Kral), "Ain't It Strange" (Smith, Kral), "Poppies" (Smith, Sohl), "Pissing in a River" (Smith, Kral). Side two: "Pumping (My Heart)" (Smith, Kral, Jay Dee Daugherty), "Distant Fingers" (Smith, Lanier), "Radio Ethiopia" (Smith, Kaye), "Abyssinia" (Smith, Kaye, Sohl). Bonus track on 1996 CD reissue: "Chicklets."

Easter (Arista, March 1978). Producer, Jimmy Iovine. Side one: "Till Victory" (Smith, Kaye), "Space Monkey" (Smith, Kral, Verlaine), "Because the Night" (Smith, Bruce Springsteen), "Ghost Dance" (Smith, Kaye), "Babelogue" (Smith), "Rock n Roll Nigger" (Smith, Kaye). Side two: "Privilege (Set Me Free)" (Mel London, Mike Leander, quoting from the 23rd Psalm), "We Three" (Smith, arranged by Verlaine), "25th Floor" (Smith, Kral), "High on Rebellion" (Smith), "Easter" (Smith, Daugherty). Bonus track on 1996 CD reissue: "godspeed" (Smith, Kral).

Wave (Arista, May 1979). Producer, Todd Rundgren. Side one: "Frederick" (Smith), "Dancing Barefoot" (Smith, Kral), "So You Want to Be (a Rock and Roll Star)" (James McGuinn, Chrirstopher Hillman), "Hymn" (Smith, Kaye), "Revenge" (Smith, Kral). Side two: "Citizen Ship" (Smith, Kral), "Seven Ways of

Going" (Smith), "Broken Flag" (Smith, Kaye), "Wave" (Smith). Bonus tracks on 1996 CD reissue: "Fire of Unknown Origin" (Smith, Kaye), "5-4-3-2-1/ Wave" (Paul Jones, Mike Hugg, Manfred Mann).

Dream of Life (Arista, June 1988). Producers, Jimmy Iovine, Fred Smith. All songs by Patti and Fred Smith. Side one: "People Have the Power," "Going Under," "Up There Down There," "Paths That Cross." Side two: "Dream of Life," "Where Duty Calls," "Looking for You (I Was)," "The Jackson Song." Bonus tracks on 1996 CD reissue: "As the Night Goes By," "Wild Leaves."

Gone Again (Arista, June 1996). Producers, Malcolm Burn, Lenny Kaye. "Gone Again" (Fred Smith, Patti Smith), "Beneath the Southern Cross" (Kaye, Smith), "About a Boy" (Smith), "My Madrigal" (Luis Resto, Smith), "Summer Cannibals" (Fred Smith, Patti Smith), "Dead to the World" (Smith), "Wing" (Smith), "Ravens" (Smith), "Wicked Messenger" (Dylan), "Fireflies" (Oliver Ray, Smith), "Farewell Reel" (Smith).

peace and noise (Arista, September 1997). Producer, Ray Cicala. "Waiting Underground" (Smith, Ray), "Whirl Away" (Smith, Kaye, Ray), "1959" (Smith, Tony Shanahan), "Spell" (Allen Ginsberg, Ray), "Don't Say Nothing" (Smith, Daugherty), "Dead City" (Smith, Ray), "Blue Poles" (Smith, Ray), "Death Singing" (Smith), "Memento Mori" (Smith, Kaye, Ray, Daugherty, Shanahan), "Last Call" (Smith, Ray).

The Patti Smith Masters: The Collective Works (Arista, June 1996). Box set of first five albums, with bonus tracks included at the end of each album and a sixth CD of "selected songs."

Gung Ho (Arista, March 2000). Producer, Gil Norton. "One Voice" (Smith, Daugherty), "Lo and Beholden" (Smith, Kaye), "Boy Cried Wolf" (Smith), "Persuasion" (Patti Smith, Fred Smith), "Gone Pie" (Smith, Shanahan), "China Bird" (Smith, Ray), "Glitter in Their Eyes" (Smith, Ray), "Strange Messengers" (Smith, Kaye), "Grateful" (Smith), "Upright Come" (Smith, Ray), "New Party" (Smith, Shanahan), "Libbie's Song" (Smith), "Gung Ho" (Daugherty, Kaye, Ray, Smith, Shanahan).

Land (1975–2002) (Arista, 2002). Two-disc greatest-hits/rarities compilation. Disc one: "Dancing Barefoot," "Babelogue," "Rock n Roll Nigger," "Gloria," "Pissing in a River," "Free Money," "People Have the Power," "Because the Night," "Frederick," "Summer Cannibals," "Ghost Dance," "Ain't It Strange," "1959," "Beneath the Southern Cross," "Glitter in Their Eyes," "Paths That Cross," "When Doves Cry" (Prince). Disc two: "Piss Factory" (Smith, Sohl), "Redondo Beach" (demo), "Distant Fingers" (demo), "25th Floor" (live, Eugene, Oregon, 1978), "Come Back Little Sheba" (Kaye, Smith), "Wander I Go" (Smith, Ray), "Dead City" (live, Denmark, 2001), "Spell" (live, Portland, Oregon, 2001), "Wing" (live, Paris, 2001), "Boy Cried Wolf" (live, Paris, 2001), "Birdland" (live, Los Angeles, 2001), "Higher Learning" (Daugherty, Kaye, Ray, Shanahan, Smith, the Rev. Frank Ray), "Notes to the Future" (Smith, live, St. Mark's Church, New York, 2002).

Trampin' (Columbia, April 2004). Producers, Patti Smith and band. "Jubilee" (Smith, Kaye, Daugherty), "Mother Rose" (Smith, Shanahan), "Stride of the Mind" (Smith, Ray), "Cartwheels" (Smith, Kaye), "Gandhi" (Smith, Kaye, Daugherty, Shanahan, Ray), "Trespasses" (Smith, Daugherty), "In My Blakean Year" (Smith), "Cash" (Smith, Ray), "Peaceable Kingdom" (Smith, Shanahan), "Radio Baghdad" (Smith, Ray), "Trampin'" (traditional).

Horses/Horses, Legacy Edition (Arista, November 2005). Commemorative 30th-anniversary reissue of *Horses,* including the original album plus a second CD with a live recording of the album performed at the 2005 Meltdown Festival at the Royal Festival Hall in London on June 25, 2005.

twelve (Columbia, April 2007). Producers, Patti Smith and her band. "Are You Experienced?" (Jimi Hendrix), "Everybody Wants to Rule the World" (Roland Orzabal, Ian Stanley, Chris Hughes), "Helpless" (Neil Young), "Gimmie Shelter" (Mick Jagger, Keith Richards), "Within You Without You" (George Harrison), "White Rabbit" (Grace Slick), "Changing of the Guards" (Bob Dylan), "The Boy in the Bubble" (Paul Simon), "Soul Kitchen" (The Doors), "Smells Like Teen Spirit" (Nirvana), "Midnight Rider" (Gregg Allman, Robert Payne), "Pastime Paradise" (Stevie Wonder).

SINGLES/EPS

"Hey Joe" (Smith, Billy Roberts)/"Piss Factory" (Smith) (Mer Records, 1974).

"Gloria in Excelsis Deo"/"My Generation" (Arista, 1976).

"Pissing in a River"/"Ask the Angels" (Arista, 1976).

"Pissing in a River"/"Pumping (My Heart)" (Arista, 1976).

"Hey Joe"/"Radio Ethiopia" (Arista, 1977).

"Hey Joe"/"Piss Factory" (Sire, 1977).

Set Free EP (Arista, 1978); "Privilege (Set Me Free)," "Ask the Angels," "25th Floor," (live, Paris, 1978); "A Poem Babelfield" (Smith, live, London, 1978).

"Because the Night"/"Godspeed" (Arista, 1978).

"Frederick"/"Frederick" (live) (Arista, 1979).

"So You Want to Be (a Rock and Roll Star)"/"5-4-3-2-1 Wave"/"A Fire of Unknown Origin" (Arista, 1979).

"People Have the Power"/"Where Duty Calls"/"Wild Leaves" (Arista, 1988).

"Looking for You (I Was)"/"Up There Down There" (Arista, 1988).

Summer Cannibals 2-CD EP (Arista, 1996). Disc one: "Summer Cannibals"/ "Come Back Little Sheba" (acoustic), "Gone Again" (live), "People Have the Power." Disc two: "Summer Cannibals," "People Have the Power" (live), "Beneath the Southern Cross," "Come On in My Kitchen" (Robert Johnson).

"1959" (Arista, 1997).

"Glitter in Their Eyes" (Arista, 2000).

"Jubilee" (Columbia, 2004).

"Qana"/ "Without Chains." Free singles available via download from www. pattismith.net.

"Gimmie Shelter" (Columbia, 2007).

Notes

INTRODUCTION

1. Zippy McDuff, "Eye on the Scene," *Metro Pulse*, August 3, 2000, p. 18.
2. Gillian G. Gaar, *She's a Rebel: The History of Women In Rock 'n' Roll*, 2nd ed. Emeryville, CA: Seal Press, 1992.
3. Smith, *Patti Smith Complete*, p. 25.

CHAPTER 1

1. Patti Smith, "We Can Be Heroes," *Details*, July 1993.
2. Dave Hickey, *Air Guitar: Essays on Art & Democracy* (Art Issues Press, 1997), pp. 15–17.
3. Victor Bockris and Roberta Bayley, *Patti Smith: An Unauthorized Biography* (Simon & Schuster, 1999), p. 52.
4. Patti Smith, *Patti Smith Complete, 1975–2006* (Harper Perennial, 2006), p. 25.
5. Paul Lester, "Icon, Me?" *The Scotsman*, April 7, 2007.
6. Bockris and Bayley, *Patti Smith*, p. 19.
7. Bockris and Bayley, *Patti Smith*, pp. 19–20.
8. Sharon Delano, "The Torch Singer," *New Yorker*, March 11, 2002.
9. Delano, "Torch Singer," p. 56.
10. Patti Smith, "Ain't It Strange," *New York Times*, March 12, 2007, and Smith, *Patti Smith Complete*, pp. 18–19.
11. Smith, *Patti Smith Complete*, p. 19.
12. Delano, "Torch Singer," p. 56.
13. Mick Gold, "Patti in Excelsis Deo," *Street Life*, May 29, 1976.
14. Terry Gross, interview on *Fresh Air*, National Public Radio, June 24, 1996.
15. Nick Tosches, "A Baby Wolf with Neon Bones," *Penthouse*, April 1976.

16. Amy Gross, "I'm Doing a Revenge for Bad Skin," *Mademoiselle*, September 1975.

17. Tosches, "Baby Wolf."

18. Tosches, "Baby Wolf."

19. Tosches, "Baby Wolf."

20. Smith, "We Can Be Heroes."

21. Bockris and Bayley, *Patti Smith*, p. 36.

22. Gold, "Patti in Excelsis Deo."

23. Bockris and Bayley, *Patti Smith*, pp. 36–37.

24. Scott Cohen, "How a Little Girl Took over a Tough Gang: The Hard-Rock Poets," *Oui*, July 1976.

25. Penny Green, "Patti Smith," *Interview*, October 1973.

26. Delano, "Torch Singer," pp. 53–56.

27. Bockris and Bayley, *Patti Smith*, p. 40.

28. Smith, "We Can Be Heroes."

29. Smith, "Jag-arr of the Jungle," *Creem*, January 1973.

30. Bockris and Bayley, *Patti Smith*, pp. 43–44.

31. Dave Marsh, "Her Horses Got Wings, They Can Fly," *Rolling Stone*, January 1, 1976.

32. Bockris and Bayley, *Patti Smith*, p. 46.

33. Bockris and Bayley, *Patti Smith*, p. 47.

34. Michael Gross, "Misplaced Joan of Arc," *Blast*, August 1976.

35. Bockris and Bayley, *Patti Smith*, p. 48; Delano, "Torch Singer," p. 57.

36. Joanna Pitman, "Elegy for a Lost Soulmate," *TimesOnline*, September 6, 2006.

37. Marc Stevens and Diana Clapton, "Patti Smith Peaking: The Infinite Possibilities of a Woman," *Club Quest*, January 1977.

38. Smith, *Patti Smith Complete*, p. 21.

39. Ben Edmonds, "The Rebel," *Mojo*, August 1996.

40. Lisa Robinson, "The High Priestess of Rock and Roll," *Hit Parader*, January 1976.

41. Bockris and Bayley, *Patti Smith*, p. 66.

42. Gross, "Misplaced Joan of Arc."

43. Delano, "Torch Singer," p. 57.

44. Bockris and Bayley, *Patti Smith*, p. 61.

45. Delano, "Torch Singer," p. 57.

46. Delano, "Torch Singer," pp. 57–58.

47. Nick Tosches, "Eat Lead, Dog of Mediocrity," *Creem*, September 1978.

48. Bockris and Bayley, *Patti Smith*, pp. 13–18.

49. Delano, "Torch Singer," p. 58.

50. Bockris and Bayley, *Patti Smith*, p. 17.

51. Delano, "Torch Singer," p. 58.

52. Robinson, "High Priestess of Rock and Roll."

53. Delano, "Torch Singer," p. 58.

54. Bockris and Bayley, *Patti Smith*, p. 70.

55. Ibid., pp. 83–85.

56. Smith, *Patti Smith Complete*, p. 27.

57. Delano, "Torch Singer," p. 58.

58. Gross, "Misplaced Joan of Arc."

59. Smith, "We Can Be Heroes."

CHAPTER 2

1. Greil Marcus, *Lipstick Traces: A Secret History of the Twentieth Century* (Harvard University Press, 1989), pp. 262–66.

2. Simon Reynolds, "Patti Smith: Even as a Child I Felt like an Alien," *The Guardian Observer Music Monthly,* May 22, 2005.

3. *Larry King Live* transcript, broadcast January 22, 2002.

4. *Larry King Live* transcript, broadcast January 22, 2002.

5. Patti Smith, *Patti Smith Complete, 1975–2006* (Harper Perennial, 2006), p. 27.

6. Tosches, "Baby Wolf."

7. Tosches, "Baby Wolf."

8. Michael Bracewell, "Woman as Warrior," *The Guardian,* June 22, 1996.

9. Ben Edmonds, "The Rebel," *Mojo,* August 1996.

10. Sean O'Hagan, "American Icon," *The Observer,* June 15, 2003.

11. Edmonds, "Rebel"; Victor Bockris and Roberta Bayley, *Patti Smith: An Unauthorized Biography* (Simon & Schuster, 1999), p. 106; Evelyn McDonnell, "Because the Night," *The Village Voice,* August 1, 1995.

CHAPTER 3

1. *Billboard* magazine, http://www.billboard.com/bbcom/charts/yearend_chart_display.jsp?f=The+Billboard+Hot+100&g=Year-end+Singles&year=1975.

2. Nick Tosches, "A Baby Wolf with Neon Bones," *Penthouse,* April 1976.

3. Jon Pareles, "A Punk-Rock Institution Closes Its Doors," *New York Times,* October 16, 2006.

4. David Fricke, "Exclusive Q&A: The Final Word from Patti Smith on CBGB," *Rolling Stone* online, October 17, 2006, www.rollingstone.com/news/story/12054 256/exclusive_qa_patti_smith_remembers_cbgb.

5. Chris Barry, "Ask the Angel," *Montreal Mirror,* September 28, 2007.

6. Charles Shaar Murray, "Down in the Scuzz with the Heavy Cult Figures," *New Musical Express,* June 7, 1975.

7. Marc Stevens and Diana Clapton, "Patti Smith Peaking: The Infinite Possibilities of a Woman," *Club Quest,* January 1977.

8. John Rockwell, "Patti Smith Battles To a Singing Victory," *New York Times,* December 28, 1975.

9. Tosches, "Baby Wolf."

10. Victor Bockris and Roberta Bayley, *Patti Smith: An Unauthorized Biography* (Simon & Schuster, 1999), pp. 120–21; Dave Marsh, "Her Horses Got Wings, They Can Fly," *Rolling Stone,* January 1, 1976.

11. William S. Burroughs, "When Patti Rocked," *Spin,* April 1988; Bockris and Bayley, *Patti Smith,* p. 121.

12. Lucy O'Brien, "John Cale and Patti Smith: How We Met," *Independent on Sunday,* August 25, 1996.

13. Ben Edmonds, "The Rebel," *Mojo,* August 1996.

14. Jessica Robertson, "Patti Smith Q&A," AOL Music, http://spinner.aol.com/ rockhall/patti-smith-2007-inductee/interview.

15. Fricke, "Exclusive Q&A."

16. Simon Reynolds, "Patti Smith: Even as a Child I Felt Like an Alien," *The Guardian Observer Music Monthly,* May 22, 2005.

17. Smith, *Patti Smith Complete,* p. 32; Reynolds, "Patti Smith"; Tony Hiss and David McClelland, "Gonna Be so Big, Gonna Be a Start, Watch Me Now!" *New York Times Magazine,* December 21, 1975.

18. Marsh, "Her Horses Got Wings."

19. Reynolds, "Patti Smith."

20. Smith, *Patti Smith Complete,* p. 44.

21. Smith, *Patti Smith Complete,* p. 48.

22. Reynolds, "Patti Smith."

23. Reynolds, "Patti Smith."

24. Smith, *Patti Smith Complete,* p. 25.

25. Jenny Turner, "Patti Smith and Richard Hell: Two Punks Don't Make a Summer," *New Statesman,* July 5, 1996.

26. Mitchell Cohen, "Patti Smith: Avery Fisher Hall, NYC," *Phonograph Record,* May 1976.

27. Lester Bangs, "Stagger Lee Was a Woman," *Creem,* February 1976.

28. Charles Shaar Murray, "Weird Scenes Inside the Gasoline Alley," *New Musical Express,* November 1975.

29. Sean O'Hagen, "American Icon," *The Observer,* June 15, 2003.

30. Bruce Berman, "The Queen of Acid Punk Rock," *Acid Rock,* November 1977.

31. Thurston Moore, "Patti Smith," *Bomb,* Issue 54, Winter 1996.

32. Ben Edmonds, "Michael Stipe on Patti," *Mojo,* August 1996.

33. Reynolds, "Patti Smith."

34. Dave Schulps, "Tom Verlaine: In Search of Adventure," *Trouser Press,* May 1978.

35. Steve Simels, "Patti Smith," *Stereo Review,* August 1978.

36. Lisa Robinson, "Patti Smith's Intuitive Mania," *Hit Parader,* March 1978.

37. Sasha Frere-Jones, "Ring in the Old," *New Yorker,* December 25, 2006; January 1, 2007, p. 28.

38. Tosches, "Baby Wolf."

CHAPTER 4

1. Michael Bracewell, "Woman as Warrior," *The Guardian,* June 22, 1996.

2. Stephen Foehr, "The Death and the Rebirth of Patti Smith," *Shambhala Sun,* July 1996.

3. Steve Simels, "Patti Smith," *Stereo Review,* August 1978.

4. Terry Gross, interview on *Fresh Air,* National Public Radio, June 24, 1996.

5. Scott Cohen, "Patti Smith: Can You Hear Me Ethiopia," *Circus Magazine,* December 14, 1976.

6. Penny Green, "Patti Smith," *Andy Warhol's Interview,* 1973.

7. Gross, interview on *Fresh Air.*

8. Victor Bockris and Roberta Bayley, *Patti Smith: An Unauthorized Biography* (Simon & Schuster, 1999), p. 158.

9. Andy Schwartz, "Patti Smith—A Wave Hello, a Kiss Goodbye," *New York Rocker,* June/July 1979.

10. Lisa Robinson, "Patti Smith: Decoding Ethiopia," *Hit Parader,* June 1977.

11. Bruce Berman, "The Queen of Acid Punk Rock," *Acid Rock,* November 1977.

12. Lisa Robinson, "Patti Smith Talks about Radio Ethiopia," *Hit Parader,* Summer–Fall 1977.

13. Robinson, "Patti Smith Talks."

14. Foehr, "Death and Rebirth of Patti Smith."

15. Patti Smith, *Patti Smith Complete, 1975–2006* (Harper Perennial, 2006), p. 85.

16. Charles Young, "Patti Smith Catches Fire," *Rolling Stone,* March 1977.

17. Mariane Partridge, "Radio Ethiopia," *Melody Maker,* October 23, 1976.

18. Dave Marsh, review, *Rolling Stone,* March 1977.

19. K. Stein, "Radio Ethiopia," *Circus Magazine,* December 14, 1976.

20. Smith, *Patti Smith Complete,* p. 66.

21. Marc Stevens and Diana Clapton, "Patti Smith Peaking: The Infinite Possibilities of a Woman," *Club Quest,* January 1977.

22. Allan Jones, "Meet the Press," *Melody Maker,* October 30, 1976.

23. Stevens and Clapton, "Patti Smith Peaking."

24. Robinson, "Smith Talks about Radio Ethiopia."

25. Allan Jones, "Meet the Press," *Melody Maker,* October 30, 1976.

26. Bockris and Bayley, *Patti Smith,* pp. 168–70; Young, "Patti Smith Catches Fire."

27. Page from *Yipster Times* reproduced in Smith, *Patti Smith Complete,* p. 65.

28. Bockris and Bayley, *Patti Smith,* pp. 174–76.

29. Bockris and Bayley, *Patti Smith,* p. 175.

30. Vivien Goldman, "Patti Cracks Noggin, Raps on Regardless," *Sounds,* February 5, 1977.

31. Goldman, "Patti Cracks Noggin."

32. Young, "Patti Smith Catches Fire."

33. Gross, interview on *Fresh Air.*

34. Sharon Delano, "The Torch Singer," *New Yorker,* March 11, 2002, p. 59.

35. Thurston Moore, "Patti Smith," *Bomb,* Issue 54, Winter 1996.

36. Bockris and Bayley, *Patti Smith,* p. 176.

37. Young, "Patti Smith Catches Fire."

38. Delano, "Torch Singer," p. 59.

39. Young, "Patti Smith Catches Fire."

40. Smith, *Patti Smith Complete,* p. 88.

41. William S. Burroughs, "When Patti Rocked," *Spin,* April 1988.

42. John Tobler, "High on Rebellion: Patti Smith Speaks, Part 2," *ZigZag,* June 1978.

43. Lisa Robinson, "Patti Smith's Intuitive Mania," *Hit Parader,* March 1978.

44. David Fricke, "Patti Smith, Flea Bid Farewell to Iconic Punk Club," *Rolling Stone* online, October 16, 2006, http://www.rollingstone.com/news/story/12045842/patti_smith_rocks_final_cbgb_show.

45. John Tobler, "15 Minutes with Patti Smith," *ZigZag,* October 1978.

46. Bockris and Bayley, *Patti Smith,* p. 184.

47. John Tobler, "15 Minutes."

48. Smith, *Easter,* liner notes.

49. Nick Tosches, "Easter," *Creem,* June 1978.

50. Dave Marsh, "Can Patti Smith Walk on Water?" *Rolling Stone,* April 10, 1978.

51. Nick Tosches, "A Baby Wolf with Neon Bones," *Penthouse,* April 1976.

52. Patti Smith, review of Velvet Underground's 1969 live record, *Creem,* September 1974.

53. Sandy Robertson, "Mick Jagger," *Sounds,* October 29, 1977.

54. Paul Rambali, "Breaking the Shackles of Original Sin," *New Musical Express,* September 16, 1978.

55. Young, "Patti Smith Catches Fire."

56. Lester Bangs, "Dear Patti, Start the Revolution without Me," *Phonograph Record,* May 1978.

57. Tosches, "Easter."

58. Marsh, "Can Patti Smith Walk on Water?"

59. Lester Bangs, *Psychotic Reactions and Carburetor Dung,* ed. Greil Marcus (Vintage, October 1988), p. 276.

60. Smith, *Patti Smith Complete,* 96.

61. Smith, *Patti Smith Complete,* 96.

CHAPTER 5

1. Jaan Uhelszki, "Rock's First Lady," *Relix,* May 8, 2007.

2. Thurston Moore, "Patti Smith," *Bomb,* Winter 1996.

3. Uhelszki, "Rock's First Lady."

4. Victor Bockris and Roberta Bayley, *Patti Smith: An Unauthorized Biography* (Simon & Schuster, 1999), pp. 144–45.

5. Uhelszki, "Rock's First Lady."

6. Bockris and Bayley, *Patti Smith,* pp. 144–45.

7. Bockris and Bayley, *Patti Smith,* p. 207.

8. William S. Burroughs, "When Patti Rocked," *Spin,* April 1988.

9. Burroughs, "When Patti Rocked."

10. Cynthia Rose, "Ivan Kral," *Viz,* 1980, http://www.rocksbackpages.com/article.html?ArticleID=1323 (Subscription required).

11. ivankral.net.

12. Lynne Margolis, "Patti Smith Plays 'Messenger,'" *Rolling Stone,* September 30, 2002.

13. Simon Frith, "Patti: Love Conquers All," *Melody Maker,* May 5, 1979.

14. Tom Carson, "Patti Smith: *Wave,*" Rolling *Stone,* June 28, 1979.

15. Sharon Delano, "The Torch Singer," *New Yorker,* March 11, 2002, p. 59.

16. Patti Smith, *Patti Smith Complete, 1975–2006* (Harper Perennial, 2006), p. 145.

17. Evelyn McDonnell, "Because the Night," *The Village Voice,* August 1, 1995.

18. Delano, "Torch Singer," p. 59.

19. Bockris and Bayley, *Patti Smith,* p. 220.

20. Delano, "Torch Singer," p. 59.

21. Jon Pareles, "Having Coffee with Patti Smith: Return of the Godmother of Punk," *New York Times,* June 19, 1996.

22. Pareles, "Having Coffee with Patti Smith."

23. Mairead Case, "Patti Smith Talks New LP, Rock Hall, Inspiration." *Pitchfork,* April 24, 2007.

24. Burroughs, "When Patti Rocked."

25. Burroughs, "When Patti Rocked."

26. Case, "Patti Smith Talks New LP."

27. Bockris and Bayley, *Patti Smith*, pp. 187 and 221; Delano, "Torch Singer," p. 60.

28. Bockris and Bayley, *Patti Smith*, pp. 231–33.

29. John Nichols, interview with Patti Smith, *The Progressive*, December 1997.

30. Delano, "Torch Singer," p. 60.

31. Neil Strauss, "Poet, Singer, Mother: Patti Smith Is Back," *New York Times*, December 12, 1995.

32. Lisa Robinson, "The Second Coming of Patti Smith," *Andy Warhol's Interview*, May 1988, pp. 82–84.

33. Bockris and Bayley, *Patti Smith*, pp. 231–39.

34. Pareles, "Having Coffee."

35. Robinson, "The Second Coming of Patti Smith."

36. Robinson, "The Second Coming of Patti Smith."

37. Robinson, "The Second Coming of Patti Smith."

38. Nichols, interview with Patti Smith.

39. Sean O'Hagan, "American Icon," *The Observer*, June 15, 2003.

CHAPTER 6

1. Patti Smith, *Patti Smith Complete, 1975–2006* (Harper Perennial, 2006), p. 154.

2. Smith, *Patti Smith Complete*, p. 154.

3. John Nichols, interview with Patti Smith, *The Progressive*, December 1997.

4. Nichols, interview with Patti Smith.

5. Nichols, interview with Patti Smith.

6. Nichols, interview with Patti Smith.

7. Smith, *Patti Smith Complete*, p. 167.

8. Vin Scelsa, "Sounds," *Penthouse*, October 1988.

9. Robert Christgau, "Consumer Guide." http://www.robertchristgau.com/get_artist.php?name=patti+smith.

10. Victor Bockris and Roberta Bayley, *Patti Smith: An Unauthorized Biography* (Simon & Schuster, 1999), p. 246.

11. Bockris and Bayley, *Patti Smith*, p. 247; Sharon Delano, "The Torch Singer," *New Yorker*, March 11, 2002, p. 61.

12. Delano, "Torch Singer," p. 61.

13. Delano, "Torch Singer," p. 61.

14. Smith, *Patti Smith Complete*, p. 180.

15. Terry Gross, interview on *Fresh Air*, National Public Radio, June 24, 1996.

16. Jon Pareles, "Having Coffee with Patti Smith: Return of the Godmother of Punk," *New York Times*, June 19, 1996.

CHAPTER 7

1. Terry Gross, Interview on *Fresh Air*. National Public Radio, June 24, 1996. Radio interview.

2. Patti Smith, *Patti Smith Complete, 1975–2006* (Harper Perennial, 2006), p. 184.

3. Sharon Delano, "The Torch Singer," *New Yorker,* March 11, 2002, p. 61.

4. Smith, *Patti Smith Complete,* p. 185.

5. Delano "The Torch Singer," pp 48–63.

6. Evelyn McDonnell, "Because the Night," *The Village Voice,* August 1, 1995.

7. Gerrie Lim, "Before I Get Old," *Big O,* July 1995.

8. Smith, *Patti Smith Complete,* p. 184.

9. Smith, *Patti Smith Complete,* p. 184.

10. Michael Bracewell, "Woman as Warrior," *The Guardian,* June 22, 1996.

11. Delano, "Torch Singer," p. 62.

12. Ben Edmonds, "The Rebel," *Mojo,* August 1996.

13. Edmonds, "The Rebel."

14. Smith, *Patti Smith Complete,* p. 184.

15. Gross, Fresh Air interview.

16. Victor Bockris and Roberta Bayley, *Patti Smith: An Unauthorized Biography* (Simon & Schuster, 1999), pp. 269–70; official Arista 1996 biography.

17. Neil Strauss, "Pop Review: Patti Smith, with Nuances of Mourning," *New York Times,* July 29, 1995.

18. McDonnell, "Because the Night."

19. Neil Strauss, "Poet, Singer, Mother: Patti Smith Is Back," *New York Times,* December 12, 1995.

20. Bockris and Bayley, *Patti Smith,* p. 273.

21. Lisa Robinson, "Patti Smith's Fellow Traveler" *New York Post,* May 1, 1998.

22. Tom Moon, "Patti Smith Returns, Bent but Unbroken," *The Philadelphia Enquirer,* June 16, 1996.

23. David Browne, "Smith & Lessons," *Entertainment Weekly,* June 12, 1996.

24. James Wolcott, "The Bollocks," *New Yorker,* July 22, 1996, pp. 74–77.

25. Strauss, "Poet, Singer, Mother."

CHAPTER 8

1. Jim Sullivan, "Patti Smith Finds 'Peace' outside Rock," *The Boston Globe,* December 2, 1997.

2. Ann Powers, "From Gleeful to Motherly and Back Again," *New York Times,* October 30, 1997.

3. Patti Smith, *Patti Smith Complete 1975–2006: Lyrics, Reflections & Notes for the Future* (Harper Perennial, 2006), 221.

4. Sullivan, "Patti Smith Finds 'Peace.'"

5. Sullivan, "Patti Smith Finds 'Peace.'"

6. John Nichols, interview with Patti Smith, *The Progressive,* December 1997.

7. Smith, *Patti Smith Complete,* p. 227.

8. Nichols, interview with Patti Smith.

9. Stephen Foehr, "The Death and Rebirth of Patti Smith," *Shambhala Sun,* July 1996.

10. Sullivan, "Patti Smith Finds 'Peace.'"

11. Smith, *Patti Smith Complete,* p. 249.

12. Nichols, interview with Patti Smith.

13. Smith, *Patti Smith Complete,* p. 243, and Sullivan, "Patti Smith Finds 'Peace.'"

14. Ben Ratliff, "New Releases," *New York Times,* October 5, 1997.

15. Jaan Uhelszki, "Patti Smith Takes Her Wisdom to the Web," *Rolling Stone,* February 15, 2000.

16. Smith, *Patti Smith Complete, 1975–2006,* p. 280.

17. Steve Baltin, "Patti Smith Gung Ho about New Album," *Rolling Stone,* March 22, 2000.

18. David Browne, "Gung Ho," *Entertainment Weekly,* March 31, 2000. http://www.ew.com/ew/article/0,,64602,00.html.

19. Seth Mnookin, Salon.com, March 23, 2000.

20. Robert Christgau, "Consumer Guide," www.robertchristgau.com.

21. Lynne Margolis, "Patti Smith Plays 'Messenger,'" *Rolling Stone,* September 30, 2002.

22. Rock and Roll Hall of Fame and Museum biography, http://www.rockhall.com/inductee/patti-smith/.

23. Mairead Case, "Patti Smith Talks New LP, Rock Hall, Inspiration," *Pitchfork,* April 24, 2007. http://www.pitchforkmedia.com/article/news/42536-patti-smith-talks-new-lp-rock-hall-inspiration.

24. Andrew Dansby and David Fricke, "Patti Smith Takes 'Trampin'' on Tour," *Rolling Stone,* May 21, 2004.

25. Andrew Dansby and David Fricke, "Patti Smith Gets Spiritual," *Rolling Stone,* February 12, 2004, www.rollingstone.com/news/story/5937211/patti_smith_gets_spiritual.

26. John Nichols, "Patriots Can 'Wrestle the Earth from Fools,'" *The Capital Times,* October 11, 2007.

27. Louise Jury, "Patti Smith Rails against Israel and US," *The Independent,* September 9, 2006, http://enjoyment.independent.co.uk/music/news/article1431117.ece.

28. Jury, "Patti Smith Rails Against Israel and US."

29. Paul Fisher, "Street Spirits Plug In and Out," *The Japan Times,* September 26, 2006.

30. Jordan Zivitz, "Full Q and A with Patti Smith," *The Montreal Gazette,* October 2, 2007.

31. Case, "Patti Smith Talks New LP."

32. Jordan Zivitz, "Patti Smith: Still Preaching Power to the People," *The Montreal Gazette,* October 2, 2007.

CHAPTER 9

1. Jon Pareles, "A Punk-Rock Institution Closes Its Doors," *New York Times,* October 16, 2006, http://www.nytimes.com/2006/10/16/arts/music/16cnd-cbgb notebook.

2. David Fricke, "Patti Smith, Flea Bid Farewell to Iconic Punk Club," *Rolling Stone,* October 16, 2006, http://www.rollingstone.com/news/story/12045842/patti_smith_rocks_final_cbgb_show.

3. Fricke, "Patti Smith, Flea Bid Farewell."

4. Rock and Roll Hall of Fame and Museum, http://www.rockhall.com/inductee/patti-smith/.

5. thefilthandthefury.co.uk and David Sprague, "Sex Pistols Flip Off Hall of Fame," *Rolling Stone,* February 24, 2006.

6. Edmunds, Ben, "The Rebel." Mojo, August 1996.

7. Patti Smith, "Ain't It Strange?" *New York Times,* March 12, 2007.

8. Smith, "Ain't It Strange?"

9. Leah Greenblatt, Pop Watch Blog, *Entertainment Weekly,* March 13, 2007.

10. Jon Pareles, "Hip Hop Is Rock 'n' Roll, and Hall of Fame Likes It," *New York Times,* March 13, 2007.

11. Pareles, "Hip Hop Is Rock 'n' Roll."

12. Jessica Robertson, "Patti Smith Q&A," AOL Music, http://spinner.aol.com/rockhall/patti-smith-2007-inductee/interview.

13. Jordan Zivitz, "Full Q and A with Patti Smith," *The Montreal Gazette,* October 2, 2007.

14. Paul Lester, "Icon, Me?" *The Scotsman,* April 7, 2007.

15. Mairead Case, "Patti Smith Talks New LP, Rock Hall, Inspiration," *Pitchfork,* April 24, 2007.

16. Chris Barry, "Ask the Angel," *The Montreal Mirror,* September 28, 2007. http://www.montrealmirror.com/2007/092707/music2.html.

17. Jaan Uhelszki, "Rock's First Lady," *Relix,* May 8, 2007. http://www.relix.com/Features/Interviews/Patti_Smith_200705082270.html.

18. Patrick Daugherty, "Smith bottoms out with cover album," www.themaneater.com, April 27, 2007, http://themaneater.com/article.php?id=26921.

19. Christgua, *twelve,* http://www.robertchristgau.com/get_artist.php?name=patti+smith

20. Jim Bliss, The Quiet Road blog, May 17, 2007, http://numero57.net/?p=170.

21. Jim Harrington, "Patti Smith Rates a Perfect 'Twelve' at Fillmore," *Inside Bay Area,* The Concert Blog, www.ibabuzz.com/concerts/.

22. Barry "Ask the Angel."

23. Jordan Zivitz, "Patti Smith: Still Preaching Power to the People," *The Montreal Gazette,* October 2, 2007.

CONCLUSION

1. Women's Wear Daily, www.wwd.com, October 4, 2007.

2. "Tunstall's Relief at 2005 Success," BBC.com, January 4, 2006. http://news.bbc.co.uk/2/hi/entertainment/4581110.stm

3. "Tunstall's Relief at 2005 Success."

4. Shirley Manson, "Patti Smith," *Rolling Stone,* April 15, 2004. http://www.rollingstone.com/news/story/5940021/47_patti_smith

5. Kristin Hersh, "Walking Around Being a Woman," in *Idle Worship,* ed. Chris Roberts (Faber and Faber, 1995).

6. Ben Edmonds, "The Rebel," *Mojo,* August 1996.

7. Dave Hickey, *Air Guitar: Essays on Art and Democracy* (Art Issues Press, 1997), pp. 148–49.

8. Patti Smith, "Ain't It Strange" *New York Times,* March 12, 2007.

9. Jon Pareles, "A Punk Rock Institution Closes Its Doors," *New York Times,* October 16, 2006, http://www.nytimes.com/2006/10/16/arts/music/16cnd-cbgb-notebook.

10. David Fricke, "Exclusive Q&A: The Final Word from Patti Smith on CBGB," *Rolling Stone* online, October 17, 2006, www.rollingstone.com/news/story/12054256/exclusive_qa_patti_smith_remembers_cbgb.

11. Nick Tosches, "A Baby Wolf with Neon Bones," *Penthouse*, April 1976.

12. Tosches, "Baby Wolf."

13. Paul Rambali, "Breaking the Shackles of Original Sin," *NME*, September 16, 1978.

14. Gillian G. Gaar, *She's a Rebel: The History of Women in Rock & Roll*, 2nd ed. (Seal Press, 1992), p. 183.

15. Rosanne Cash, "Janis Joplin," *Rolling Stone*, April 15, 2004. http://www.rollingstone.com/news/story/5939239/46_janis_joplin.

16. Mairead Case, "Patti Smith Talks New LP, Rock Hall, Inspiration," *Pitchfork*, April 24, 2007.

17. Case, "Patti Smith Talks New LP."

18. Gaar, *She's a Rebel*, p. 93.

19. Gaar, *She's a Rebel*, p. 193.

20. Terry Gross, Interview on *Fresh Air*. National Public Radio, June 24, 1996. Radio interview.

21. Simon Reynolds and Joy Press, *The Sex Revolts: Gender, Rebellion, and Rock 'n' Roll* (Harvard University Press, 1995).

22. Reynolds and Press, *Sex Revolts*.

23. Reynolds and Press, *Sex Revolts*.

24. Camille Paglia, "Caption: What's in a Picture," *Civilization*, December 1996– January 1997.

25. Jessica Robertson, "Patti Smith Q&A," AOL Music, http://spinner.aol.com/rockhall/patti-smith-2007-inductee/interview.

26. Smith, "Ain't It Strange."

Annotated Bibliography

Arista records. Artist biography. www.aristarec.com/psmithbio.html.

Bangs, Lester. "Stagger Lee Was a Woman." *Creem*, February 1976. www.creemmag azine. com/_site/BeatGoesOn/PattiSmith/StaggerLeeWasAWoman0512.html. Review of *Horses*.

Bangs, Lester. "The White Noise Supremacists," *Psychotic Reactions and Carburetor Dung*. Edited by Greil Marcus. Vintage, October 1988. pp. 272–282. Essay on chic racism in punk rock, reprinted from *Village Voice*.

Barry, Chris. "Ask the Angel." *Montreal Mirror*, September 28, 2007. http://www. montrealmirror.com/2007/092707/music2.html.

Baltin, Steve. "Patti Smith Gung Ho about New Album." *Rolling Stone*, March 22, 2000. http://www.rollingstone.com/artists/pattismith/articles/story/5924141/ patti_smith_gung_ho_about_new_album. Article about *Gung Ho* album.

Berman, Bruce. "The Queen of Acid Punk Rock." *Acid Rock*, November 1977.

Billboard magazine. http://www.billboard.com/bbcom/charts/yearend_chart_dis play.jsp?f=The+Billboard+Hot+100&g=Year-end+Singles&year=1975 Top five singles from 1975.

Bliss, Jim. The Quiet Road blog, May 17, 2007, http://numero57.net/?p=170.

Bockris, Victor, and Roberta Bayley. *Patti Smith: An Unauthorized Biography.* Simon & Schuster, 1999). A biography culled from years of published interviews and pro- files as well as interviews of people who knew Smith over the years.

Bracewell, Michael. "Woman as Warrior." *The Guardian*, June 22, 1996.

Browne, David. "Patti Smith: *Gung Ho*," *Entertainment Weekly*, March 31, 2000. http://www.ew.com/ew/article/0,,64602,00.html. *Gung Ho* review.

Browne, David. "Smith & Lessons." *Entertainment Weekly*, June 12, 1996. http:// www.ew.com/ew/article/0,,293074,00.html. Review of *Gone Again*.

Burroughs, William S. "When Patti Rocked." *Spin*, April 1988. Interview between Burroughs and Smith before her retirement, republished by *Spin* magazine.

Carson, Tom. "Patti Smith: *Wave*," *Rolling Stone*, June 28, 1979. http://www.roll ingstone.com/artists/pattismith/albums/album/105149/review/5946343/ wave. Review of *Wave*.

Case, Mairead. "Patti Smith Talks New LP, Rock Hall, Inspiration." *Pitchfork*, April 24, 2007. http://www.pitchforkmedia.com/article/news/42536-patti-smith-talks-new-lp-rock-hall-inspiration. Interview on her induction into Rock and Roll Hall of Fame.

Cash, Rosanne. "Janis Joplin." *Rolling Stone*, April 15, 2004. http://www.rolling stone.com/news/story/5939239/46_janis_joplin Reflection on the importance of Janis Joplin to music.

Christgau, Robert. "Consumer Guide." www.robertchristgau.com. Record reviews.

Cohen, Mitchell. "Patti Smith: Avery Fisher Hall, NYC." *Phonograph Record*, May 1976. Concert review.

Cohen, Scott. "How a Little Girl Took over a Tough Gang: The Hard-Rock Poets." *Oui*, July 1976.

Cohen, Scott. "Patti Smith: Can You Hear Me Ethiopia." *Circus Magazine*, December 14, 1976.

Dansby, Andrew, and David Fricke. "Patti Smith Gets Spiritual." *Rolling Stone*, February 12, 2004. www.rollingstone.com/news/story/5937211/patti_smith_gets_ spiritual.

Dansby, Andrew, and David Fricke. "Patti Smith Takes *Trampin'* on Tour." *Rolling Stone*, May 21, 2004. Article about *Trampin'* tour.

Delano, Sharon. "The Torch Singer." *New Yorker*, March 11, 2002, pp. 48–63. Excellent profile on Smith, following her reemergence as a performer.

Edmonds, Ben. "Michael Stipe on Patti." *Mojo*, August 1996. Short Q&A with Stipe about Smith.

Edmonds, Ben. "The Rebel: Patti Smith." *Mojo*, August 1996.

"Eye on the Scene." *Metro Pulse*, August 3, 2000, p. 18. Commentary on Smith's concert in Knoxville, Tennessee, in 2000.

Filth and the Fury, Website of the Sex Pistols, http://www.thefilthandthefury.co.uk/

Fisher, Paul. "Street Spirits Plug In and Out." *The Japan Times*, September 26, 2006. http://search.japantimes.co.jp/cgi-bin/fm20060929a1.html. Article about Soul Flower Union, a band that cites the influence of Smith.

Foehr, Stephen. "The Death and the Rebirth of Patti Smith." *Shambhala Sun*, July 1996. http://www.shambhalasun.com/index.php?option=com_content&task= view&id=2080&Itemid=244. Interview after the death of her husband, with focus on religious themes.

Frere-Jones, Sasha. "Ring in the Old," *New Yorker*, December 25, 2006; January 1, 2007, p. 28.

Fricke, David. "Exclusive Q&A: The Final Word from Patti Smith on CBGB." *Rolling Stone* online, October 17, 2006. www.rollingstone.com/news/story/1205 4256/exclusive_qa_patti_smith_remembers_cbgb. Online-only interview with Smith on the closing night of CBGB.

Fricke, David. "Patti Smith, Flea Bid Farewell to Iconic Punk Club." *Rolling Stone* online, October 16, 2006. http://www.rollingstone.com/news/story/12045 842/patti_smith_rocks_final_cbgb_show. Review of final show at CBGB.

Frith, Simon. "Patti: Love Conquers All." *Melody Maker*, May 5, 1979. Review of *Wave*.

Gaar, Gillian G. *She's a Rebel: The History of Women in Rock & Roll.* 2nd ed. Emeryville, CA: Seal Press, 1992. Comprehensive book about the history of women in rock 'n' roll.

Gold, Mick. "Patti in Excelsis Deo." *Street Life*, May 29, 1976.

Goldman, Vivien. "Patti Cracks Noggin, Raps on Regardless." *Sounds*, February 5, 1977. Article about Smith's injury during a concert.

Green, Penny. "Patti Smith." *Andy Warhol's Interview*, October 1973. Interview conducted prior to Smith's rock career, focusing on her poetry.

Greenblatt, Leah. Pop Watch Blog, *Entertainment Weekly*, March 13, 2007.

Gross, Amy. "I'm Doing a Revenge for Bad Skin." *Mademoiselle*, September 1975.

Gross, Michael. "Misplaced Joan of Arc." *Blast*, August 1976.

Gross, Terry. Interview on *Fresh Air.* National Public Radio, June 24, 1996. Radio interview.

Harrington, Jim. "Patti Smith Rates a Perfect 'Twelve' at Fillmore," *Inside Bay Area*, The Concert Blog, www.ibabuzz.com/concerts/.

Hersh, Kristin. "Walking Around Being a Woman." In *Idle Worship: How Pop Empowers the Weak, Rewards the Faithful, and Succors the Needy*, edited by Chris Roberts. London: Faber and Faber, 1995, pp. 91–96. Essay about Patti Smith's influence.

Hickey, Dave, *Air Guitar: Essays on Art and Democracy.* Los Angeles: Art Issues Press, 1997.

Hiss, Tony, and David McClelland. "Gonna Be so Big, Gonna Be a Start, Watch Me Now!" *New York Times Magazine*, December 21, 1975, pp. 25–30.

Ivankral.net. Profile of Patti Smith Group guitarist from his Web site.

Jones, Allan. "Meet the Press." *Melody Maker*, October 30, 1976. Mocking coverage of a Patti Smith press conference.

Jury, Louise. "Patti Smith Rails against Israel and US." *The Independent*, September 9, 2006. http://enjoyment.independent.co.uk/music/news/article1431117.ece. Article about Smith's songs "Qana" and "Without Chains."

Larry King Live, January 22, 2002. Interview with Patty Hearst about her kidnapping and subsequent media coverage. Transcript: http://transcripts.cnn.com/TRANSCRIPTS/0201/22/lkl.00.html.

Lester, Paul. "Icon, Me?" *The Scotsman*, April 7, 2007.

Lim, Gerrie. "Before I Get Old." *Big O*, July 1995. Interview on the occasion of *Horses'* being named best record of previous 20 years by *Big O* magazine.

Manson, Shirley. "Patti Smith," *Rolling Stone*, April 15, 2004. Musician reflects on the influence of Patti Smith. http://www.rollingstone.com/news/story/5940021/47_patti_smith.

Marcus, Greil. *Lipstick Traces. A Secret History of the Twentieth Century.* Cambridge, MA: Harvard University Press, 1989. Marcus's book focuses on connections between cultural eras that culminated in the punk generation.

Margolis, Lynne. "Patti Smith Plays 'Messenger.'" *Rolling Stone*, September 30, 2002. http://www.rollingstone.com/artists/pattismith/articles/story/5933516/patti_smith_plays_messenger. Review of art show opening at Andy Warhol Museum in Pittsburgh.

Marsh, Dave. "Can Patti Smith Walk on Water?" *Rolling Stone*, April 10, 1978. http://www.rollingstone.com/artists/pattismith/albums/album/120255/review/5944596/easter. Review of *Easter.*

Marsh, Dave. "Her Horses Got Wings, They Can Fly," *Rolling Stone*, January 1, 1976.

Marsh, Dave. "Patti Smith: *Radio Ethiopia*" *Rolling Stone*, March 1977. http://www.rol
lingstone.com/artists/pattismith/albums/album/227777/review/5941548/
radio_ethiopia. Review of *Radio Ethiopia*.

McDonnell, Evelyn. "Because the Night." *The Village Voice*, August 1, 1995. One
of the first interviews with Smith after her return to music after Fred Smith's
death.

Mnookin, Seth. "Sharps & Flats," Salon.com, March 23, 2000. *Gung Ho* review.
http://archive.salon.com/ent/music/review/2000/03/23/smith_mitchell/
index.html.

Moon, Tom. "Patti Smith Returns, Bent but Unbroken." *The Philadelphia Enquirer*,
June 16, 1996. Review of *Gone Again*.

Moore, Thurston. "Patti Smith." *Bomb*, Issue 54, Winter 1996. Guitarist from Sonic
Youth interviews Smith about her career, influence, and husband.

Murray, Charles Shaar. "Down in the Scuzz with the Heavy Cult Figures." *New Musical Express*, June 7, 1975. Article about CBGB scene, focusing on Smith and
Television.

Murray, Charles Shaar. "Weird Scenes Inside the Gasoline Alley," *New Musical Express*,
November 1975. Review of *Horses*.

Nichols, John. "Patriots Can 'Wrestle the Earth from Fools.'" *The Capital Times*,
October 11, 2007.

Nichols, John. "Patti Smith." *The Progressive*, December 1997. Interview that focuses
on Smith's political leanings.

O'Brien, Lucy. "John Cale and Patti Smith: How We Met." *Independent on
Sunday*, August 25, 1996. http://findarticles.com/p/articles/mi_qn4158/is_
19960825/ai_n14069644.

O'Hagan, Sean. "American Icon." *The Observer*, June 15, 2003. http://observer.
guardian.co.uk/magazine/story/0,11913,976010,00.html.

Paglia, Camille. "Caption: What's in a Picture." *Civilization*, December 1996–
January 1997. Essay about the cover illustration of *Horses*.

Pareles, Jon. "A Punk-Rock Institution Closes Its Doors," *New York Times*, October 16, 2006. www.nytimes.com/2006/10/16/arts/music/16cnd-cbgbnote
book. Smith comments on the importance of CBGB when it closes its doors.

Pareles, Jon. "Having Coffee with Patti Smith: Return of the Godmother of Punk."
New York Times, June 19, 1996. Interview with Smith after her return to
music.

Pareles, Jon. "Hip Hop Is Rock 'n' Roll, and Hall of Fame Likes It," *New York Times*,
March 13, 2007.

Partridge, Mariane. "Radio Ethiopia," *Melody Maker*, October 23, 1976. Harsh
review of *Radio Ethiopia*.

Patti Smith Babelogue, http://www.oceanstar.com/patti/, Website maintain by Patti
Smith fans which was invaluable in tracking down source materials.

Powers, Ann. "From Gleeful to Motherly and Back Again." *New York Times*, October
30, 1997. http://query.nytimes.com/gst/fullpage.html?res=9C0CE0DE1031
F933A05753C1A961958260&scp=1&sq=patti+smith+ann+powers.

Rambali, Paul. "Breaking the Shackles of Original Sin." *New Musical Express*, September 16, 1978.

Ratliff, Ben. "New Releases." *New York Times*, October 5, 1997. http://query.nytimes.
com/gst/fullpage.html?res=9B0CE7D8163DF936A35753C1A961958260&s
cp=1&sq=patti+smith+ben+ratliff. Review of *peace and noise*.

Reynolds, Simon. "Patti Smith: Even as a Child I Felt Like an Alien." *The Guardian Observer Music Monthly*, May 22, 2005. http://observer.guardian.co.uk/omm/story/0,,1486833,00.html.

Reynolds, Simon, and Joy Press. *The Sex Revolts: Gender, Rebellion, and Rock 'n' Roll.* Cambridge, MA: Harvard University Press, 1995, pp 355–362. Book about gender roles in rock 'n' roll.

Robertson, Jessica. "Exclusive Interview with Patti Smith." AOL Music. http://spinner.aol.com/rockhall/patti-smith-2007-inductee/interview. Online interview with Smith on her induction into Rock and Roll Hall of Fame.

Robertson, Sandy. "Mick Jagger," *Sounds.* October 29, 1977. Interview with Mick Jagger in which he famously trashed Smith.

Robinson, Lisa. "The High Priestess of Rock and Roll." *Hit Parader*, January 1976.

Robinson, Lisa. "Patti Smith: Decoding Ethiopia." *Hit Parader*, June 1977. Interview about *Radio Ethiopia*.

Robinson, Lisa. "Patti Smith's Fellow Traveler." *New York Post*, May 1, 1998. Interview with Michael Stipe on the release of his book, *Two Times Intro: On the Road with Patti Smith.*

Robinson, Lisa. "Patti Smith's Intuitive Mania." *Hit Parader*, March 1978. Interview as Smith reemerged following her fall from stage.

Robinson, Lisa. "Patti Smith Talks about Radio Ethiopia." *Hit Parader*, Summer–Fall 1977. Part two of interview about *Radio Ethiopia*.

Robinson, Lisa. "The Second Coming of Patti Smith," *Andy Warhol's Interview*, May 1988, pp 82–84. One of few interviews conducted during Smith's period away from the music industry in the 1980s.

Rock and Roll Hall of Fame and Museum. Biography. http://www.rockhall.com/inductee/patti-smith/.

Rockwell, John. "Patti Smith Battles to a Singing Victory." *New York Times,* December 28, 1975, p. 31.

Rose, Cynthia. "Ivan Kral." *Viz*, 1980. Article about Patti Smith's guitarist, http://www.rocksbackpages.com/article.html?ArticleID=1323 (Subscription required).

Schulps, Dave. "Tom Verlaine: In Search of Adventure." *Trouser Press*, May 1978. Interview with Verlaine in which he talks about Smith's influence on punk rock.

Scelsa, Vin. "Sounds," *Penthouse*, October 1988. Review of *Dream of Life.*

Schwartz, Andy. "Patti Smith—A Wave Hello, a Kiss Goodbye." *New York Rocker,* June/July 1979.

Simels, Steve. "Patti Smith." *Stereo Review*, August 1978. Interview.

Smith, Patti. "Ain't It Strange?" *New York Times*, March 12, 2007. Op-ed on her induction into the Rock and Roll Hall of Fame.

Smith, Patti. *Creem*, September 1974. Review of Velvet Underground's 1969 live record.

Smith, Patti. "Jag-arr of the Jungle." *Creem*, January 1973. Essay on Smith's discovery of the Rolling Stones and her sexual response to them.

Smith, Patti. *Patti Smith Complete, 1975–2006.* Harper Perennial, 2006. Collection of Smith's lyrics and liner notes, along with excerpts from her journals and reflections and photographs from her career.

Smith, Patti. "We Can Be Heroes." *Details*, July 1993. Essay by Smith on her early fan worship and how it transformed her.

Sprague, David. "Sex Pistols Flip Off Hall of Fame," *Rolling Stone*, February 24, 2006. http://www.rollingstone.com/news/story/9385165/sex_pistols_flip_off_hall_of_fame.

Stein, K. "Radio Ethiopia," *Circus Magazine*, December 14, 1976. Review of *Radio Ethiopia*.

Stevens, Marc, and Diana Clapton. "Patti Smith Peaking: The Infinite Possibilities of a Woman." *Club Quest*, January 1977.

Strauss, Neil. "Poet, Singer, Mother: Patti Smith Is Back." *New York Times*, December 12, 1995. Interview on Smith's return to the music industry.

Strauss, Neil. "Pop Review: Patti Smith, with Nuances of Mourning." *New York Times*, July 29, 1995. http://query.nytimes.com/gst/fullpage.html?res=990C E5DA143AF93AA15754C0A963958260&scp=1&sq=patti+smith+nuances+of+mourning. Review of concert in Central Park.

Sullivan, Jim. "Patti Smith Finds 'Peace' outside Rock." *The Boston Globe*, December 2, 1997. Interview.

Tobler, John. "15 Minutes with Patti Smith." *ZigZag*, October 1978. Interview focusing on Smith's hostility with the music press.

Tobler, John. "High on Rebellion: Patti Smith Speaks, Part 2." *ZigZag*, June 1978. Interview after Smith recovers from her concert injury.

Tosches, Nick. "A Baby Wolf with Neon Bones." *Penthouse*, April 1976. An early career interview where Smith discusses sexuality, poetry, feminism, and rock 'n' roll.

Tosches, Nick. "Easter." *Creem*, June 1978. Record review.

Tosches, Nick. "Eat Lead, Dog of Mediocrity." *Creem*, September 1978.

"Tunstall's Relief at 2005 Success." BBC.com, January 4, 2006. Interview with KT Tunstall about the song "Suddenly I See." http://news.bbc.co.uk/2/hi/entertainment/4581110.stm.

Turner, Jenny. "Patti Smith and Richard Hell: Two Punks Don't Make a Summer." *New Statesman*, July 5, 1996. Book review of the *Coral Sea* and reflections on the origin of the punk aesthetic.

Uhelszki, Jaan. "Patti Smith Takes Her Wisdom to the Web." *Rolling Stone*, February 15, 2000. http://www.rollingstone.com/artists/pattismith/articles/story/5923835/patti_smith_takes_her_wisdom_to_the_web.

Uhelszki, Jaan. "Rock's First Lady." *Relix*, May 8, 2007. http://www.relix.com/Features/Interviews/Patti_Smith_200705082270.html.

Wolcott, James. "The Bollocks," *New Yorker*, July 22, 1996, pp. 74–77.

Women's Wear Daily, www.wwd.com, Oct. 4, 2007. Article about fashion show, which references Smith's look.

Young, Charles. "Patti Smith Catches Fire." *Rolling Stone*, March 1977. Profile on Smith quoting Smith's incendiary comments on race.

Zivitz, Jordan. "Full Q and A with Patti Smith." *The Montreal Gazette*, October 2, 2007.

Zivitz, Jordan. "Patti Smith: Still Preaching Power to the People," *The Montreal Gazette*, October 2, 2007.

Index

About the Author

JOE TARR is a journalist and critic with almost 15 years experience working for the daily and alternative presses and television. He's written extensively about popular culture and music. In recent years, Tarr has worked as a freelancer, writing scripts for the Oxygen network's hit true crime show, *Snapped!*